Doing Grammar

....

Doing Grammar

Fourth Edition

MAX MORENBERG
Miami University

New York   Oxford

OXFORD UNIVERSITY PRESS

2010

Oxford University Press, Inc., publishes works that further Oxford University's
objective of excellence in research, scholarship, and education.

Oxford   New York
Auckland   Cape Town   Dar es Salaam   Hong Kong   Karachi
Kuala Lumpur   Madrid   Melbourne   Mexico City   Nairobi
New Delhi   Shanghai   Taipei   Toronto

With offices in
Argentina   Austria   Brazil   Chile   Czech Republic   France   Greece
Guatemala   Hungary   Italy   Japan   Poland   Portugal   Singapore
South Korea   Switzerland   Thailand   Turkey   Ukraine   Vietnam

Published by Oxford University Press, Inc.
198 Madison Avenue, New York, New York 10016

http://www.oup.com

Oxford is a registered trademark of Oxford University Press

Library of Congress Cataloging-in-Publication Data
Morenberg, Max, 1940–
Doing grammar / Max Morenberg.—4th ed.
p.   cm.
Includes index.
ISBN 978-0-19-538729-2
1. English language—Grammar.   2. English language—Grammar—Problems,
exercises, etc.   I. Title.
PE1112.M64 2009
428.2—dc22

                                                            2009026673

Printing number: 9 8 7 6 5 4 3 2 1

Printed in the United States of America
on acid-free paper

My children have become successful adults.

They grew up with a father who put a lot of time into academic projects.

I offer them my love, respect, and the spirit that remains in this book of all those mostly forgotten projects that kept me from spending more time with them as children.

Ara
Cori
Adam

CONTENTS
....

CHAPTER 5   **Rearranging and Compounding**   89

PREFACE

I doubt whether any school subject is so universally dreaded and loathed by students and remembered with as much discomfort by adults. The term "grammar" will generally make people grimace and snarl. When I want to free myself from a particularly obnoxious person at a cocktail party, all I have to do is tell him that I'm a grammarian. Without fail, he'll lower his head and sidle away, mumbling into his shirt collar, "I never did well at that in school." When I like the person and want to continue the conversation, I say I'm a linguist.

If you're one of those who would rather eat lint than "do grammar," I know how you feel, because I hated grammar as a kid. I even failed eleventh-grade English because of my animosity for the subject. Grammar classes seemed an endless repetition of silly rules and mindless diagrams that took up a portion of every year from third grade to twelfth grade. The lessons never stuck in my mind because nothing about grammar ever seemed to make sense. Grammar was something you had to endure, like the awful-tasting cough syrup that was supposed to be good for you.

It's odd that so many of us hate studying grammar. It's like cats hating to stalk prey. Or dolphins learning to dislike swimming. Humans are as much language animals as cats are stalking animals and dolphins are swimming animals. We are born to love language and everything associated with it—rhythm, rhyme, word meanings, grammar. If you want to make a three-year old child roll on the floor laughing, just tell her a riddle, or alliterate words, or read her Dr. Seuss' lilting rhythms and rhymes about cats in hats or elephants who are "faithful, one hundred percent" or Sam I Am eating green eggs and ham on a boat with a goat. Listen to a child in a crib entertaining himself by repeating sounds and syllables, playing with language. Think about the games you played in kindergarten by creating strange words like Mary Poppins' "supercalifragilisticexpialidocious." Keep a ten-year-old entertained on a car trip by producing odd sentences in a "Mad Libs" game. Then ask an eighth grader what subject she hates most. The answer will invariably be grammar. We're born to love grammar. We are taught to hate it.

I was taught to hate it by well-meaning teachers who presented grammar as morality lessons of do's and don'ts, linguistics etiquette. I learned only the most trivial lessons—that you shouldn't end sentences in prepositions or start sentences with conjunctions or write fragments. When I found professional writers who used fragments, who ended sentences with prepositions, or who began them with conjunctions, I was told that it's all right for professional writers to break the rules because they know them. Not a satisfactory answer. It made me disdain the subject even more.

Then, in a junior-level grammar class at Florida State University, Kellogg Hunt introduced me to Paul Roberts' *English Sentences,* and I began to see grammar in a new way. Before I read Roberts' book, grammar was just an endless list of pointers and admonitions to me: Do this, don't do that. Roberts said that grammar is "something that produces the sentences of a language." He went on to explain that grammar is a system that puts words into an understandable order. Roberts illustrated the point with a simple game. You put words on 25 cards, one word to a card, and place the cards in a hat. The words are **face, my, never, his, dog, usually, car, struck, the, liked, a, washed, window, sometimes, seldom, George, stroked, he, she, Annabelle, her, goldfish, often, Sam, touched.** If you pick the cards from the hat, one at a time, and place them in rows of five, you'll probably never produce an English sentence. You'll get nonsense like **struck the she Sam touched.** But if you first arrange the cards into stacks following the pattern **Sam never stroked his window,** and pick them in order starting with the **Sam** stack, you'll always produce a five-word sentence like **George usually struck my goldfish** or **Annabelle sometimes touched her dog.** In fact, there are hundreds of such sentences in the hat. What you've done by arranging the cards is to sort words into classes and then put the classes in order. If you play long enough with the sentences, you discover important facts about the ordering of words—that words make constituents, units like **his window, washed his window, seldom washed his window,** and **Sam seldom washed his window.** You find that a noun phrase can fit within a verb phrase, that the new verb phrase can pattern with another noun phrase to make a sentence: you've learned that constituents form hierarchies. You may also discover that some noun phrases can't function as subjects for some verb phrases and that some noun phrases can't function as objects with some verbs. **My window never stroked she** isn't an English sentence, though it follows the pattern Noun Phrase + Adverb + Verb + Noun Phrase.

Roberts' game is a pretty simple idea. But it was a revelation to me: grammar is like a machine that fabricates sentences according to a set of discernible principles. When we speak or write, we don't throw words into sentences at random: we order them according to a discernable system. We build constituents and relate them to one another within hierarchical frameworks. Grammar made sense to me.

The next revelation was that you can take the simple sentences produced by such a grammar machine and put them together into new and different combinations, because the grammar of a language keeps recycling material, using the same constituents over and over in new combinations. In this way, grammar produces an infinite number of sentences from a small number of core constituents, or modules.

To introduce beginning linguistics students to this idea, I ask them to combine two sentences into one in as many ways as they can. My favorite two sentences for this exercise are **It surprised me** and **Jane arrived late,** sentences that my colleague Andy Kerek made up several years ago. If you try the exercise, remember that you can add words like **and,** or **when,** or **if,** and you can change the forms of words—for example, from **arrive** to **arriving** or **arrival.** Students will typically come to the next class with 50 or 60 combinations. The all-time champ was a mathematically inclined student who ran a factor analysis on the combinations and produced 467 new sentences, stopping, he said, not because he couldn't continue but because he finally got bored with the task.

Those two ideas, the grammar machine and the combining exercise, inform everything in this book. Chapter 1 introduces you to six verb types that are central to the core sentences and determine what structures and functions can exist within them. Chapter 2 defines categories like noun, adjective, adverb, and preposition and shows how those categories build into constituents that fit together within hierarchies. Chapters 3 and 4 expand the concepts of verb phrases and noun phrases. Chapter 5 shows how you can rearrange or compound components of the core sentences. Chapter 6 explains how you combine core sentences into relative clauses, while Chapter 7 describes how to reduce those clauses to phrases. Chapter 8 demonstrates how you combine core sentences into substitutes for nouns—noun clauses, gerunds, and infinitives. Chapter 9 explores ways you combine sentences into nonrestrictive modifiers. Finally, Chapter 10 shows that your knowledge of grammar can enhance your understanding of literary style and may even help you improve your writing.

Mastering the technical vocabulary and concepts in *Doing Grammar* demands the kind of studying you'd put into a science or math course. Go through the book slowly and methodically. Underline important concepts and write notes in the margins. Don't move ahead until you understand what you're reading. But don't be afraid of doing grammar, either. You already know more grammar than you suspect. You speak, write, and understand language without ever thinking about the identity and function of grammatical constituents.

The best that a textbook like this can do is make you conscious of how language operates to produce sentences. Grammar works by putting words, phrases, and clauses together into sentences. Any native speaker of English can make **It surprised me** and **Jane arrived late** into **It surprised me that Jane arrived late**, **Jane surprised me by arriving late**, or **When Jane arrived late, I was surprised**. When you complete *Doing Grammar,* you should be able to identify **that Jane arrived late** as a noun clause which functions as a logical subject, **arriving late** as a gerund phrase that functions as the object of the preposition **by,** and **when Jane arrived** as an adverb clause of time.

We all put sentences together. The grammarian's job is to take those structures apart, identify them, and explain how the parts relate to one another. Putting together is natural; taking apart and labeling is learned.

The idea behind *Doing Grammar* is that if you can see how you put sentences together, you understand how to take them apart. It takes practice to learn grammatical analysis. So, besides the explanations, each chapter has lots of sentences for you to analyze. I hope you find them appealing as well as challenging. I've devoted a great deal of time and effort to finding example sentences that are interesting. Besides hating mindless grammar exercises, I always hated the sentences in grammar books because they were so lifeless that you could be sure they occurred nowhere else but grammar books. The sentences in *Doing Grammar* are real sentences—vivid and detailed.

Doing Grammar is not tied to one ideology. Its terminology is traditional. It draws upon both traditional and generative grammars for its basic concepts. It is rooted in the traditional principles of Otto Jespersen as well as in the contemporary formulations of Noam Chomsky, with an admixture of Kenneth Pike's Tagmemics and Robert Allen's Sector Analysis. It is nurtured through the textbook explanations of Paul Roberts and the language development research of Kellogg Hunt. When I have questions, I usually look for answers in Quirk, Greenbaum, Svartvik, and Leech's *A Comprehensive Grammar of the English Language*. Nowadays, I also look in Huddleston and Pullum's *The Cambridge Grammar of the English Language*. I also find questions and answers in cyberspace, particularly from the listserv for the Assembly of Teachers of English Grammar. The scholarly works, the textbooks, and other linguists and grammarians I've learned from through the years form the book's academic credentials.

I have attempted to make the technical and obscure clear and sensible. The book assumes, loosely, that a small number of core sentences composed of basic classes of constituents can be rearranged or combined into new, more elaborate sentences. It also assumes that if you learn to analyze the structures and relationships in the core sentences, you will be able to analyze the structures and relationships in the new combinations. After working through *Doing Grammar,* you should be able to read and understand a traditional grammar text or be prepared to begin the study of linguistic theory. And you should be able to reflect more thoughtfully on how writers, including yourself, use language to create stylistic effects.

Changes in the Fourth Edition

The first edition of *Doing Grammar,* about 20 years ago, was little more than the mimeographed manuscript I used as the syntax text in my junior-level class on the structure of the English language. Like Paul Roberts' *Syntactic Structures,* it covered only syntactic issues in a narrow way, explaining some verbs and some core sentences and a few modified sentences—compounds, relative clauses, and the like. The next two editions grew to include more combinations, parts of speech, and style, becoming a more complete introductory grammar book. But when I read through it to revise for the fourth edition, I thought it was a bit clunky.

For that reason, I trimmed as much as I added for this edition. I removed what I thought was bloated and confusing, sentences and paragraphs here, whole sections there. I made the fourth edition leaner, more focused.

I replaced Chapter 10's section on clarity with a few more examples of student writing, to introduce the issue of how students who understand grammar write more interesting sentences.

Throughout the book, I changed example sentences that seemed to me out of date. At least once, an out-of-date sentence became an historic one—when I changed a Vg sentence about Brad Pitt buying Jennifer Anniston a diamond necklace to one about Clark Gable buying Carole Lombard a ranch. Lombard won't switch to Angelina Jolie. Anyway, I love movies from the thirties, forties, and fifties, and many of my example sentences reflect that. I'd rather talk about Gable and Lombard than use a generalization like "the movie star" and "his wife." I always aim for details: the Chilean crash survivors who planned to eat their dead pilot, for instance. It takes a long time to find good examples that have both universality and specificity.

In addition to slimming down and updating examples, I cleared up some explanations. I added a brief summary to the explanation about Vc verbs that better explains the difference between the two types of Vc verbs, those that consider and those that produce results. I found a good example of our intelligence services using grammatical analysis to sort through and understand clandestine cell phone and email messages. The code-breakers who look for specific words discovered they could find them faster in messages when they sorted through syntax. Swirls of words without syntax, as Hamlet realized, are simply insane.

I also fixed a few inconsistencies in the Answer Key. For instance, in the 14th sentence in Chapter 9, I changed one *NP* to *NP:Obj/Prep*. Boy, it's easy to lose yourself in those diagrams. There were more small problems like that than I imagined.

Perhaps the most noticeable addition is the glossary. Several reviewers of the third edition remarked that a glossary would be helpful to students. And I realized after revising the book, rereading it in detail, that the reviewers were right. When I started revising, I thought I knew what was in each chapter, that I could if I wanted open immediately to the discussion of parsing, for instance. I couldn't. Obviously, readers must have an even tougher time finding definitions. Writing the definitions for the glossary helped me in other ways as well. It made me formulate specific definitions for lots of issues I assumed I'd been clear about. I hadn't always been—for instance, with phrases like "sentence nucleus." The glossary helped me, and it will help readers. The glossary is a good addition.

I liked the third edition of *Doing Grammar*. But I think I improved it. I hope you find the fourth edition more clear, more focused and useful, and more detailed.

I can't promise that you will love grammatical analysis because you studied this book as I learned to love grammatical analysis after I studied Paul Roberts' *English Sentences* as an undergraduate. I hope you will. But you'll understand the English language better after putting together and taking apart sentences and thinking about what you're doing within the system we explore.

You learn to understand grammar by doing grammar.

Doing Grammar finally has a teacher's manual. The manual supplies quizzes, worksheets, exams, discussion questions, information on developing a syllabus, teaching tips, online resources, and the second half of the Answer Key. Written by Charles MacQuarrie of the University of California at Santa Barbara, the teacher's manual provides a meaningful addition to the text.

Acknowledgments

A published book is always the work of many people beyond the author.

The Oxford University Press editors are as good as textbook editors get. Jan Beatty, Executive Editor, acquired the book and gave final approval to what Cory, Jaimee, and I produced. Cory Schneider, Associate Editor, provided a non-grammarian's view of a difficult text and helped make it more readable and useful. He became a guide and friend as I revised and refined the text. Jaimee Biggins, Production Editor, coordinated the designers, copyeditors, and others who turned a bland typescript into a book with some esthetic integrity.

The many reviewers provided ideas and insights as teachers and scholars. They are Edwin Eleazer, Francis Marion University; David Flanagan, Ithaca College; Lori Garner, University of Illinois at Urbana-Champaign; Laura Halliday, Southern Illinois University,

Carbondale; Vivian Lindhardsen, George Mason University; Michelle Moosally, University of Houston – Downtown; Marshall Myers, Eastern Kentucky University; Dwayne Strasheim, Hastings College; and Ed Zoerner, California State University – Dominguez Hills.

Additionally, Charlie MacQuarrie, California State University at Santa Barbara, who began as one of those reviewers, became the author of the new instructor's manual. His knowledge of grammar and his teaching experience created a welcome addition to this book. And his sense of humor allowed him to put up with my suggestions.

Finally, my children supported me through a difficult emotional time.

M.M.

CHAPTER 1

Identifying Verbs and Core Sentences

Preview

This chapter identifies the six verb types and their associated noun, adjective, and adverb phrases, which together compose the core sentences. These six core sentence types are the building blocks from which we construct all the other sentences in the language. By building larger and more varied sentences out of smaller basic sentences, identifying all the parts, and showing how the words, phrases, and clauses fit together, we'll build a GRAMMAR: a system that puts words together into meaningful units—phrases, clauses, and sentences.

What Grammar Does

As a graduate student at Florida State University, I took courses in French and German designed specifically to teach graduate students enough of those languages to pass a reading knowledge test. I appeared for the German exam one Saturday morning with a graduate student friend of mine, Joe Smith.

After several hours of translating German, Joe and I left the exam room together for the short walk home. "Wasn't that a funny paragraph about the Virgin Mary in a monastery?" he asked as we stepped into the bright Tallahassee sunshine. The exam had taxed my knowledge of German, and I didn't remember anything funny about it—certainly not the paragraph about monks scurrying around a medieval monastery, trying to save various statues and religious objects as they worked to put out a fire. "What do you mean funny?" I replied. Joe looked at me, hoping I would verify his interpretation of the paragraph. "Wasn't the Virgin Mary running around setting fires in the monastery?" he asked. "No, Joe," I replied. "One monk was carrying a statue of Mary while he ran around trying to put out the fires."

Obviously, Joe had misread something. He had the statue performing an action, not simply being carried around.

If you've studied a foreign language in school, you've probably been in a situation like Joe's, where you've known the meaning of the words and still misinterpreted the sentence. What's missing in this situation is a knowledge of the grammar, the system that puts words together into meaningful units. Grammar tells you who does what to whom. It tells you who is dousing the fires and what is being carried around by that person.

Grammar and Our View of Language

Since grammar is a system that puts words together into meaningful units, we will study grammar in order to analyze those units and their relationships. Analyzing sentences is called PARSING. Our goal is to understand how sentences are constructed out of words, phrases, and clauses. One of the earliest English grammar books, Robert Lowth's *A Short Introduction to English Grammar,* published in 1762, said that the purpose of English grammar was to teach us to "express ourselves with propriety" and to "judge of every phrase and form of construction whether it be right or wrong."

Many grammar texts have followed Lowth's goals—to teach students to express themselves in socially acceptable ways and to make judgments about correct and incorrect usage. Grammar books concerned with such issues of "right" and "wrong" spend a lot of time telling you that "he don't eat salads" or "between you and I" are ungrammatical because they don't meet certain standards of acceptable usage. Books that provide such prescriptive rules often include lists of errors.

Doing Grammar is not concerned with prescribing rules that will make you a "socially correct" speaker or writer. It has no list of errors. It aims to make you aware of the structure of the English language. It takes the view that grammar is the structured system that underlies our language and that the basic unit of language structure is the sentence.

For us, doing grammar means studying the structured system that is the English language. You study grammar, in this view, in order to determine how your language works, just as you study anatomy to determine how your body works.

We are primarily concerned with describing and analyzing language, with understanding how sentences are structured. Grammar is a system that puts sentences together; grammarians are analysts who take sentences apart (they parse sentences), just as botanists are scientists who take plants apart, or physicists are researchers who take atoms apart.

But grammarians don't analyze sentences just to analyze sentences, any more than botanists analyze plants just to analyze plants or physicists analyze atoms just to analyze atoms. Grammarians analyze sentences in order to understand how language works. What kind of verbs can be made passive? How can you make a sentence with an adverb of manner into a question? What's the difference between a direct object and an indirect object? Why do you have to add an extra auxiliary verb to many question sentences? These are among the questions of language structure we'll look at in this book.

After grammarians examine how sentences are constructed, we also study sentences in social, psychological, or literary contexts. In the final chapter of *Doing Grammar,* we'll explore how sentences function in literature and in our own writing so that we can become more thoughtful writers and readers, more knowledgeable teachers of writing and reading, or more discerning editors. Doing grammar in the way suggested in this book will make you a more perceptive observer of language.

My daughter Cori majored in botany in college. I'm always amazed at how much more she sees in trees and bushes and grass than I do. I see a tree, or perhaps a pine tree or an oak. That's the end of my knowledge. Cori knows things that allow her to understand the botanical world more acutely. One day we were walking the dog in a local woods, when I said, "Aren't those maples like the two in our backyard?" "No, Dad," she replied. "They're maples, okay. But we have sugar maples. These are silver maples. See how the leaves on these are different? They're serrate and a little different shape, not as broad." Cori looks at trees and bushes and grass like a botanist, thoughtfully and knowledgeably. It is her knowledge of plants that made her for some years a valuable aide to medical researchers at a botanical garden.

After you work through this book, you should be able to examine the English language in a more thoughtful and knowledgeable way, like a grammarian. Perhaps you'll see that a passive sentence you've read lacks an agent, so it isn't making as strong a connection with the reader as it might. Or you may recognize that a participial phrase in the passage you're writing may be just the structure to enhance the sense of movement you're trying to invoke.

A journalism student came into my office one day excited because she could understand that in order to emulate the "punchy" language from *Rolling Stone,* she had to write a lot of fragments. Nonrestrictive modifiers punctuated as sentences. An insight from her grammar course. She became a better reader and a better writer when she understood how writers use grammar to produce different stylistic effects. She began to see how writers craft language when they construct sentences.

Verbs and Core Sentences

To begin our study of grammar, we'll define six verb types. These six verb types establish a core of sentences that are basic to the structure of the English language. The core sentences contain fundamental components and relationships. If you learn the basic structures within core sentences and learn how to build larger, more complex sentences by rearranging constituents and combining these core sentences in various ways, you will understand how English grammar structures and organizes our language.

Verbs: The Basic Sentence Components

Verbs are basic to sentences. They determine the other constituents and define the relationships among those constituents. Verbs tell you, for instance, that certain noun phrases function as subjects and that others function as objects, predicate nouns, or object complements.

If you can identify the six types of verbs that define the core sentences, you can identify the basic structures and relationships in English sentences, no matter how long or complex those sentences become. In a sense, grammatical structures are like body parts. They have great variety but few constituents. And both DNA and grammar are constructed according to basic patterns, DNA according to the double helix, grammar according to the hierarchy. In the next chapter, we'll look at how the hierarchy underlies grammatical structures. Now, we're differentiating verbs.

You differentiate a verb type by two criteria: the constituent that follows immediately to its right and its relationship to that constituent. With the exception of an intransitive verb, which may sometimes be followed by a blank space, verbs must be followed immediately by either a noun phrase, an adjective phrase, or an adverb phrase.

Intransitive Verbs

I've already mentioned that INTRANSITIVE verbs may be followed by blank space. Unlike other verbs, intransitives don't need nouns or adjectives immediately to their right. They can end sentences, like

> The mayor **spoke**.
> The roach **died**.
> Garfield **slept**.

Spoke, died, and **slept** are intransitive because they are not followed by other words. Here are a few more verbs that are intransitive because they end sentences:

> Birds **fly**.
> The yeast **rose**.
> The window **broke**.

But intransitive verbs don't have to end sentences. They may be followed by adverbs—words and phrases that answer questions like how? where? why? when? and how often? In the sentences

> The baby panda **cried** *softly*.
> Toni Morrison **writes** *exquisitely*.

the intransitive verb **cried** is followed by the single word adverb *softly* and **writes** is followed by the adverb *exquisitely*. Both adverbs tell you how. In the next examples, the intransitive verbs **sank, jumped, disappeared, climbed,** and **erupted** are all followed by adverb phrases:

> The Titanic **sank** *in 1912*.
> The stuntman **jumped** from the third-floor balcony.
> Amelia Earhart's plane **disappeared** on a transcontinental
>   flight.
> ABC's ratings **climbed** *higher than NBC's*.
> The volcano **erupted** with the destructive force of an atomic
>   bomb.

In all the previous examples, the verbs can either end sentences or be followed by adverbs. But that's not always the case for intransitive verbs. Some intransitive verbs cannot end sentences: they must be followed by adverbs. The verb **act** in the next example is one of those intransitives.

> Cadillac's seating system **acts** *like a shock absorber.*

You can't say

> *Cadillac's seating system **acts.***

without an adverb phrase such as *like a shock absorber.* (Note: An asterisk before a phrase or sentence in this book means it is ungrammatical; the sentence cannot occur.)

To summarize, intransitive verbs may end sentences or they may be followed immediately by adverbs. Some students find it useful to write such facts into a formula like the following, where parentheses mean that a structure may or may not occur. NP means noun phrase and VI means intransitive verb.

> NP VI (Adverb)

Linking Verbs

In contrast to intransitives, LINKING VERBS cannot end sentences, nor can they be followed immediately by adverbs. They must be followed by either nouns or adjectives, one or the other; those nouns and adjectives may be single words or multiple-word phrases. In addition, linking verbs constitute a small class of probably no more than a few dozen verbs, including **seem, remain, appear, become,** and the verbs of the senses, such as **feel, look, smell, sound,** and **taste. Turned** and **stayed** can be linking verbs when they are followed by adjectives, as in

> The meeting **stayed** *productive.*
> The cheese **turned** *rancid.*

In the same way, **looks** and **tasted** are linking verbs followed by adjectives:

> The president **looks** *weary.*
> Mom's lasagna **tasted** *scrumptious.*

The linking verbs **remained** and **becomes** in the next two sentences are followed by nouns, *an honest man* and *Wonder Woman*.

Silas **remained** *an honest man.*
Diana Prince **becomes** *Wonder Woman.*

Adjectives and nouns that follow linking verbs are closely associated with their subject noun phrases. An adjective that follows a linking verb generally summarizes some characteristic of the subject noun. In the above examples, weariness is a characteristic of the president; it's why other people perceive him to be weary (he **looks** *weary*). Scrumptiousness is a characteristic of Mom's lasagna; that's why it **tasted** *scrumptious*. A noun that follows a linking verb refers to the same person or thing that a subject noun refers to. Diana Prince and *Wonder Woman* are the same person and so are Silas and *an honest man.*

Sentence constituents have both structure and function. Adjective phrases (structures) that follow linking verbs function (relate to the other sentence components) as PREDICATE ADJECTIVES. Noun phrases that follow linking verbs function as PREDICATE NOUNS.

In brief, linking verbs are followed by nouns or adjectives; the nouns function as predicate nouns, and the adjectives function as predicate adjectives. The following formula says the same thing more concisely. Curly brackets mean that one or the other structure within them must occur. Structures occur before a colon, functions after. So NP: PredN means that the noun phrase functions as a predicate noun.

$$\text{NP} \quad \text{VL} \quad \left\{ \begin{array}{l} \text{NP: PredN} \\ \text{Adj: PredAdj} \end{array} \right\}$$

Transitive Verbs

Like intransitive verbs, transitive verbs make up a huge set that contains thousands of verbs. Transitive verbs must be followed immediately in sentences by noun phrases. But unlike the noun phrases that may follow linking verbs, the nouns that follow transitives do not rename their subjects; they are usually not related to them at all. They function as DIRECT OBJECTS. Often the object of a transitive verb has something "done" to it by the subject—as in the following examples, in which the letter is typed (by the secretary), the Milk-Bone is crunched (by Jamal's Doberman), and the Medicare bill was supported (by President Johnson).

The secretary **typed** *the letter.*
Jamal's Doberman **crunched** *the Milk-Bone.*
President Johnson **supported** *the Medicare bill.*

Here is a fact about transitive verbs that can help you identify them: sentences with transitive verbs can usually be turned into passive sentences. The three examples above, for example, can all be inverted to become

The letter was **typed** by *the secretary.*
The Milk-Bone was **crunched** by *Jamal's Doberman.*
The Medicare bill was **supported** by President Johnson.

PASSIVE SENTENCES invert normal subject and object noun phrases. Here are some more examples:

Coyotes **killed**
↓
The sheep were **killed** by coyotes.

Satellites **monitor** *the Saudi pipel*
↓
The Saudi pipeline is **monitored** by satellites.

Snopes.com **dispels** *urban legends.*
↓
Urban legends are **dispelled** by snopes.com.

If a sentence can be made passive, you can be sure the verb is transitive.

To summarize, transitive verbs are followed by noun phrases that function as direct objects. Sentences with transitive verbs can almost always be inverted to form passive sentences. Here is the transitive verb formula:

NP VT NP:DObj

Two-Place Transitive Verbs

We'll look at two more transitive verb types. Both are called TWO-PLACE TRANSITIVE VERBS because they are followed by two related constituents: a noun phrase direct object and either another noun phrase, a prepositional phrase, or an adjective phrase. The first two-place transitive we'll examine is called a Vg (vee gee) verb.

Vg Verbs

Vg VERBS act like **give** in the following sentence:

> The school board **gave** the teachers *a raise.*

or like **buy** in

> Clark Gable **bought** Carole Lombard *a ranch.*

When Vg verbs are followed immediately by two noun phrases, as in the previous examples, the first noun phrase functions as an indirect object, the second as a direct object.

> The school board **gave**   the teachers   *a raise.*
>   NP:IObj   NP:DObj

> Clark Gable **bought**   Carole Lombard   *a ranch.*
>   NP:IObj   NP:DObj

INDIRECT OBJECTS receive the noun that is the direct object. In the examples, the teachers receive *a raise,* and Gable's wife, Carole Lombard, received *a ranch.* Indirect objects have one more important characteristic: with few exceptions, they can perceive as well as receive. In other words, indirect objects are almost always animate; usually they are human. Vg verbs create a business scenario, giving and receiving.

Sentences with Vg verbs have an alternate form. You can often rearrange the noun phrases in a sentence with a Vg verb, placing the indirect object in a prepositional phrase introduced by **to** or **for**.

> The school board **gave** *the teachers* a raise.
> ↓
> The school board **gave** a raise *to the teachers.*

> Clark Gable **bought** *Carole Lombard* a ranch.
> ↓
> Clark Gable **bought** a ranch *for Carole Lombard.*

Notice that the nouns in the prepositional phrases remain the receivers of the direct object nouns. Even in prepositional phrases, they are indirect objects. Vg verbs have both direct and indirect objects, whether the indirect objects precede their direct objects or follow *to* or *for* in prepositional phrases. The *to* or *for* in such prepositional phrases mark the noun phrases as receivers, as indirect objects. The prepositional phrases *to the teachers* or *for Carole Lombard* function as adverbs of reception.

In the following sentences, **fed** and **provides** are Vg verbs because they contain both direct objects (*caloric goo* and *perfect nutrition*) and indirect objects (*the rats* and *dogs*). The *to* and *for* mark the indirect objects, *the rats* and *dogs*.

> Researchers **fed** a caloric goo *to the rats.*
> Purina's Nutrient Management food **provides** perfect nutrition *for dogs.*

Not all *to* and *for* prepositional phrases occur with Vg verbs or contain indirect objects. In the following sentence, **sent** is a Vg verb because the prepositional phrase *to her husband* contains the indirect object *her husband* (*to her husband* functions as an adverb of reception).

> The florist **sent** the roses *to her husband.*

But in the next sentence,

> The florist **sent** the roses *to Cincinnati.*

To Cincinnati is a prepositional phrase that functions as an adverb of place. Unless you personify Cincinnati, making it humanlike, Cincinnati is simply a location, a city along the Ohio River. Because *to Cincinnati* functions as an adverb of place, the verb **sent** in that sentence is a VT verb, a regular transitive verb, not a Vg verb.

We'll discuss adverbs in more detail in the next chapter. For now, just remember that you determine adverb types by asking questions about them. An adverb of place answers the question *where?* Manner answers *how?* Frequency answers *how often?* And reception answers *to whom?* In the first florist sentence, *to her husband* answers *to whom;* you can also change it to

> The florist **sent** her husband the roses.

It's clearly a two-place transitive sentence. **Sent** is a Vg verb. In the second florist sentence, *to Cincinnati* answers *where?* And you cannot move *Cincinnati* into the indirect object position. In the Cincinnati sentence, **sent** is a VT verb.

Determine for yourself whether the next two examples are VT or Vg verbs.

Thomas Jefferson **left** a marvelous legacy for Americans.

The truck **delivered** the bricks to the building site.

In the first sentence, you can move *Americans* after the verb **left**. And you can ask *for whom?* of the prepositional phrase. **Left** is a Vg verb. But you must ask of the second sentence, "Where did the truck deliver the bricks?" **Delivered** is a VT verb.

Occasionally, a Vg verb will have an inanimate direct object:

The Jiffy Lube station **gave** a quick oil change to my Jeep.

I'm not suggesting that Jeeps are more animate than other cars. But you can change the sentence to

The Jiffy Lube station **gave** my Jeep a quick oil change.

And though you can't ask *to whom?* neither can you ask *where?* So *to my Jeep* isn't a place. You might grimace a bit, but Vg seems a much better answer than VT for the kind of verb **gave** is in the oil change sentence.

Let's summarize. A Vg verb is a two-place transitive that must be followed by both an indirect object and a direct object, whether the indirect object is in a *to* or *for* phrase or whether it sits next to the verb. That's what the formula says.

$$\text{NP} \quad \text{Vg} \quad \left\{ \begin{array}{ll} \text{NP: IObj} & \text{NP: DObj} \\ \text{NP: DObj} & \left\{ \begin{array}{l} \text{To} \\ \text{For} \end{array} \right\} \text{NP: IObj} \end{array} \right\}$$

Vc Verbs

The second two-place transitive verb is called Vc (vee cee). A Vc verb is followed by a direct object noun phrase, then by either another noun phrase, an adjective phrase, or an infinitive phrase. These phrases function as OBJECT COMPLEMENTS.

Vc verbs often act like the verb **consider** in

Republicans **consider** Democrats *big spenders.*
OR
Some rock fans **consider** Bob Dylan *old-fashioned.*
OR
Thomas Jefferson **considered** the Missouri Compromise to be the death of the nation.

In the first example, **consider** is followed by *Democrats,* a noun phrase functioning as a direct object, which is followed by *big spenders,* a noun phrase that functions as an object complement. In the second example, *Bob Dylan* is the direct object, and the adjective *old-fashioned* is the complement. In the third example, the noun phrase *Missouri Compromise* is the direct object; the infinitive phrase *to be the death of the nation* is the complement.

The term "complement" in grammar refers to a constituent that completes a phrase or clause. In the example above, Republicans don't just consider Democrats; they **consider** Democrats *big spenders.* Similarly, rock fans don't consider Bob Dylan; they **consider** Bob Dylan *old-fashioned.* Nor did Jefferson consider the Missouri Compromise; he **considered** it *to be the death of the nation.* These noun, adjective, and infinitive phrases in sentences with Vc verbs function as object complements because they complete the idea of the verb and follow a direct object.

The second point to help you identify complements to Vc verbs is that object complements have some of the same characteristics as the predicate nouns and predicate adjectives that follow linking verbs. Nouns that function as object complements refer to the same person or thing as their objects, just as predicate nouns refer to the same person or thing as the subjects in a sentence with a linking verb. In the examples above, *big spenders* renames *Democrats.* Adjectives that are object complements give characteristics of their direct objects. So, if some rock fans are correct, *Bob Dylan* is *old-fashioned.*

In the following examples, **think, found,** and **deem** are Vc verbs in two-place transitive sentences:

Mr. Wilson **thinks** Dennis a terror.
Princess Diana **found** the royal crown to be a prison.
Most historians **deem** Lincoln complex.

Some Vc verbs act more like **make** or **elect** than **consider.** In a sense, these verbs "create" their object complements from their objects. Here are three sentences with Vc verbs like **make:**

Sportswriters **nicknamed** Julius Erving *Dr. J.*
The sexual revolution **makes** some people *uncomfortable.*
Marx Brothers' movies **get** my dad *to laugh.*

Notice how these last three Vc verbs have a sense of making their objects into something—making Julius Erving into Dr. J., making some people uncomfortable, making my dad (to) laugh.

But Vc verbs all have three-part predicates: a verb, an object, and a complement, whether the complement is a result of the verb's action or is considered by it. Here is the formula for sentences with Vc verbs.

$$\text{NP} \quad \text{Vc} \quad \text{NP:DObj} \quad \left\{ \begin{array}{l} \text{NP:ObjComp} \\ \text{AdjPh:ObjComp} \\ \text{InfPh:ObjComjp} \end{array} \right\}$$

Two-Place Transitives as Transitives

It is important to remember that two-place transitive verbs, both Vc and Vg, are indeed transitive. They have direct objects and you can make sentences with them into passives.

Sportswriters **nicknamed** *Julius Erving* Dr. J.
↓
Julius Erving **was nicknamed** Dr. J. by sportswriters.

In fact, you can make either version of a Vg sentence into a passive.

Researchers **fed** *the rats* a caloric goo.
↓
The rats **were fed** a caloric goo by the researchers.

Researchers **fed** *a caloric goo* to the rats.
↓
A caloric goo **was fed** to the rats by the researchers.

The Verb BE

Many grammar books include the verb BE with the linking verbs because it is like the linking verbs in several ways. But for reasons that will become apparent in later chapters, it is more efficient to list BE as a separate verb category. For one thing, listing BE as a separate category simplifies many of the statements that we make about verbs. If we put BE and linking verbs into one category, we have to say some of the linking verbs can be followed by noun and adjective phrases and some can be followed by adverbs of place as well. By separating the linking verbs from BE, we simply say that linking verbs are followed by noun phrases or adjective phrases. You can move BE to the front of a sentence to make a question (Are the children happy?) You can't move **seem** or another linking verb.

The verb BE is followed by either noun phrases, adjective phrases, or adverbs of place. And it's easy to recognize the verb BE. BE has eight forms: **be, is, are, am, was, were, been, being**. Like the linking verbs, BE can be followed by noun or adjective phrases that function as PREDICATE NOUNS or PREDICATE ADJECTIVES:

> Marilyn Monroe **was** *insecure.*
> Alfred Hitchcock's "Psycho" **is** *the classic horror film.*

Unlike the linking verbs, BE may be followed immediately by an adverb of place, as in

> My mother **was** *in the next room.*
> The post office **is** *down the block.*

An adverb that follows BE is sometimes called a PREDICATE ADVERB, though we'll call it an adverb of place to be consistent with our adverb labeling practice. Grammarians often classify adjectives, nouns, and adverbs that follow BE as SUBJECT COMPLEMENTS. Remember that complements complete constructions.

Here is the formula for sentences with BE verbs:

$$ \text{NP} \quad \text{BE} \quad \begin{Bmatrix} \text{NP:PredN} \\ \text{Adj:PredAdj} \\ \text{Adv-pl:PredAdv} \end{Bmatrix} $$

Verbs and Slots and Sentence Nuclei

You can think of sentences as composed of verbs and SLOTS (positions) that are filled by structures that also have functions. Looked at in this way, a linking verb is followed by a slot that is filled by an adjective followed by a predicate adjective or a noun phrase functioning as a predicate noun. A transitive verb is followed by a noun phrase functioning as a direct object. A Vg verb is followed by two slots, and so on. Verbs are also preceded by noun phrases functioning as subjects.

A verb and its slots make up a basic sentence unit we call a SENTENCE NUCLEUS. Sometimes a sentence has only the slots that form its nucleus, as we've shown in the sentences in this chapter. But we can add adverbs and other structures to sentence nuclei. A sentence usually continues beyond its nucleus. For instance, here is a VT nucleus with several adverb structures added to it:

> Lee Harvey Oswald shot President Kennedy on November 22, 1963, from a window overlooking the Dallas motorcade route.

The sentence nucleus is **Lee Harvey Oswald shot President Kennedy**. *On November 22, 1963* is a prepositional phrase functioning as an adverb of time. *From a window overlooking the Dallas motorcade route* is a prepositional phrase functioning as an adverb of place. The nucleus of the next example is **Sally Hemings was the mother of seven of his children**. The core sentence has a BE verb; **the mother of seven of his children** is a noun phrase that functions as a predicate noun.

> Sally Hemings, a slave, Thomas Jefferson's lifelong concubine, was the mother of seven of his children.

Adding structures to a sentence nucleus does not change the relationships within the nucleus. The slots within the nucleus determine the verb type.

Verbs Change Types

One important point to remember in identifying verbs is that verbs become different types when they are in different environments. We saw that earlier with the sentence in which the florist sent the flowers to her husband or to Cincinnati. When she sent the flowers to her husband, **sent** was a Vg verb. When she sent them to Cincinnati, **sent** was a VT verb. Suppose, now, that instead of occurring in the sentence

> The president **looked** *weary*.

where it is a linking verb because it precedes an adjective, **looked** occurred in the sentence

> The president **looked** *toward the reporters*.

Then **looked** would be intransitive, because *toward the reporters* is a prepositional phrase that functions as an adverb of place. In the sentence

> Toni Morrison **writes** *exquisitely*.

the verb **writes** is intransitive, followed by an adverb of manner. In the sentence

Toni Morrison **writes** *lyrical novels.*

the verb **writes** is transitive, followed by a noun phrase object, *lyrical novels.* In the sentence

GM **makes** the *dream yours.*

makes is a Vc verb followed by a noun phrase direct object the *dream* and a noun phrase object complement *yours.* But in the sentence

GM **makes** cars and trucks.

makes is a VT verb, followed by a noun phrase direct object *cars and trucks.*

The point is that, because verbs are defined by what follows them, the same verb can become a different type in a different circumstance.

Reference Material

The six verb types presented in this chapter account for most of the verbs you'll come across in your reading, writing, and speaking, though perhaps not every one. After all, this book is an introduction to the system of English grammar. Its job is to show you how English grammar works, not to explain, as an encyclopedic reference grammar might, every verb type in the language.

So we don't build sections on semi-transitive verbs like **weigh**, **cost**, and **resemble** that can't be made passive, such as

Sumo wrestlers **weigh** a ton.
Hummers **resemble** military vehicles.

Nor do we include subsets of Vg verbs whose indirect objects fit into prepositional phrases beginning with *of,* like

The Steelers' quarterback **asked** a question *of the line judge.*

or ergative verbs that can occur as transitive or intransitive, making their transitive-form direct objects into subjects when they are intransitive:

Rover **tore** our couch.
↓
Our couch **tore**.

When you need more information, there are several good reference grammars, including some by older grammarians like Hendrik Poutsma, George O. Curme, and Otto Jespersen. The two most complete one-volume reference grammars of English are:

Rodney Huddleston, Geoffrey K. Pullum, Laurie Bauer, and others, *The Cambridge Grammar of the English Language* (New York: Cambridge University Press, 2002).

Randolph Quirk, Sidney Greenbaum, Geoffrey Leech, and Jan Svartvick, *A Comprehensive Grammar of the English Language* (New York: Longman, 1985).

And of course, there's the Web. The Internet has a lot of good information and a lot of bad. Before you Google for grammar information, find out how to differentiate good Web sites from bad Web sites and talk to your instructor about the sites you find. I discovered, for instance, a good YouTube video that introduces passive sentences (www.youtube.com/watch?v=1xTreaklNr8). I also found some YouTube clips about gerunds that would probably confuse students. Be careful!

Knowledge and Practice

Like math and science, grammar is a cumulative subject. That is, what you learn in one chapter or lesson affects what you learn in the next. You have to remember the information about verb types in Chapter 1 in order to navigate through the lessons on analyzing sentences in Chapter 2. And you need the information you acquire in Chapters 1 and 2 to make it through Chapter 3, and so on. To understand Chapter 10, you'll have to understand the information in the previous nine chapters.

So learning the information in this text is important, very important. But knowing information alone won't make you proficient. You'll need to do more than read the chapters and memorize patterns and definitions in order to master grammatical analysis. If you know the old joke about the Midwestern tourist who gets lost in Manhattan and stops an old woman to ask for directions to Carnegie Hall, you know what more you need to do. Here's the joke, for those who aren't familiar with it.

"How do you get to Carnegie Hall?" asks the Midwesterner. The old woman looks sternly at the young man, shakes her umbrella in his direction, and says, "Young man, you have to Practice! Practice! Practice!"

Like many old jokes, this one teaches an important lesson. Practice will make you proficient at grammatical analysis as well as get you to Carnegie Hall. To encourage you to "get to Carnegie Hall" grammatically, each chapter in this book has lots of exercises for you to test your knowledge and try out your new skills. So—Practice! Practice! Practice! Knowledge and practice together are the essence of doing grammar.

Verbs and Slots

Knowing the six core verbs gives you a solid beginning for learning how to identify all the parts of a sentence nucleus. If you can identify the type of verb, you know the slot or slots that follow it. If you know, for instance, that **remains** is a linking verb in the sentence

Dracula **remains** a popular literary character.

then you know that the phrase *a popular literary character* must be either an adjective phrase or a noun phrase. Those are the only two structures that can immediately follow a linking verb. Since *Dracula* and *a popular literary character* refer to the same person, you know *a popular literary character* is a noun phrase functioning as a predicate noun.

If you can identify the structure and function of the words in the slots following a verb, you know the kind of verb. For instance, in the sentence

Billy Joel **sang** "The Star-Spangled Banner."

the phrase "*The Star-Spangled Banner*" is a noun phrase; thus the verb **sang** must be a transitive verb, a linking verb, or a form of BE. Only those three verbs can precede a single noun phrase. Obviously, **sang** isn't a form of BE. Since Billy Joel and "*The Star-Spangled Banner*" don't refer to the same person or thing, **sang** can't be a linking verb. By process of elimination, it must be transitive. If you want more evidence, turn the sentence into a passive:

The "*Star-Spangled Banner*" **was sung** by Billy Joel.

Understanding the six core verbs allows you to identify all the parts of a sentence nucleus.

Chapter Summary: The Six Verb Types

- Grammar is a system that puts words together into meaningful units.
- The way we define grammar shapes our view of language.
- This chapter identifies six core verbs—intransitive, linking, VT, Vg, Vc, and BE.
- Intransitive verbs can end sentences or be followed by adverbs
- Linking verbs must be followed by either noun phrases that function as predicate nouns or adjective phrases that function as predicate adjectives.
- Transitive verbs are followed by noun phrases that function as direct objects.
- Vg verbs are two-place transitives followed by both direct and indirect objects.
- Indirect objects can follow the verb immediately or be part of a *to* or *for* prepositional phrase. They typically receive and perceive.
- Vc verbs are two-place transitives followed by direct objects and object complements—either noun phrases, adjective phrases, or infinitive phrases that complete the meaning of the verb.
- Two-place transitive verbs are indeed transitive.
- The verb BE is followed by an adjective phrase, a noun phrase, or an adverb of place.
- The verbs and slots defined in this chapter identify sentence nuclei.
- Sentence nuclei constitute the building blocks of language.
- A verb is identified by the constituent that follows it and the relationship between the verb and the constituent.
- The same words can become different verb types in different environments.
- A large reference grammar would include more verb types.
- Knowledge and practice together are the essence of doing grammar.
- If you can identify the verb in a core sentence, you know what slot or slots must follow it; if you can identify the slot(s), you know the core verb.

EXERCISES

I. Identifying Verb Types

Each of the following sentences is a nucleus of a core sentence. Identify the verbs in these sentences, and label the slots that accompany them. Explain how you decided that a verb is intransitive, linking, transitive, Vg, Vc, or a form of BE.

EXAMPLE
The referee awarded the Dolphins the touchdown.

Explanation: In this sentence, I'm sure **awarded** is a two-place transitive Vg verb. For one thing, it is followed by two noun phrases, *the Dolphins* and *the touchdown*. Since the Dolphins can both perceive and receive the direct object (the touchdown), the Dolphins must be the indirect object. I am even more sure because I can move the Dolphins into a prepositional phrase to the Dolphins:

The referee awarded the touchdown to the Dolphins.

Sentences

1. Seat belts save lives.
2. Bungee jumping is a dangerous sport.
3. Disney World offers visitors family entertainment.
4. Roosevelt named Eisenhower Supreme Allied Commander.
5. The soccer fans grew rowdy.
6. Spreadsheets make business analysis easy.
7. The president's dog jumped into the ambassador's lap.
8. Yellowstone is a national treasure.
9. Alcoholism shatters dreams.
10. Geese rose from the marsh.
11. The city council bought SUVs for the police department.
12. Business colleges prepare students to be entrepreneurs.
13. The cocaine supply seems limitless.
14. Katrina destroyed New Orleans.
15. Alaska remains a wilderness.
16. The Internet makes everyone equal.
17. Several Vietnamese dishes are on the menu.
18. Florida executed Theodore Bundy.
19. Young readers find J. K. Rowling a great writer.

20. Michael Phelps won Olympic accolades.
21. Psychologist Stanley Coren calls border collies the smartest dogs.
22. Savings accounts provide investors security.
23. Muhammad Ali walked through the mall.
24. God rested on the seventh day.
25. Teenage drug addiction remains grim.
26. The Dodgers sprinted to their locker room.
27. Some rebellious teens become runaways.
28. Beagle pups are noisy.
29. Rattlesnakes scare most people.
30. A glade is a forest clearing.
31. Many American schools are overcrowded.
32. The Cordillera Sarmiento Mountains are in Chile.
33. Kids enjoy *The Simpson*'s humor.
34. A German submarine sank the *Lusitania*.
35. The *Lusitania* lies in 295 feet of water.
36. War breeds technological innovation.
37. A brilliant moon painted the iceberg a fuchsia pink.
38. Libertarians oppose big government.
39. A steel band's sound is hypnotic.
40. Oedipus became a patricide.
41. School resumes Monday.
42. Lincoln signed the Emancipation Proclamation.
43. Rachel Maddow found Oprah an interesting guest.
44. The doorman found Oprah a cab.
45. The *Titanic*'s captain was uninformed.
46. Crack changed the drug scene.
47. Paul Newman died at 83.
48. Racism remains inexplicable.
49. Racism remains in our society.
50. Autism is a mystery.

CHAPTER 2

Relating Words, Phrases, and Slots

Parts of Speech

The ultimate constituents of sentences are words, individual words that merge into larger and larger constituents. To understand how to analyze sentences, you need a basic understanding of word categories. These categories, called PARTS OF SPEECH, are nouns, verbs, adjectives, adverbs, pronouns, prepositions, auxiliaries, determiners, and conjunctions. In this chapter, we'll define nouns, verbs, adjectives, adverbs, and prepositions. Then we'll look at how these constructions fill phrase slots within sentences.

Nouns, verbs, adjectives, and adverbs are content words. CONTENT WORDS refer to actions, objects, and ideas in the everyday world. Determiners, auxiliaries, pronouns, and conjunctions are function words. FUNCTION WORDS generally refer to concepts within the grammatical text; they express grammatical features like mood, definiteness, and pronoun reference. Or, they facilitate grammatical processes like rearrangement, compounding, and embedding.

Prepositions have characteristics both of content words and of function words, though we consider them as function words.

Perhaps the most obvious difference between content words and function words is that content words are OPEN CLASSES and function words are CLOSED CLASSES. You can make up new open-class words— nouns, verbs, adjectives, and adverbs—as Lewis Carroll did in his poem

"Jabberwocky." Here's one stanza from the poem, with the content words boldfaced:

> 'Twas **brillig** and the **slithy toves**
> Did **gyre** and **gimble** in the **wabe**;
> All **mimsy** were the **borogoves,**
> And the **mome raths outgrabe.**

Notice how Caroll used common English pronouns (**it**), articles (**the**), conjunctions (**and**), and prepositions (**in**). But he created verbs like **gyre** and **gimble**, nouns like **wabe** and **tove**, and adjectives like **brillig** and **slithy**. He was so good at it that we seem to understand these words. Surely a **tove** must be some sort of animal, don't you think? After all, it can **gyre** and **gimble**.

In many grammar books, the content words are defined strictly by meaning. Nouns, for instance, are said to name people, places, or things, while verbs supposedly define actions, existence, or occurrence. While there's a certain truth to such definitions, explanations of their meanings won't always help you identify nouns, verbs, adjectives, and adverbs. To those semantic definitions, we'll add definitions related to the forms of words, and we'll consider their distribution—where they occur in relation to other words and phrases.

What Nouns Do

Let's take a look at nouns first. If we limit our definition of NOUNS to those words which name people, places, or things, we quickly run into problems. A **chair** is a thing; the **president** is a person; the **university** is a place. The definition works fine with those words. But what about the nouns **rain** or **fight**? Rain is both a thing and an action. According to *The American Heritage Dictionary* on my computer, **rain** is "water condensed from atmospheric vapor and falling in drops." A **fight**, too, is as much an action or an occurrence as a thing. One definition my dictionary gives for **fight** is "to wage or carry on (a battle)." Are **fight** and **rain** verbs because they refer to actions? No. They're nouns. There are lots of nouns that objectify actions or events. We also have trouble using people, places, or things to define abstract nouns like **liberty**, **sobriety**, or **truthfulness**. In short, the semantic definition of nouns as people, places, or things is limited. It isn't how we know a **wabe** is a noun. We know it because of grammatical clues in the text—where the word occurs and what form it takes.

To get a more complete sense of nouns, let's look at their distribution, where they occur. Notice that **rain** and **fight** can both follow determiners like *the, a(n), his, our, her, this,* or *that: the* **rain**, *a* **fight**. **Truthfulness, liberty,** or **sobriety** can follow determiners as well (*his* **truthfulness,** *our* **liberty,** *her* **sobriety**). **Chair, president,** and **university** can also follow determiners (*this* **chair,** *the* **president,** *that* **university**). It turns out that defining nouns as those words that follow determiners gives you more scope than trying to contain the category within a small set of meanings. Whatever **wabe** means, it follows *the*. That fact alone identifies it as a noun. Determiners not only identify nouns, they can make words (whether real or made-up) into nouns. For instance, **red** and **experienced** are normally adjectives. But place *the* in front of them and the adjectives become nouns.

> Mom prefers *the* **red**.
> *The* **experienced** make better administrators.

Besides defining nouns by how they pattern with determiners, we can find clues to their nounness in their form. With a small number of exceptions like **deer, fish, child, alumnus,** and **octopus,** nouns that you can count are made plural by adding **-s** or **-es**:

> flag → flags
> beach → beaches
> accordion → accordions

You know Lewis Carroll was talking about more than one **borogrove** because the word occurs as **borogroves,** with a plural **-s** ending.

If you use all three definitions—meaning, distribution, and form—you should be able to identify any noun you encounter. The same is true for verbs, adjectives, and adverbs; you can get closer to a full definition of these content categories if you define them in grammatical terms as well as by their meaning. Let's take a look at verbs next.

Verbs, Modal Auxiliaries, and Tense

VERBS generally express action, as in

> The sniper **killed** the terrorist.

or a state of being, like

> The president **is** in Alaska.

This definition of their meaning identifies a lot of verbs, but not all. Action or state of being doesn't seem to characterize **underwent** in

> The Marlins' pitcher **underwent** surgery.

Nor does it characterize **sleep** or **hear**. So let's look at the distribution of verbs and their forms to get more ways of identifying them.

Verbs can follow modal auxiliaries like **can** or **would**.

can hear	**would** cherish
can undergo	**would** vegetate
can dream	**would** seem
can scan	**would** languish
can be	**would** write

Putting words after **can** or **would** is a good way to identify them as verbs. Another way is to remember that verbs can be made into past and present tense forms:

comb → **combed** → **comb(s)**
sit → **sat** → **sit(s)**
drive → **drove** → **drive(s)**

Verbs, then, not only show action or state of being but also follow modals and have past and present tense forms.

Adjectives and Noun Characteristics

ADJECTIVES often limit, qualify, or specify characteristics of nouns, as in a **small** chair, the **tardy** girl, a **beige** paint. Or they function as predicate adjectives or object complements. Most adjectives are gradable; that means you can put them on a scale from less to more. If you can grade an adjective, you can add a comparative -**er** suffix and a superlative -**est** suffix to it; you can introduce it with *more* or *most;* or you can intensify it with an intensifying adverb (an INTENSIFIER) like *very, pretty, awfully,* or *incredibly:*

> bright, brighter, brightest, very bright
> grungy, grungier, grungiest, awfully grungy
> nervous, more nervous, most nervous, incredibly nervous

In terms of distribution, most adjectives can follow the verb **seem**:

> The tangerine **seems** *ripe.*
> The disk **seems** *fragmented.*
> The football scores **seem** *lopsided.*

Typically, you use intensifiers to amplify the impact of adjectives.

> The condom issue turned *damned* **nasty.**
> The jury seemed *incredibly* **bored.**

Adjectives occur in different forms, can modify nouns in several ways, are usually gradable, can often follow **seem**, and can themselves be modified by intensifiers.

Adverbs Orient Readers and Listeners

Probably the most difficult category to pin down, ADVERBS often modify verbs. You can expand any sentence by adding adverbs to the nucleus. Adding adverbs does not change the verb type or the relationships within the nucleus. Here are an adverb, adverb phrases, and an adverb clause added to various verb types:

> The baby cried **loudly.** (Adverb)
> The Soviet Union remained our enemy **throughout the cold war.** (Phrase)
> The robotic plane is pterodactyl-shaped **for agility.** (Phrase)
> The new outfielder hit two homers **to prove his value.** (Phrase)
> L.L. Bean sent the package to Mom **by mistake.** (Phrase)
> The senator called the president foolish **when the White House proposed the trade agreement.** (Clause)

Often you can add two, three, or even more adverbs to the nucleus of a sentence:

> L.L. Bean sent the package to Mom **[in Tucson] [by mistake].**

> The new outfielder hit two homers **[into the red seats] [before the seventh inning] [to prove his value].**

Among other things, adverbs tell you how, when, where, why, through what means, to what extent, how often, how far, and under what condition. By giving you such information, adverbs specify relationships and help orient readers and listeners to what is going on in a sentence. "Orient" is the important word here. Adverbs put the content of a sentence into the proper context, like time, place, manner, reason, condition, and extent. That's the sense in which they orient readers and listeners: adverbs tell them such things as where, through what means, how far, how often, why, and when.

Though what they do is straightforward, adverbs are difficult to pin down. In his book on the relationship of linguistics to school grammar texts, Brock Haussamen calls adverbs "one of the most complex and slippery categories in all of grammar." Haussamen continues that the important point to convey to students is "the great range of descriptive possibilities that the adverb provides." Adverbs are complex and slippery. You should remember that they put the content of a sentence into the proper context.

Now let's look at some of the ideas adverbs can convey and the variety of forms they can assume. (Don't worry about all the forms yet; you won't have to identify infinitive phrases or adverb clauses, for instance, until several chapters down the road.) Take a look at the example sentences above. In the first sentence, **loudly** is an adverb of manner; it's a single word that tells how. In the second, **throughout the Cold War** is an adverb of duration; it is a prepositional phrase that tells for how long. **To prove his value** is an adverb of reason (or purpose); it's an infinitive phrase that explains why. **By mistake** is an adverb of cause; it's a prepositional phrase that tells the motive (or cause). And **when the White House proposed the trade agreement** is an adverb of time; it's a clause that tells when. There are also adverbs of instrument (The carpenter hit the nail **with a hammer**), means (The firefighter reached the second floor **by the stairs**), agency (The tree was trimmed **by the gardener**), association (The senator votes **with the Democrats**), frequency (Ara types those reports **all day**), condition (The health care bill would go nowhere **without the Surgeon General's help)**, and extent (DiMaggio hit the ball **as far as possible**). These are the most common adverb relationships, but they don't exhaust all the possibilities.

Adverbs are difficult to define and sometimes difficult to identify. They are difficult to define because they show so many different kinds of relationships; they are difficult to identify because they are "realized" by so many different kinds of structures. Here are some examples of the kinds of structures you will most frequently find as adverbs. We commonly make adverbs out of adjectives by adding -ly:

loud → loudly
bright → brightly
frequent → frequently
quick → quickly
hasty → hastily

We sometimes use nouns and noun phrases as adverbs:

last summer
the day before yesterday
Tuesday

We often use prepositional phrases as adverbs:

in the middle
by the bridge
with the British
because of his disability
during the game

We use whole clauses as adverbs:

because the terrorist refused to surrender
after the attorney general accepted blame
although the plumber guaranteed his work
in case it rains
if the Republicans continue to filibuster

And we use other structures as adverbs as well, structures like participles, absolute phrases, and infinitives. We'll talk about these in later chapters. Try not to let all this confuse you. There are lots of different structures that can function as adverbs, and there are lots of different kinds of adverb relationships. While it is true that adverbs can be daunting, it is also true that most of the time they're simple and straightforward. By far the greatest number of adverbs deal with manner, place, time, reason, frequency, and extent. As you work through the book, you'll discover how adverbs fit into the overall grammatical picture.

Prepositions Precede Noun Phrases

You may have learned in elementary school that PREPOSITIONS show what a flying airplane can do to a cloud: the plane can fly **through** the cloud, **into** the cloud, **over** the cloud, **under** the cloud, **around** the cloud, **toward** the cloud, or **by** the cloud. Actually, prepositions are much more diverse than the airplane/cloud mnemonic device suggests. Among other things, they tell us when (**after** the dance), how long (**for** the summer), why (**because of** the stock market collapse), how (**like** a sailor), or what condition (**despite** his ability). Prepositions are usually one word, like **out**, **on**, or **with**. But they can sometimes be two or more words, like **except for, together with, as for, with regard to, in spite of,** or **in lieu of**. There are about 100 single-word prepositions and 60 complex prepositions.

Prepositions never appear alone. As their name implies, prepositions are **pre**-positions. They precede the noun phrases with which they form constituents. A noun phrase that follows a preposition functions as an OBJECT OF A PREPOSITION; sometimes objects of prepositions are called OBLIQUE OBJECTS, to differentiate them from objects of verbs, which are direct objects. A preposition, along with its noun phrase object, constitutes a PREPOSITIONAL PHRASE. Prepositional phrases often function as adverbs. Here is a sentence with a prepositional phrase (**through the Danish Straits**) that functions as an adverb of place:

> The patrol boat followed the submarine **through the Danish straits**.

And here is a sentence with a prepositional phrase (**from the coal smoke**) that functions as an adverb indicating a cause.

> My eyes stung **from the coal smoke**.

Prepositions are function words, but they have some characteristics of content words. Prepositions refer to real-world concepts like direction (*up* the staircase, *around* the block); they also stand for grammatical properties like genitive case (the head *of* the class). But they are a closed class: you cannot create new prepositions.

Words and Grammar

Words alone or in dictionary lists or crossword puzzles can amuse and intrigue you. But they can't add up to much unless they're put together into grammatical units, as Shakespeare illustrated in *Hamlet*. When he wants to appear mad to members of the court, Hamlet enters the stage reading a book. Polonius asks what Hamlet is reading, and the melancholy prince replies, "Words, words, words."

Hamlet's answer makes it seem as if the words come from the page free of grammar, the system that builds them into meaningful units. How better to appear insane than to read words without understanding the system that holds them together? The words become a swarm of objects flying at you every which way. Words without grammar would be odd indeed. We never read, write, speak, or hear words that explode before us like lava from a volcano. Because words merge with one another into phrases and clauses, in organized, systematic ways, we can take phrases and clauses apart in order to study the system of grammar.

Grammatical Slots Identify Phrases

In the first chapter, we referred to noun phrases and verb phrases and adjective phrases as the constituents that we have to identify along with verbs. Why not refer simply to individual words, not phrases, when we're doing grammatical analysis?

To answer that question, let's look at the relationship between nouns and pronouns. Pronouns refer to nouns. The pronouns **he** and **they** in the following sentences refer to the nouns *Truman* and *dolphins* in the sentences that precede them.

> Truman won the presidential election in 1948. Despite criticism from much of the press at the time, **he** has become one of the most honored presidents of the twentieth century.
> Dolphins are intelligent creatures. **They** communicate with each other and even with their human keepers.

In these sentences, pronouns refer to single-word nouns. But take a look at the next sentences.

> The Cincinnati Bengals lost more games than they won in 1999. **They** lacked a take-charge quarterback and an effective offensive line.
> You add a bit of the bayou to your menu when you serve this tongue-tingling seafood gumbo. Prepare **it** with shrimp, crabmeat, okra, and Cajun spices.

In these sentences, the pronouns **they** and **it** refer not to single-word nouns but to whole phrases, **the Cincinnati Bengals** and **this tongue-tingling seafood gumbo**. In brief, a single-word noun or pronoun can fill the same grammatical space as a multiple-word noun phrase. This same phenomenon is true for adjectives, verbs, and adverbs: single words can all fill the same grammatical spaces as larger phrases. Thus, we refer to all noun, verb, adjective, and adverb constituents within sentences as phrases, whether they're single words or much longer strings of words. In fact, it's the spaces that these phrases fill—the grammatical slots within sentence nuclei—that are important for identifying verb types. And it is slots—spaces filled by single words or phrases—that are important in grammatical analysis. That is, it doesn't matter whether a noun (or verb or adjective or adverb) phrase slot is filled by one word or by one hundred. What matters is that a slot is filled by a constituent that can legitimately fill that slot.

Slots in effect "make" constituents what they are. Gerunds in Chapter 8, for instance, are -**ing** verbs that fill noun phrase slots. Hence, they are verbs that have become nouns, and these verbal nouns function as subjects, direct objects, or objects of prepositions, exactly as any other noun can function. We know that a prepositional phrase functions as an adverb when it fills the slot after an intransitive verb,

The abolitionist movement emerged **in the 1830s**.

But we'll see in Chapter 7 that, when it fills a slot within a noun phrase, a prepositional phrase functions as an adjective:

Political movements **in the 1830s** anticipated the Civil War.

The Hierarchy

The large constituents like clauses (sentences are INDEPENDENT CLAUSES, clauses that can stand alone), noun phrases, and verb phrases break down into smaller constituents. This fact—that larger constituents contain smaller constituents—points to the major structural pattern of language: the hierarchy. A HIERARCHY is a pattern in which structures fit within structures. Hierarchies define the basic structural principle of clauses and phrases.

You can liken this hierarchical system of language to the nested dolls you might have played with as a child. When you opened one doll, there was a smaller, exact duplicate within it, and so on until you reached the last one. That's the way with sentences. No matter how large or complicated they become, if you take them apart one piece at a time, you'll find familiar constituents fitting inside one another. It sounds complicated, but when you understand this basic structural principle of language, you are able to do any kind of grammatical analysis.

Constituents as Hierarchies

Words merge into phrases that merge into larger phrases and clauses. Let's look at how the merging works to fit parts within parts as hierarchies. In the sentence

 Citizen Kane is the best American movie.

the adjective **American** and the noun **movie** merge to make the noun phrase **American movie**.

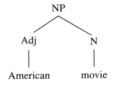

Then the adjective **best** merges with **American movie** to make a larger noun phrase **best American Movie**.

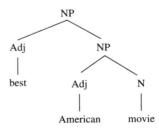

The merges with **best American movie** to complete the noun phrase **the best American movie**.

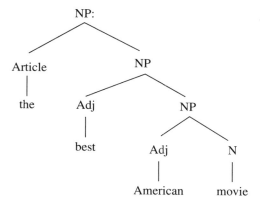

That noun phrase constituent merges with the verb **is** to form a verb phrase constituent **is the best American movie**. Since it follows a BE verb, the noun phrase functions as a predicate noun.

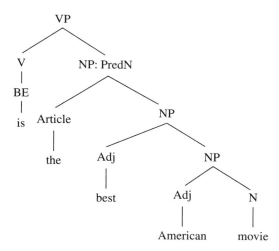

Finally, **is the best American movie** merges with the noun phrase *Citizen Kane* to complete the sentence *Citizen Kane* **is the best American movie.**

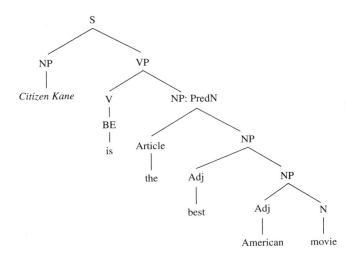

No matter how complicated the sentence, the principle of words and phrases merging into larger phrases and clauses still holds true. Grammar is a system that builds constituents as hierarchies.

Grammatical Analysis and Chicken Parts

Noun phrases that function as subjects and verb phrases that function as predicates are the two main constituents of sentences. A CONSTITUENT is an individual word or a group of words that fill a single slot. Whether one word, a phrase several words long, or a clause dozens of words long, the parts of a constituent form one unit.

Since sentences are composed of constituents, grammatical analysis is a little like cutting a chicken into parts. If you do it correctly, each part will be a recognizable component—a wing, a breast, a thigh, a leg.

The chicken metaphor points to the essence of the issue. Some years ago, a popular food chain ran a TV commercial that showed customers of another chicken restaurant dismayed when they looked into their buckets and found unrecognizable parts counted as complete pieces of chicken—legs cut in two, for instance. When they questioned the clerk, he replied brashly, "pieces is pieces." When the scene switched to the popular restaurant chain, the customers happily looked into their buckets to find parts they recognized as proper constituents of chickens—complete legs, thighs, breasts, and wings.

Like the happy customers, you'll find only recognizable constituents when you do grammatical analysis—nouns, verbs, adjectives, and adverbs. No strange-looking parts cut in half. However long or short, grammatical constituents will always be complete parts. In grammatical analysis, as in chicken cutting, it's not true that "pieces is pieces." Pieces are constituents—recognizable units. Constituency is the most important issue in grammatical analysis. You have to understand which words work together as units before you can establish relationships among the units.

Heads and Attributes

When words build into phrases, those constituents break down into heads and attributes. ATTRIBUTES "cluster around" or "aggregate around" heads. The HEAD of a phrase constituent is central to the phase. It is always a word that the constituent structure is named for: the head of a noun phrase is a noun; the head of a verb phrase is a verb; the head of an adjective phrase is an adjective; the head of a prepositional phrase is a preposition. You get the picture. In the *Citizen Kane* sentence, the head of the noun phrase **the best American movie** is the noun **movie**. The attributes **American, best,** and **the** all cluster around the noun **movie** in constituents within constituents. The verb **is** heads the verb phrase **is the best American movie.**

Basic Sentence Structure

A sentence (an independent clause) is composed of two main constituents: a noun phrase that functions as a subject and a verb phrase that functions as a predicate. A SUBJECT generally defines a topic, and a PREDICATE generally makes a comment about the topic. A subject occurs before a predicate.

To analyze sentences, you identify sentence components both by the class they fall into (their STRUCTURE) and by how they relate to one another (their FUNCTION). It is important to differentiate structures from functions. Here are examples of the six core sentence types, with slashes separating subjects from predicates. Notice that when we analyze sentences, we label components by both their structure (before the colon) and their function (after the colon), as in NP:Subj and VP: Pred. VP means verb phrase.

Small businesses / thrive in French towns.
NP:Subj   VP:Pred
The Internet / became a porno district.
NP:Subj   VP:Pred
Native Americans / used echinacea for medicinal purposes.
NP:Sub   VP:Pred
The students / handed the teacher their quizzes.
NP:Subj   VP:Pred
Early colonists / considered tomatoes toxic.
NP:Subj   VP:Pred
The Hawaiian Islands / are coral atolls.
NP:Subj   VP:Pred

The Yes/No Question Test

Before we go any further, let's look at one method that many students find helpful for identifying subjects and predicates. This method is based on two facts about sentences. The first fact is that most sentences make statements, like

The president **will** visit Moscow in June.
American priorities **have** changed since the collapse of the
     Soviet Union.
The researchers who discovered the oncogene **are** working on a
     new cancer drug.

The second fact is that you can change any statement into a yes/no question, as in the following:

The president **will** visit Moscow in June.
Will the **president visit Moscow** in June?
American priorities have changed since the collapse of the
     Soviet Union.
Have American priorities changed since the collapse of the
     Soviet Union?
The researchers who discovered the oncogene **are** working on
     a new cancer drug.
Are the researchers who discovered the oncogene working on a
     new cancer drug?

To make a sentence into a yes/no question, you can move an auxiliary verb like **will**, **have**, or **are** to the front of the sentence. Auxiliary verbs signal the beginning of the predicate. The subject is the word or phrase that you move them around in order to form a question. So the above examples break into subjects and predicates in the following way:

Predicate	Subject
visit Moscow in June.	The president
changed since the collapse of the Soviet Union.	American priorities
working on a new drug for cancer.	The researchers who discovered the oncogene

If the predicate begins with a verb rather than an auxiliary word like **will**, **have**, or **are**, then you make a yes/no question by putting **do**, **did**, or **does** at the beginning of the sentence:

Harriet's mother works at Wal-Mart.
↓
Does Harriet's mother work at Wal-Mart?

With **do**, **did**, or **does**, you can test for subjects and predicates by going in the other direction. Move the **do**, **does**, or **did** in order to make the sentence an emphatic statement:

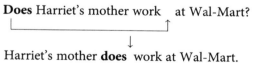

Harriet's mother **does** work at Wal-Mart.

The subject is the phrase you move the do-word around; the predicate begins at the verb you move the do-word next to. In the example, **Harriet's mother** is the subject of the original statement; **works at Wal-Mart** is the predicate.

This yes/no question test to find subjects and predicates is almost foolproof, whether you're working with short simple sentences or long complex sentences.

Tree Diagrams

Some people find it helpful when they're doing grammatical analysis to show the constituents and their relationships visually, as diagrams. There are several ways to diagram sentences. The type we used to build the *Citizen Kane* sentence is called a TREE DIAGRAM because it shows constituents "branching off" from one another. Tree diagrams clearly illustrate the structure of constituents and how constituents relate to one another as hierarchies.

The following tree diagrams show the six core sentences diagramed to reflect the constituents and functions we've discussed so far.

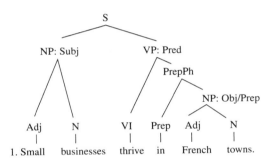

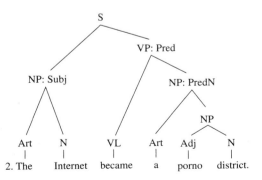

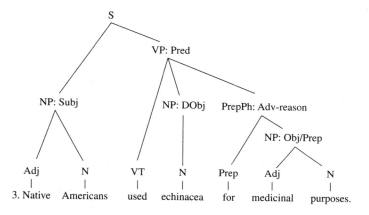

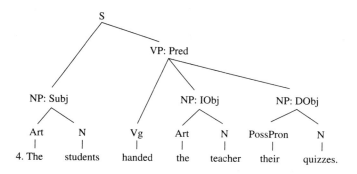

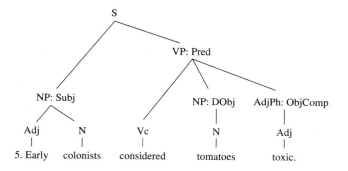

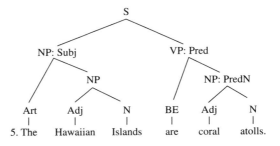

S

NP: Subj   VP: Pred

NP   NP: PredN

Art   Adj   N   BE   Adj   N
| | | | | |
5. The   Hawaiian Islands are   coral   atolls.

Diagrams as Tools

You can show the same information by enclosing constituents in LABELED BRACKETS, one inside the other.

[[Native] [Americans]] [[used] [echinacea] [[for] [[medicinal] [purposes.]]]]
   Adj   N   VT   N   Prep   Adj   N
NP:Subj   NP:DObj   NP:Obj/Prep
                                                   PrepPh:Adv-reason
                    VP:Pred

You can draw TRADITIONAL DIAGRAMS (often called Reed-Kellogg diagrams), with lines going off in all directions.

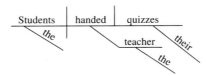

Among the problems associated with these traditional diagrams is that they neither show hierarchies nor label major phrase constituents as structures or functions—major weaknesses, indeed.

Or you can draw diagrams as I do in the appendix by naming constituents and drawing lines around them.

The   Internet   became   a   porno   district.
Art   N   VL   Art   Adj   N
—NP: Subj—   ——NP——
                          —NP: PredN—
                        ———VP: Pred———

These show hierarchies (upside down) and label constituents. They're also relatively easy to construct in a computer writing program.

How often you diagram, what kind of diagrams you use, and how detailed you make your diagrams depend on how helpful you find diagraming. Because they capture the relationships between constituents and reflect hierarchies in the structure of constituents, I often use tree diagrams in this book to illustrate how to analyze sentences. You have to keep in mind that we're working with fairly simple sentence structures in these first few chapters. Any diagraming system works to some extent with such sentences. When sentences become long and complicated, particularly with disjoined constituents, any diagraming system becomes too tangled to give you much help.

I had a poster in my office at Miami University that diagrams a 958-word stretch of text from French author Marcel Proust's *Cities of the Plain*. The label on the poster claims it is "the longest sentence." The poster is wrong; the 958 words from Proust do not make "the longest sentence." It's not the longest sentence anyone has written; nor is it the longest sentence anyone could write. But that's another issue.

The issue we're concerned with is the usefulness of the diagram. It isn't very useful, but it was much admired. The traditional diagram that outlines Proust's "sentence," with lines going off every which way to fill the 3' x 5' poster, was marveled at by almost everyone who came into my office for the first time. "Wonderful," some would say, or, "I wish I could do that." They were wrong to have valued the diagram so much. It didn't help the diagramer understand that he or she was diagraming a long fragment, though the diagramer did know when to draw lines horizontally, when to draw them vertically, when to draw whole lines, and when to draw dotted lines. The diagram on the poster has so many lines coming off it in so many different ways that it wasis useless as a visual aid. The monster diagram is what it is: an interesting conversation piece in a grammarian's office. It was useless for any other purpose that I could ever figure out. It certainly wouldn't help anyone to understand the structure of the Proust "sentence." The diagram is complicated and intimidating.

The point to remember about diagraming is simple: if it helps you to visualize the structure and function of constituents, use diagrams. But don't get too caught up in them. No diagraming system will help when sentences become much more involved than those we're analyzing in these first few chapters of this book. And diagraming is neither a virtue nor a central goal of grammatical analysis. Diagraming is at best a tool that can sometimes help you visualize constituents and their relationships. Diagrams are tools, not goals.

The goal of grammatical analysis is to recognize constituents, hierarchies, and relationships. That's how we understand sentences. So it shouldn't be a surprise that parsing sentences has become a useful tool for the CIA and large corporations. Such parsing allows the CIA to identify and track potential terrorists. The intelligence services collect enormous amounts of electronic data, and they analyze that data by parsing it into grammatical units and looking for nouns, verbs, adjectives, and adverbs that mention issues of interest The corporations look for business-related issues in their calls and online messages. Finding individual words isn't enough, as Hamlet and my graduate student friend Joe Smith realized. Real understanding demands parsing the words into proper grammatical units—clauses and phrases that relate to one another in hierarchies.

Multiple-Word Verbs

When we looked at verbs in the last chapter, we recognized only one-word verbs. Now that we've explained constituency, we can see that two or more words often work together as a single verb constituent. In the following sentences, for instance, the two-word phrases **took on** and **bawled out** function as single constituents; they are two-word transitive verbs.

> Franklin Roosevelt **took on** the presidency in 1933.
> The D.I. **bawled out** the recruit.

To test whether **took on** and **bawled out** are transitive verbs, you can make the sentences passive, moving the subject noun phrases into **by**-phrases and the object noun phrases into the first position:

> Franklin Roosevelt **took on** the presidency in 1933.
> ↓
> The presidency **was taken on** *by Franklin Roosevelt* in 1933.

> The D.I. **bawled out** the recruit.
> ↓
> The recruit **was bawled out** *by the D.I.*

When multiple-word verbs are transitive, you can often move the VERB PARTICLE—the words like **up**, **down**, and **out** that form constituents with the verbs—around the object noun phrase.

> Conan O'Brien **pulled off** the scam.
>
> ↓
>
> Conan O'Brien **pulled** the scam **off**.
>
> The librarian **looked up** the author in *Who's Who*.
>
> ↓
>
> The librarian **looked** the author **up** in *Who's Who*.

In fact, if the object of a multiple-word transitive verb is a pronoun, the particle must occur after it.

> Conan O'Brien **pulled** it **off**.
> The librarian **looked** it **up** in *Who's Who*.

You can't say

> *Conan O'Brien **pulled off** it.
> *The librarian **looked up** it in *Who's Who*.

Multiple-word verbs are not always transitive; they can be intransitive as well. In the next examples, **blew up**, **played around**, and **broke down** are intransitive verbs.

> The silo **blew up**.
> John Kennedy **played around** before his marriage.
> The defendant **broke down** after the verdict.

Verb particles are often confused with prepositions. They differ from prepositions, though, because they make constituents with verbs, not with noun phrases. Notice the difference between the following two sentences.

> The senator **called up** the president.
> The senator **called** up the stairs.

To begin with, when you read them aloud, you say them differently because of their different constituency. In the first, you pause slightly before the noun phrase **the president**. In the second, you pause before **up**. That's because **up the stairs** makes a single constituent in the second sentence; it is a prepositional phrase that functions as an adverb of place. **Up the stairs** answers the question "where did the senator call?" So **call** is an intransitive verb followed by an adverb of place. And **up** is a preposition, forming a constituent with the noun phrase **the stairs**. In the first sentence, **call up** is a single constituent, a two-word transitive verb followed by a noun phrase direct object, **the president**. **Up** is a verb particle because it forms a constituent with the verb, not with the following noun phrase. As a further test that **call up** is a transitive verb constituent in the first sentence, you can turn that sentence into a passive:

The senator **called up** the president.

↓

The president was **called up** by the senator.

You would diagram the two sentences differently to show their different constituencies.

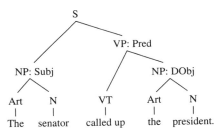

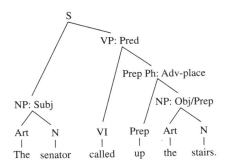

When you consider the differences between multiple-word verbs (verbs that form constituents with particles) and prepositional phrases (prepositions that form constituents with noun phrases), you can see why constituency is such a central principle in grammatical analysis.

Chapter Summary: Words, Hierarchies, and Constituents

This chapter defines nouns, verbs, adjectives, adverbs, and prepositions according to their meaning, form, and distribution. It then shows how phrases and single words both fill the same slots and how words form as hierarchies into constituents. Here are the main points of the chapter.

- Word categories are called parts of speech.
- Nouns, verbs, adjectives, and adverbs are content words, open classes.
- Determiners, auxiliaries, pronouns, conjunctions, and prepositions are function words, closed classes.
- Nouns do more than name things; they can follow determiners and form plurals.
- Verbs can follow modal auxiliaries and be made past and present tense.
- Adjectives often specify characteristics of nouns; many are gradable.
- Adverbs help to orient readers and listeners; they show many relationships and are realized by many structures.
- Prepositions must precede noun phrases and make prepositional phrases with them.
- Words get their force from grammar.
- Grammatical slots are important for identifying verb types.
- Grammar builds constituents as hierarchies.
- Grammatical analysis is like cutting a chicken into parts properly, into recognizable constituents.
- Phrases break down into heads and attributes.
- A sentence is composed of a noun phrase slot that functions as a subject and a verb phrase slot that functions as a predicate.
- The yes/no question test will help you find subjects and predicates.
- Diagrams are tools, not goals.
- Two or more words often work together as a single verb constituent.

EXERCISES

I. Identifying Sentence Constituents

First, identify the verb types in the following sentences. Then, analyze the sentences as far as you are able, labeling both structures and functions. Identify, as well, heads of phrases and sentence nuclei. If it helps your analysis, diagram the sentences. When appropriate, comment on how you came to decisions about constituents or labels.

EXAMPLE
   Oncology nurses care for dying patients.

Explanation: Only six words but a tough sentence. **Oncology nurses** is the noun phrase subject; **nurses** is the head of the phrase. The yes/no-question test assures me of that. I can make the sentence into a question by adding **do**:

   Do oncology nurses care for dying patients?

And I can move the **do** around **oncology nurses** to produce

   Oncology nurses **do** care for dying patients.

So **care for dying patients** is the verb phrase that functions as the predicate. Now comes the tough part. The verb is either a two-word transitive (**care for**) or a single-word intransitive (**care**) followed by a prepositional phrase (**for dying patients**) that functions as an adverb. I'll choose **care for** as a two-word transitive verb. For one thing, I think I say **care for** as a single unit, without pausing between the words. For another thing, I can turn the sentence into a passive, moving the object noun phrase (**dying patients**) to the front and the subject noun phrase (**oncology nurses**) into a prepositional phrase:

   Dying patients are cared for by oncology nurses.

Patients is the head of the object noun phrase; **care for** is the head of the verb phrase. The sentence diagramed:

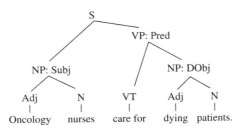

Sentences

1. The boiler exploded with a loud bang.
2. A dancer's body is her living voice.
3. Americans love informal dining.
4. The aircraft commander behaved prudently.
5. Sagebrush carpets western terrain.
6. Dr. Jekyll became a different person after his experiment.
7. The groom showed up in a brocade tuxedo.
8. Stephen King gives readers scary stories.
9. Our local yards turned brown because of the drought.
10. Literary historians call Joel Chandler Harris an American regionalist.
11. The International Olympic Committee returned Jim Thorpe's medals to his family in 1983.
12. Holocaust Museum visitors find their experience unsettling.
13. Amelia Earhart disappeared in 1937 during a global flight.
14. Spring is hiking season in Idaho.
15. The chef made the young couple a mango-basil soup.
16. The Senate came up with a compromise bill despite White House opposition.
17. AIDS was a big city plague until the 1990s.
18. The 1948 Chrysler Town and Country makes an unforgettable impression at car shows.
19. New York's Cotton Club made African American entertainment popular during the 1920s.
20. Early TV sitcoms seem naive nowadays.
21. The Blue Ridge Parkway runs through a magic land.
22. Nepal's government declared their nation a republic in 2008.
23. Huck is an unreliable narrator.
24. Midwesterners moved to California in large numbers after World War II.
25. A peaceful world proved a fleeting dream in the 1990s.
26. The green tea extract reduced appetites significantly.
27. Cowhands consider the Calgary Stampede a rip-roaring party.
28. *Hamlet* ends in a bloody melee.
29. Gardening clothes became fashionable during the 1980s.
30. Thoreau offered advice to young people in *Walden*.
31. Anne Frank died in a concentration camp.
32. Soviet economic policy was ineffective in the technological age.

33. The convicted Klansman turned in his accomplices.
34. A human being breathes 500 million times during an average lifetime.
35. General Grant's determination made him victorious.
36. Leadville, Colorado, is America's highest incorporated city.
37. Distance comes from a balanced golf swing.
38. The shuttle *Columbia* carried Gene Roddenberry's ashes into space.
39. Some curries taste sweet.
40. Lead-based paint remains a danger in older housing projects.
41. Terrorism shatters dreams.
42. One fitness guru dubbed couch potatoes "vidiots."
43. Orlando is the world's biggest tourist attraction.
44. The *Roe vs. Wade* decision gave women an option.
45. The IRS sends taxpayers their refunds within six weeks.
46. The Tagua palm grows in the Ecuadorean rain forest.
47. Ethiopia's situation turned nightmarish after the drought.
48. The inanimate world appears static because of our limited senses.
49. A great burger is great because of its prime beef.
50. Many elderly people see their lifestyles diminished after retirement.

....

CHAPTER 3

Expanding Verb Phrases

Tense, Modality, and Aspect

In this chapter, we'll look at the components of the MAIN VERB—the verb phrase constituent that contains the verb along with the elements that mark the categories *tense, modality,* and *aspect.* These three concepts indicate the status of a verb. Many grammar books lump the three into one category that they call *tense,* and then these books equate tense with real-world time. In contrast, we'll look at tense, modality, and aspect as separate but closely related grammatical concepts that overlap with real-world time but aren't always the same thing. We'll also take a close look at how we indicate tense and at the constituents that make up modality and aspect: modal auxiliaries, the auxiliary markers HAVE and BE, verb past participle forms, and verb present participle forms.

If you keep an open mind to the idea of separating the three concepts into distinct but closely related categories that differ from each other in both form and meaning, you should find the ideas in the chapter interesting and enlightening. Once you've worked through the chapter, you'll see that it's simpler to look at the status of a verb as composed of three concepts rather than one.

Status of the Main Verb

When they categorize tense, modality, and aspect under the single cover term *tense,* grammar books conjugate verbs into such categories as past tense (played), future tense (will play), past conditional tense (might play), present perfect tense (has played), or present progressive tense (is playing). Then they ask you to memorize long, complicated conjugation lists. Lots of grammarians, myself included, don't think that it's correct to dump all three concepts into one large category called "*tense*"; nor is it useful to memorize long lists.

Defining tense as one large category that includes tense, modality, and aspect and that corresponds exactly to real-world time obscures important characteristics of verb phrases. Memorizing long lists of conjugations wastes time and energy: native English speakers already know how to conjugate the verbs in their own language. And they can learn to name the various concepts if they understand how the system works to create verb status.

Let's look at why it's more productive to think of tense, modality, and aspect as three separate grammatical categories indicating the STATUS of a verb. The main reason to think of them as separate categories is that tense, modality, and aspect occur as distinct forms: they are marked in three different ways. Here, for instance, is how the verb **play** changes to show tense, modality, and aspect. The past tense form of **play** is shown by the -**ed** ending in **played**. The condition or modality of the verb is revealed by the word **might** in **might play** or by **will** in **will play**. The perfective aspect is expressed in the phrase **has played** by the word **has** plus the verb form **played**. And the progressive aspect is shown by the word **is** along with the verb form **playing** in the phrase **is playing**. Underlying these changes from tense to mood (modality) to aspect is a system that works in a regular manner for all but a small set of verbs (the key words here are **system** and **regular**).

Just as tense, modality, and aspect are different from each other because they are realized by different forms, they are different from real-world time concepts, with which they correspond only partially. Though they sometimes overlap with our sense of time in the real world, tense, modality, and aspect are grammatical concepts not bound to real time.

The verb, along with the forms that show its tense, modality, and aspect, is called the MAIN VERB. The forms that show tense, modality, and aspect (the **might** or **will**, **has**, and **is** in the examples above) constitute the AUXILIARY elements of the main verb.

In the sections that follow, we'll explain separately the aux-iliary elements that create tense, modality, and aspect, then we'll look at how these auxiliary elements can fit together into larger patterns.

Verb Form

TENSE determines the physical form of a verb. This point is impor-tant to note because, for reasons buried in the history of our language, English verbs exhibit only two tense forms—which we call PAST and PRESENT. (Remember that we're talking about the grammatical concept tense, not real-world time, and we're focusing on the form-changing characteristic of tense, the fact that it inflects verbs—INFLECT in this case meaning to change the form of. The English language has perfectly adequate ways to show future time and other real-world time concepts.) Don't let the names *past* and *present* confuse you; the two verb forms could just as easily be called Form 1 and Form 2 (this discussion would probably be less confusing if that were the case).

Grammarians have long differentiated tense from time. In a 1924 *English Journal* article, "The Teaching of Grammar," Otto Jespersen, one of the important English grammarians, commented on the difficulty of relating time and tense in English: "we have different grammatical tenses, but these correspond only roughly to the divisions of natural time, and it is therefore a pity that we are obliged to use [the same terms to refer to tense and time]" (p. 167).

That the two tense forms relate to time in different ways is easy enough to demonstrate. If you were asked, "What did your neighbor do last night?" you could answer

My neighbor **walked** her dog.

The past tense form **walked** clearly indicates the action took place in the past. But the present tense form, **walks**, does not necessarily mean that the action of the verb is taking place at the present time. The present form often means that the action of the verb is a common practice, that it is something which happens habitually. For instance, if you were asked, "What does your neighbor do for exercise?" you'd likely answer with **walks**, as in

My neighbor **walks** her dog.

By using the present tense form, you state that it is a common practice for your neighbor to walk her dog for exercise. She might not be out walking her dog at the present moment; nonetheless, she walks the dog frequently enough that you consider it is routine for her to do so. So the present tense form often means that an action takes place habitually.

Here's another example of how the present tense doesn't have to relate to present time. If we say,

Superman **defeats** Lex Luthor again and again.

the verb **defeats** is in present tense form. Yet we might use the present tense form to mean a past time idea, as the next two sentences illustrate:

In early comic books, Superman **defeats** villain after villain. But in a recent book-length comic, a villain kills Superman.

It's even possible to use the present tense form to indicate future time. Imagine being asked, "When does your plane leave?" You would likely answer with a present tense verb form:

My plane **leaves** in three hours.

The next diagrams show how you indicate the main verb constituent and its tense. Notice that the status of the main verb, past and present in these sentences, is noted after the colon, MV:Past or MV:Pres. Possessive pronouns (like **my** and **her**) are defined in the next chapter. The past tense form more clearly relates to past time than the present tense form relates to present time.

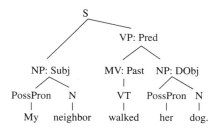

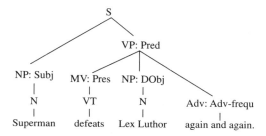

Finiteness

Tense is the only one of the three main verb concepts that *must* occur in the verb phrase predicate of a sentence. In fact, without tense, a verb phrase can't be a predicate. Because tense is necessary for a verb phrase to be a predicate, we can now expand our definition of a sentence from the first two chapters. A SENTENCE is not simply a noun phrase subject plus a verb phrase; it is a noun phrase subject plus a verb phrase that shows tense.

Remember, if there is no tense, there is no predicate; therefore, there is no sentence. A verb that inflects for (exhibits) tense is FINITE. In contrast, a verb that is not inflected for tense is an INFINITIVE because it is nonfinite. Some grammarians call the nonfinite form the BASE FORM.

Mood and Purpose

We often classify sentences according to their purpose or intent. Sentences generally make statements (Polynesians ruled Hawaii until 1791. They can ask questions (Why does cancer frustrate microbiologists?). They can order or command (Turn in your homework by noon Friday). Or sentences can indicate possibility or eventuality (Women athletes can compete against men in most sports). These notions about purpose or intent—to make statements, to ask questions, to issue commands, or to indicate possibility—are called MOOD, or MODALITY. When a sentence makes a statement, it is in the INDICATIVE mood: this is the normal (unmarked) mood. When it asks question, it is in the INTERROGATIVE mood. When it makes a command or request, it is in the IMPERATIVE mood. And when it indicates possibility, it is in the CONDITIONAL mood.

Conditional Mood

The mood, or purpose, of a sentence is related to the form of the main verb. In this section, we're interested in how to construct the conditional mood. Normally, we make sentences conditional by adding a word like **may**, **should**, or **must** to the main verb. These words are called MODAL AUXILIARIES or simply MODALS. Some books call them HELPING VERBS. The most common modal auxiliaries are

Base/Present Form	Past Form
can	could
shall	should
will	would
may	might
must	

Phrases like **ought to, used to, dare to, seem to, need to, happen to, want to, be able to,** and **have to** can also act as modal auxiliaries; they are sometimes called SEMIMODALS.

When they occur in a sentence, modal auxiliaries (or semimodals) always occur at the beginning of the main verb constituent, as in:

Photography promotes visual awareness.
Photography **might** promote visual awareness.

The president's speech reassured the public.
The president's speech **has to** reassure the public.

Since they occur at the beginning of the main verb, they inflect for past or present tense. **Might** is the past form of **may**. **Has to** is the present form of **have to**. So the first example sentence is in the *past* conditional mood; the second example sentence is in the *present* conditional. **Might promote** and **has to reassure** are the main verbs of these sentences, as you can see in the diagrams.

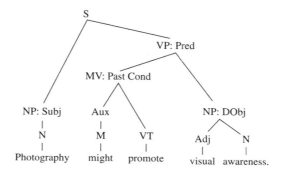

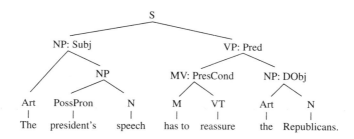

Conditional Mood and Possibility

The meaning of the conditional mood is always concerned with possibility (and the related notions of certainty, obligation, desire, necessity, promise, permission, and even threat). Look at the example sentences again. The first notes the possibility that photography promotes visual awareness (it **might**). The second indicates the necessity that the president's speech reassure the public (it **has to**). Because they are related to possibility, conditional concepts are concerned with events that haven't happened but might happen in the future. After all, something that is possible or necessary would have to happen at some point down the road. Since the concepts expressed by the conditional mood overlap with the real-world concept of futurity, modals are sometimes said to express futurity.

The next example may be viewed as a promise of some future engagement by the singer:

Mary Chapin Carpenter **will** perform in the civic auditorium.

The actual time for the performance is unspecified (just a vague promise) unless you add an adverb that indicates time more exactly. In the next sentence, the prepositional phrase **on Friday** functions as the adverb of time that specifies when Mary Chapin Carpenter will perform.

Mary Chapin Carpenter **will** perform in the civic auditorium **on Friday**.

This sentence does indicate future time, but it does so with an adverb.

Before we leave the conditional mood, we should note one more fact about its construction. The verb following a modal auxiliary is always nonfinite, as are **promote, reassure**, and **perform** in the previous examples. Tense changes the form of only one word in a main verb: the first word. This is a terribly important concept to remember when you have to identify the principal parts of words in the main verb, as you will have to later in the chapter.

Future Time and Conditional Mood Again

It's probably worthwhile addressing the question about future tense more than once in this chapter, since this question troubles some students and arises frequently in class. I haven't manipulated the language to rid it of future tense, as we saw in the 1924 Jespersen article I cited earlier. For at least 150 years, grammarians who study the history of the language have noted that one of the differences between Germanic languages and other Indo-European languages is that verbs in Germanic languages exhibit only two tense forms (English is a Germanic language, like German, Dutch, Swedish, and Norwegian). Grammarians from every school of grammar—traditional to tagmemic—readily acknowledge the fact that English has only past and present tense forms. The key word here is **form**. Tense in English is an inflectional form as well as a temporal idea.

In short, that English has two tense forms is well accepted in grammatical studies (except in some high school and junior high textbooks). The idea of two tenses takes nothing away from the language. Speakers of English can indicate future time easily enough. Generally we indicate future time, as the previous section notes, by making the main verb conditional and by adding an adverb of time to the sentence, like this:

> *Gourmet* magazine **will publish** ten chocolate cake recipes **next month**.

If it takes nothing away from our language, acknowledging the two-tense structure of verbs doesn't complicate our grammatical system either. In fact, it probably simplifies the way we can explain the relationships between tense, modality, and aspect. In essence, recognizing that English has two tense forms allows us to look at verb phrases in a more analytic way than some textbooks present them.

Aspect

ASPECT indicates that the action of a verb is either completed or continuing; the action flows or it stops. Aspect occurs in two varieties—perfect or progressive.

Perfect Aspect

PERFECT ASPECT indicates that the action of a verb is completed. Perfect aspect is shown by the auxiliary HAVE followed by a PAST PARTICIPLE (**had predicted** and **have unraveled** in the examples that follow).

> The astrologist **had predicted** an earthquake in May.
> Political relationships **have unraveled** in Russia.

Because the auxiliary HAVE in the first example is in the past tense form, **had predicted** is past perfect, while **have unraveled** in the second example is present perfect. Don't let the terms *past perfect* and *present perfect* confuse you. Remember that both versions of the perfect aspect relate to completed action. The *past* and *present* designations refer only to the tense form of the auxiliary HAVE, as the diagrams indicate.

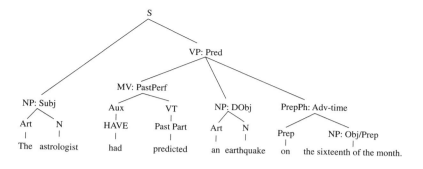

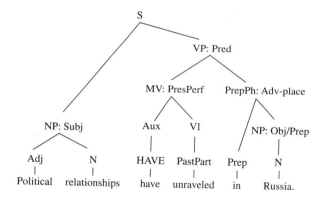

Past Participles

Before moving on to progressive aspect, let's stop and talk about past participles. The word *past* in *past participle* does not refer to time; it refers only to a verb's form, as *past* does in *past tense*. A past participle is the form of a verb that can follow HAVE. The past participle of a regular verb is the same as the past tense form of the verb, like **predicted** or **unraveled** in the examples above. Past participle forms of irregular verbs vary with the verb. Some add **-n** or **-en** to the basic form:

drive → driven
write → written

Some change a vowel:

> drink → drunk
> sing → sung

Other don't change spelling or pronunciation from their base form:

> become → become
> quit → quit

However complicated the variations from basic form to past participle may seem, verb forms are so fundamental to the language that you can depend on your knowledge of English to find the past participle of a verb, whether it's regular or irregular. To show yourself how basic it is, change the italicized verb after the **have, had,** or **has** below to the correct past participle.

> I **had** *print* the botany paper before class.
> You **have** *bite* the pencil into pieces.
> She **has** *find* Michelle's jacket.
> They have *sleep.*

For the vast majority of verbs in English, you'll know the past participle, the verb form after **have, has,** or **had.** If you answered **printed, swallowed, bitten, found,** and **slept,** you're correct.

> I had ***printed*** the botany paper before class.
> You have ***bitten*** the pencil into pieces.
> She has ***found*** Michelle's jacket.
> They have ***slept.***

For a very few verbs, probably no more than a half dozen or so that are in the process of changing their forms—like *swim* (**swum**), *dive* (**dived** or **dove**), *wake* (**waked**), or *strive* (**strived** or **striven**)—you might have to look up the correct past participle.

Progressive Aspect

Just as the perfect aspect denotes completed action, the PROGRESSIVE ASPECT refers to continuing action. Progressive aspect is composed of an auxiliary BE followed by a PRESENT PARTICIPLE, as in

> John Travolta **was dancing** at a disco ballroom.
> The Web **is reconnecting** families.

Because the auxiliary **was** in the first example is in the past tense form, the status of **was dancing** is past progressive, while the status of **is reconnecting** in the second example is present progressive. The "past" and "present" designations refer only to the tense form of the auxiliary BE, just as "past" and "present" refer to the tense form of the auxiliary HAVE in the perfect aspect. The present participle, by the way, is always an **-ing** form of the verb. There are no exceptions.

develop → developing
provide → providing
respond → responding
throw → throwing
dive → diving

The two example progressive sentences are diagramed below.

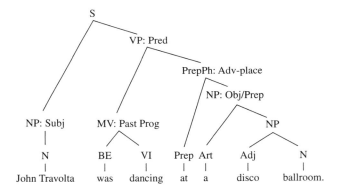

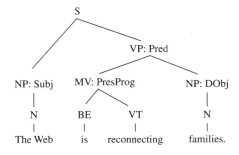

Present Participles

You should be aware that, though a present participle is always an **-ing** form, not every word ending in **-ing** is a present participle. In the following sentence about Julia Roberts, for instance, the word **charming** is an adjective, a predicate adjective; it is preceded by the past tense form of the verb **BE**. In this example, Julia Roberts seems charming to the reporters. "Charmingness" thus is a characteristic of Julia Roberts; that's why **charming** is an adjective here.

> Julia Roberts was **charming** to the **reporters**.

Contrast the adjective **charming** with the present participle **charming**.

> The pope was **charming** his American audience.

In the second example, the pope was doing something to his American audience—entertaining them. Since **charming** is a verb in the second example, the phrase **was charming** is in the past progressive aspect (the past tense form of the auxiliary **BE** plus the present participle form of the verb **charm**. You can also intensify the adjective or compare it.

> Julia Roberts was very **charming** to the reporters.
> Julia Roberts was more **charming** to the reporters than
> Eminem.

You can't intensify or compare the verb **charming**. If you try, you'll get ungrammatical sentences.

> *The pope was very **charming** his American audience.
> *The pope was more **charming** his American audience than the
> Venezuelan president.

The fact that **charming** can be an adjective in one circumstance and a present participle in a different circumstance is simply another instance of a word changing from one category to another. It's a common occurrence in grammar, as we've already seen.

Conditional, Perfective, and Progressive

You've already seen that tense is shown by the verb itself or by the first word in the main verb: either the modal (conditional mood), HAVE (perfect aspect), or BE (progressive aspect). Conditional mood, perfect aspect, and progressive aspect can occur separately or in various combinations with one another. Here are several examples:

> William R. Ferris directed the Center for the Study of Southern Culture. (Past tense)
> You **can catch** Lyme disease from ticks. (Present conditional)
> The president **might have changed** his position before the senate vote. (Past perfect conditional)
> Mick Jagger **has been dabbling** in real estate for years. (Present perfect progressive)
> States **should have been spending** more on schools during the past decade. (Past perfect progressive conditional)

Tense Form of Main Verb

Notice that tense appears only once in a main verb (this is a particularly important point to remember); tense changes the form of the first word of the main verb—whether the word is a verb, a modal auxiliary, the auxiliary BE, or the auxiliary HAVE. In the first example above, the verb **directed** is in the past tense form; in the second example, the modal **can** is in the present tense form; in the third, the modal **might** is in the past tense form; in the fourth, the auxiliary **has** is in the present tense form; in the fifth, the modal **should** is in the past tense form. All the words in the main verb except the first word are in one or another nonfinite form—infinitive (**catch**, **have**), past participle (**changed**, **been**), or present participle (**spending**, **dabbling**). It's worth repeating in order to summarize the central idea in this paragraph: only the first word in the main verb is a tense form; the rest of the words in the main verb are nonfinite forms. We'll go over this point again after discussing principal parts.

Principal Parts

As you've seen in the discussion of the status of main verbs, every verb has five forms: infinitive (or base), past tense, present tense, present participle, and past participle. These five forms are called PRINCIPAL PARTS. Some grammar books give long lists of verbs with their principal parts and instruct readers to memorize those lists. You don't have to memorize long lists of verbs and their principal parts. You can make your own list of the principal parts of every verb in the language if you remember just the following six things about verb forms.

1. The base form of a verb (the infinitive form) does not show tense. (Often, though, it looks exactly like the present tense form that takes a plural subject.)
2. The present tense form that takes a singular third-person subject (like he/she/it) ends in -s or -es, for just about every verb in the language, regular or irregular.
3. The past tense form for most verbs (the regular ones) ends in -d or -ed.
4. The present participial form always ends in -ing. This is true for regular and irregular verbs.
5. The past participial form of regular verbs is the same as their past tense form.
6. Past participles can always follow **have**, as in "I (They) **have/has** _____ (it)." The form of the verb that can fill the blank is the past participle.

Here are some verbs and their principal parts:

Base/Infinitive	write	use	float	sing	remember
Present Tense	write(s)	use(s)	float(s)	sing(s)	remember(s)
Past Tense	wrote	used	floated	sang	remembered
Present Participle	writing	using	floating	singing	remembering
Past Participle	written	used	floated	sung	remembered

The Words in the Main Verb

Now, with this information about principal parts, let's look again at the main verb constituent. We've noted that the first word in the main verb, *only* the first word, is in past or present tense form. The rest of the words in the main verb are in different forms (one of the other principal parts). Here, for instance, is a sentence in which the status of the main verb is past perfect progressive conditional:

The candidate's staff **should have been planning** more than one campaign strategy.

The modal **should** is in the past tense form. **Have** is in the base (infinitive) form since it follows a modal. **Been** is in the past participle form (it follows **have**). And **planning** is in the present participle form. The status of the main verb in the next sentence is present perfect.

Princess Diana **has become** a tragic figure.

The auxiliary **has** is in the present tense form (it's the first word in the main verb); **become** is a past participle (it follows **has**). When you analyze the main verb constituent, you're always looking for (1) the forms (the principal parts) of the individual words as well as (2) how the words combine with one another to create the status of the main verb.

Here is a diagram of the main verb of the Mick Jagger sentence (Mick Jagger **has been dabbling** in real estate for years), with its principal parts marked:

Lets look at the principal parts and how they fit together. The first word in the main verb, **has**, is in the present tense form; **has** is followed by **been**, a past participle. Together, they make perfect aspect. **Been** and the present participle **dabbling** make progressive aspect. The present tense of **have**, the past participle of **be**, and the present participle of **dabble** combine to make the present perfect progressive status.

A Main Verb May Contain Tense, Modality, Perfective Aspect, and Progressive Aspect

Though the main verb constituents occur in the order **tense + modality + perfective aspect + progressive aspect**, you always describe status beginning with the tense form of the first word of the main verb, then the perfect aspect (if it occurs), then the progressive (if it occurs), then the modality (if a modal occurs or if the mood is imperative or interrogative). We typically don't mention the mood if it is indicative, though you can, if you wish to. You say "past perfect progressive conditional" when you describe the status of

> States **should have been spending** more on schools during the past decade.

It begins with the modal **should**, a past tense form. **Have,** an infinitive form, plus **been,** a past participle, makes perfect aspect. **Been** plus the present participle **spending** makes progressive aspect.

If you look at the main verb as separate parts that compose the status in a regular, organized way, you should do fine.

Here is a schematic of the possible combinations of tense, modality, and aspect within the main verb (parentheses indicate a construction is optional; it may or may not occur).

Tense + (Modal) + (Perfect) + (Progressive) + Verb

To emphasize that tense must occur in the main verb, the schematic shows tense as a freestanding unit, though tense actually becomes part of the modal, HAVE, BE, or verb that is the first word of the main verb. The schematic should help you remember the ways to expand a main verb. It indicates that a main verb must contain a verb as well as tense. A main verb may have, in various combinations, a modal, perfect aspect, or progressive aspect. Remember that tense occurs only once in the main verb constituent; it changes the form of the first word in the main verb.

How to Expand a Main Verb

The following schematics indicate that you may expand a main verb in eight ways:

1. Tense + Verb
2. Tense + Modal + Verb
3. Tense + Perfect + Verb
4. Tense + Progressive + Verb
5. Tense + Modal + Perfect + Verb
6. Tense + Modal + Progressive + Verb
7. Tense + Perfect + Progressive + Verb
8. Tense + Modal + Perfect + Progressive + Verb

Regular Verbs

Most verbs in English are REGULAR VERBS, which means that their past tense form ends in -**d** or -**ed** and that their past participle form is the same as their past tense form. Here are some examples of regular verbs.

Base/Infinitive		Past Tense		Past Participle
accept	→	accepted	→	accepted
call	→	called	→	called
formulate	→	formulated	→	formulated
render	→	rendered	→	rendered
slow	→	slowed	→	slowed
grieve	→	grieved	→	grieved
rave	→	raved	→	raved

A verb that either does not form its past tense with -**d** or -**ed** or that has a past participle that is not the same as its past tense is called IRREGULAR. There are only about one hundred irregular verbs in English. Here are some examples.

Base/Infinitive		Past Tense		Past Participle
choose	→	chose	→	chosen
drive	→	drove	→	driven
fight	→	fought	→	fought
be	→	was/were	→	been
bring	→	brought	→	brought
swim	→	swam	→	swum
sit	→	sat	→	sat

Chapter Summary: Components of the Main Verb

We've examined the components of the main verb—the verb phrase constituent which contains the verb along with the elements that mark the categories tense, modality, and aspect. These three categories indicate the status of a verb. We've explained tense, modality, and aspect as separate but closely related grammatical concepts that overlap with real-world time but aren't always the same thing. We've looked at the constituents that make up tense, modality, and aspect: modal auxiliaries, the auxiliary markers HAVE and BE, verb past participle forms, and verb present participle forms. And we've considered the five principal parts of verbs. Here are the main points of Chapter 3.

- Tense, modality, and aspect are separate concepts.
- Tense, modality, and aspect define the status of the main verb.
- Tense determines the physical form of a verb.
- A sentence is a noun phrase plus a finite verb phrase.
- Mood denotes the purpose of a sentence.
- Modal auxiliaries indicate conditional mood (possibility).
- English speakers indicate future time with adverbs and the conditional mood.
- Aspect indicates that the action of a verb is completed or continuing.
- Auxiliary HAVE plus a past participle make perfect aspect.
- Auxiliary BE plus a past participle make progressive aspect.
- Not every word ending in **-ing** is a present participle.
- Conditional, perfective, and progressive can occur together.
- Only the first word in the main verb is a tense form.
- Verbs have five forms, called principal parts.
- The words in the main verb occur in different forms.
- A main verb may contain tense, modality, perfective aspect, and progressive aspect.
- A main verb may be expanded in eight ways.
- Most English verbs are regular, which means their past tense ends in **-d** or **-ed** and their past participle does the same.
- The main verb marks tense, mood, and aspect.

EXERCISES

I. Changing Main-Verb Forms
Make the main verbs of the following sentences into the forms indicated in parentheses.

EXAMPLE
Police battle against the odds. (Present progressive)
Police are battling against the odds.

1. Ovophobes switch to egg substitutes to avoid cholesterol. (Present progressive)

2. Richard Gere is shy. (Present conditional)
3. Mercedes-Benz is the epitome of luxury. (Past perfect)
4. The weather forecaster predicted rain for the area next week. (Present progressive conditional)
5. Oil prices had been worrying the White House. (Past indicative)

II. Identifying Verb Status and Analyzing Sentences

Identify the status of the main verbs in the following sentences, and label the other constituents in the sentences, both their structures and functions. Explain how you identified the status of the main verbs.

EXAMPLE

Woody Guthrie has become a music icon since the sixties.

Explanation: In this sentence, **has become** is the main verb. **Has** is the mark of the perfect and **become** is a past participle. Since **has** is in the present form, the status of the main verb is present perfect. **Woody Guthrie** is a noun phrase that functions as the subject. **Has become a music icon since the sixties** is a verb phrase functioning as a predicate.

The verb **become** is linking; it is followed by a noun phrase (**a music icon**) that functions as a predicate noun: **a** is an article, **music** is used as an adjective, and **icon** is a noun. **Since the sixties** is a prepositional phrase: **since** is a preposition, **the sixties** is a noun phrase functioning as the object of the preposition. **The** is an article, and **sixties** is a noun.

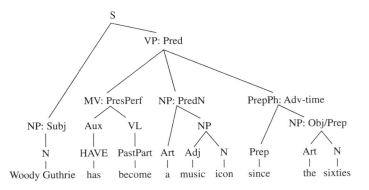

Sentences

1. The state legislature might offer parents school vouchers soon.
2. Student Senate denied funding to the gay rights organization.
3. Females are initiating dates nowadays.
4. Daiker College will have a splendid chemistry building next year.
5. Springfield would have built a police station with the federal grant.
6. The Navy can finance your college education.
7. Edna Buchanan has set her novels in south Florida.
8. Winston Churchill was a complicated giant on the world stage.
9. Franklin Roosevelt had understood the Nazi threat before World War II.
10. Elvis may be history's biggest star.
11. My history class is reading *The Diary of Anne Frank*.
12. Stingrays could have been cruising near the beach.
13. The prince may complete his education at Harvard.
14. Paul Simon's lyrics have become political.
15. The environment will suffer because of rising temperatures.
16. The silo might have blown up.
17. Lawsuits can cripple medical practices.
18. My roommate's nervousness was becoming a burden.
19. Eddie Murphy was being vulgar during the interview.
20. A poor Christmas season could shut down smaller stores.
21. Miami Beach has turned into the American Riviera.
22. Cable outlets are challenging phone companies for computer hookups.
23. The architecture students have to come up with a functional home design.
24. Education can be a potent weapon.
25. Suburbanites are pouring their creative juices into Halloween celebrations.
26. Concert tickets will be available at the Coliseum tonight.
27. Skillful play has brought media attention to Tiger Woods.
28. Kennedy faced down Khrushchev during the Cuban Missile Crisis.
29. The primatologist may be gambling away her welcome among the chimp family.
30. Language-immersion programs are flourishing in elementary schools.
31. Humidity can make my dog uncomfortable.
32. The prizefighter had come to after the knockout.

33. Communism seems to be dying around the world.
34. Superman was fighting the Axis during World War II.
35. The Weather Bureau had been playing Chicken Little with the coastal residents.
36. Raskolnikov could hear the murdered man's voice in his dreams.
37. The Russian fans were booing the French skater during her performance.
38. Congress has made problems for the president since the election.
39. Joseph Conrad had become fluent in English.
40. Portfolios can document your writing ability.
41. Mary Cassatt seems to have given financial assistance to an important French art dealer.
42. Some women athletes are using the word "babe" in a new way.
43. Washington ought to downsize soon.
44. A contemporary Hemingway may be waiting in the wings.
45. Parasites can make host organisms deathly ill.
46. The dean's committee had been examining our undergraduate program.
47. Diplomacy has been Obama's passion.
48. Orville wanted to make the design public.
49. The DVD has shaken up the home video market.
50. A banjo player was playing in front of Radio Shack.

CHAPTER 4

Exploring Noun Phrases

Noun Phrase Components

In this chapter, we classify nouns. Then we look at determiners and pronouns as well as inflective and phrasal genitive constructions.

Proper and Common Nouns

Grammarians classify nouns in various ways: as common (the **pope**) or proper (**John XXIII**); concrete (**teacher**) or abstract (**pedagogy**); as countable (**bottle**), noncountable (**water**), or collective (**team**). Noun classes overlap. So a noun like **team** in

The **team** met to watch the game films

is at the same time common, concrete, countable, and collective. Since there is so much overlap among the classes, noun classification schemes can quickly become too complicated to be useful for beginning students. You should be aware of the different noun classes, though the only ones we'll be concerned with in any detail are proper and common. This classification is perhaps the most obvious way to differentiate noun types.

PROPER nouns refer to unique people, places, or things; they are sets of one and typically name something or someone, like **God, the Statue of Liberty, Ohio, Chicago, Leonardo DiCaprio,**

Cheerios, Miami Beach High School, President Truman, or *Moby Dick*. Proper nouns are often two or more words long, like **the Louvre, the Empire State Building, the Rio Grande**, or **Florida State University**, and many proper nouns include the definite article **the**. Typically, we capitalize proper nouns. By their nature, proper nouns are singular, but there are situations that allow you to make proper nouns plural, especially when you use a proper noun to indicate a whole class, like:

> If there were more **Trumans** in national politics, Americans might have a higher regard for politicians.

> There don't seem to be any new *Moby Dicks* on the literary horizon.

All the nouns that are not proper are COMMON, like **divine being, statue, state, city, movie star, cereal, high school, former president**, and **novel**. You don't need special situations to make common nouns plural: **divine beings, statues, states, cities, movie stars, high schools, former presidents, novels**.

Determiners

Most noun phrases consist of a noun alone or a noun together with an article, a possessive, a demonstrative, a number, or a prearticle. These structures belong to a larger category called DETERMINERS. The determiners occur so routinely with nouns that you can use determiners to test whether a word is a noun. As we saw in Chapter 2, if an article makes a constituent with a word or phrase, you can be sure that constituent is a noun.

Determiners are so closely identified with nouns that they can even make other kinds of words into nouns. Perhaps the most famous literary example of this is the title of Stendahl's novel *The Red and the Black,* in which the article **the** makes words that are normally adjectives, **red** and **black**, into nouns. You don't have to be a world-renowned author to say, "I like **the purple** rather than **the light violet**." Articles, possessives, demonstratives, numbers, and prearticles are so frequently a part of noun phrases that it's easy to overlook their significance.

Some grammar books don't differentiate between determiners and adjectives, which also make constituents with nouns. But determiners and adjectives are different. As we saw in Chapter 2, adjectives are content words, open-class words. Determiners are function words, closed-class words.

Definite Articles

The articles are **a**, **an**, and **the**. **The** is DEFINITE, while the two other articles are INDEFINITE. The difference between definite and indefinite refers to whether a noun phrase expresses SHARED INFORMATION. Definite articles indicate that the speaker/writer and listener/reader share information. In some grammar books, shared information is called OLD INFORMATION. Indefinite articles do not express shared information.

Let's take a closer look at this idea of shared information. Imagine that your friend Janet called and asked you to her apartment for dinner. She might add, "Would you bring the chair with you? We don't have enough seating." If she made the request using the noun phrase **the chair**, she would be indicating that you know what chair she is referring to; in other words, you and she share old information about a chair. By using **the**, Janet shows that she expects you to bring a particular chair that you and she both know about.

In contrast, notice what would happen if Janet used an indefinite article in her request: "Would you bring a chair with you? We don't have enough seating." If she made the request with the noun phrase **a chair**, she would be indicating that you could bring any chair you wanted to bring. You and she don't share information about a chair.

Articles, like other determiners, make close, natural relationships with nouns. Here are diagrams of three noun phrase constituents with articles:

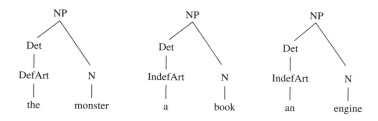

Demonstratives

This, **that**, **these**, and **those** are DEMONSTRATIVES. Like definite articles, demonstratives indicate old information. But they do something more as well. They also point to things: **this** computer, **that** telephone, **these** books, **those** marbles. You can hardly say a noun phrase that includes a demonstrative without raising your hand to point. The grammatical concept of pointing is called DEIXIS. **This** and **these** point to things that are near; **that** and **those** point to things that are farther away. **This** and **that** are singular; **these** and **those** are plural.

Possessive Pronouns

Some POSSESSIVE PRONOUNS are determiners; they form phrases with the nouns they precede. Some possessive pronouns are independent; they fill noun phrase slots. Here are the eight determiner-possessive pronouns and the diagrams to show how they pattern.

Singular	**Plural**
my	our
your	your
his, her, its	their

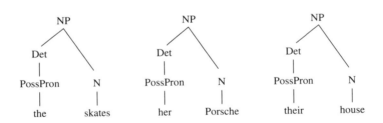

Independent possessive pronouns are not determiners; they stand alone in noun phrases. I introduced them here with the determiners because they're related to the determiner-possessive pronouns. The eight independent possessive pronouns are:

Singular	**Plural**
mine	ours
yours	yours
his, hers, its	theirs

These independent possessive pronouns derive from the determiner-possessive pronouns. **My** adds an **n** sound (**my** → **mine**); **her, our, your,** and **their** add an **s** (**her** → **hers, our** → **ours, your** → **yours,** and **their** → **theirs**); **his** and **its** do not change form.

This locker is **hers.** That's **yours.**

The Smiths' house was destroyed by the tornado. **Ours** remained standing.

Here is a diagram of the first example.

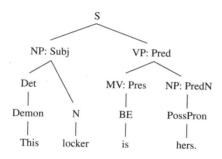

Numbers

We consider NUMBERS determiners when they precede nouns, as in *ten* **giraffes** or **mom's** *first* **balloon trip.** Numbers fall into two classes: CARDINAL (**one, two, three,** etc.) or ORDINAL (**first, second, third,** etc.; also **next, last**). Ordinal numbers generally follow articles or possessives.

> his **third** date
> the **next** explosion

The next diagrams show numbers patterning with nouns and articles or possessives to form noun phrases.

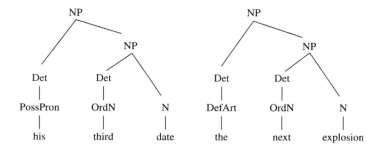

Numbers that do not precede nouns are generally considered nouns themselves, as in

My granddad will be **seventy-five** on his next birthday.

In this example, **seventy-five** functions as a predicate noun.

Prearticles

Several word classes can precede articles, including partitives, quantifiers, multipliers, and fractions. In order to simplify the discussion, we'll classify them all under PREARTICLES, since they occur before articles or possessives. Here are some examples of the quantifiers and partitives:

some (of)	(a) little (of)
any (of)	plenty (of)
no	a lot of
none (of)	a good deal of
each (of)	a small quantity of
every	an item of
either (of)	a slice of
neither (of)	a bowl of
many (of)	a quart of
(a) few (of)	a pound of
several (of)	a jar of

Remember that you include them under prearticles, as the diagrams on page **77** indicate.

The multipliers and the fractions are self-explanatory. The fractions are phrases like **a third, two-fifths,** and **three-eighths.** Like the other prearticles, the fractions may be followed by **of: a third of, two-thirds of,** and **three-eighths of.**

Multipliers include such words and phrases as **once, twice,** or **three times.** They're not followed by **of,** but they are often followed by **a, every,** or **each.** These words that follow multipliers are determiners that form constituents with the following nouns. The **a** is, of course, an indefinite article; **each** and **every** we'll just consider unspecified determiners. Some grammarians classify them as adjectives. Some grammarians call them semiadjectives. Since they act more like function words than content words, I think it's more consistent to include **each** and **every** among determiners and leave it at that.

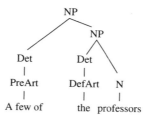

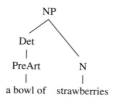

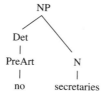

The diagrams on page **78** shows some multipliers and fractions diagramed. Following our practice to simplify the classification of prearticles, I've listed them all simply as prearticles. Notice that **each** in the phrase **twice each month** is a determiner that makes a constituent with **month** before **each month** makes a constituent with **twice**.

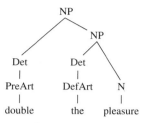

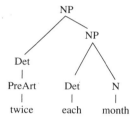

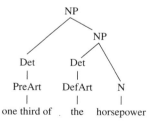

The word **of** often appears with prearticles—fractions, partitives, and quantifiers. When it does, **of** forms a constituent with the prearticle; it does not form a constituent with the following noun. So **of** is not a preposition when it occurs with prearticles, though some grammar books and teachers call it a preposition. This point about **of** is important to notice because it is part of the difference between phrases composed of prearticles plus nouns and phrases composed of nouns and phrasal genitives, which we'll look at after the section on post-noun modifiers.

Postnoun Modifiers

All and **both,** among others, can occur after nouns as well as before them. It is possible to explain postnoun modifiers as prearticles that have been moved after the noun—as in the first example below, where **all the students** becomes **the students all.** For simplicity, we won't rearrange determiners or even consider postnoun modifiers as part of the determiner system. Here are two examples of the two noun phrases in question followed by two diagrams.

> The students **all** participated in the election.
> Ted Kennedy's brothers both died tragically.

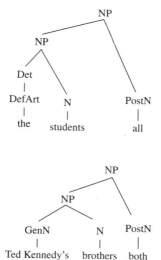

Genitives

Possessive nouns occur in two forms—**'s** and **of phrases**. Though possessive nouns are not determiners, they act like possessive pronouns, so I've included them at the end of the section about determiners. Inflected possessive nouns always end in **'s,** as in the following examples:

The **reporter's** assignment was inner-city gangs.
Mark Twain tells a **boy's story** in *The Adventures of Tom Sawyer.*

Possessives also occur as prepositional phrases:

General MacArthur defied the authority **of President Truman.**
The music **of Bach** heralds the modern age.

Phrasal possessives can usually be turned into inflected forms. For instance, you can change the prepositional phrases **of President Truman** and **of Bach** into inflected nouns:

General MacArthur defied **President Truman's** authority.
Bach's music heralds the modern age.

Sometimes you can't turn possessives back and forth from phrases to inflectives or from inflectives to phrases: you can't make **my mom's new car** into *the new car of my mom.** And sometimes when you move a noun from the prepositional phrase to the front of the head noun, the moved noun won't inflect:

patterns of **behavior**
↓
behavior patterns

a network of **computers**
↓
a computer network

Because such possessives are not exactly determiners and because they don't all pattern alike, some grammar books label possessive nouns, whether phrasal or inflective, as adjectives. We'll call only those uninflected nouns that precede other nouns adjectives, like **computer** in **computer network** or **college** in **college reunion**. That is, they are nouns that function as adjectives, as the next diagram shows.

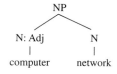

"Genitive" Rather than "Possessive"

We've been calling inflected nouns and **of phrases** possessives. But we'll begin calling them GENITIVES; genitive is the old term for the case of the noun we now indicate by the **'s** or the **of phrase**. Similarly, what we've called possessive pronouns should probably be called genitive pronouns as well. Genitive is a more accurate term than possessive for these structures, since about 60 percent of so-called possessives do not indicate possession. The term "genitive" more accurately indicates that a noun with either the **'s** form or the **of phrase** may show a relationship other than simple possession. After all, the phrase **J. K. Rowling's book** may denote a book that belongs to the author J. K. Rowling but which she did not write, as in

>   That dictionary is **J. K. Rowling's book.**

or it may denote a book that she wrote but does not own, as in

>   *Harry Potter and the Goblet of Fire* is **J. K. Rowling's book.**

In the same way, the destruction **of Warsaw** (or **Warsaw's** destruction) in the next example is not in any way a destruction that belonged to the city but a destruction that was levied against Warsaw. In these examples, Warsaw is actually the object of **destroyed** (the verb form of **destruction**).

>   The German air force destroyed Warsaw.
>   ↓
>   the destruction **of Warsaw** by the German air force
>   OR
>   **Warsaw's** destruction by the German air force

In the inflected genitive **her parents'** or the phrasal genitive **of her parents** in the next examples, **her parents** are doing the consenting; they are the actors (the subjects of **consented**). They don't "possess" the consent.

>   Her parents consented.
>   ↓
>   the consent of her parents
>   OR
>   her parents' consent

In some cases, like

> a good **night's** sleep
> OR
> ten **dollar's** worth of gas

the genitive noun measures the following noun.

Sometimes the genitive phrase can be unclear about who performs an action and who is acted upon. In a sentence like

> The shooting **of the terrorists** bothered the townspeople.

we can't be sure whether the terrorists did the shooting or were themselves shot.

When you parse noun phrases with inflected genitives, you treat the genitives much as you would possessive pronouns, though you don't include them under determiners. The following diagrams indicate the correct analysis of noun phrases with inflective genitives.

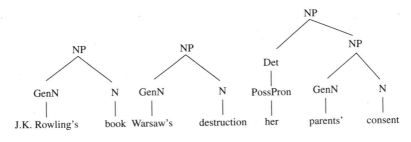

Phrasal genitives are prepositional phrases. Be careful not to confuse noun phrases like

> **some of** the audience

with noun phrases like

> the joy of the audience

In the first, **some of** is a prearticle and **audience** is the head of the noun phrase **some of the audience**. In the second, **of the audience** is a prepositional phrase that functions as a genitive within the noun phrase **the joy of the audience**; its head is **joy**.

When you parse phrasal genitives, you should indicate both their structure (PrepPh) and function (Gen). If you draw diagrams, you should also show that the phrasal genitive makes a noun phrase constituent first with the noun head before this noun phrase makes a larger noun phrase constituent with an article, as in the next diagram.

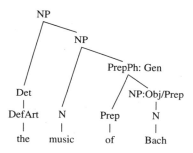

Personal, Reflexive, and Indefinite Pronouns

Several different kinds of pronouns fill noun phrase slots. Those you encounter most frequently are the personal pronouns, the reflexive pronouns, and the indefinite pronouns.

The PERSONAL PRONOUNS occur in subject and object forms:

Subject Forms	Object Forms
I	me
you	you
he, she, it	him, her, it
we	us
you	you
they	them

The personal pronouns refer to previously mentioned nouns. The nouns they refer to may be in their own clause or in a previous clause:

The president had a bad day with congressional leaders. He couldn't get them to support the tax package.

The senator voted against the bill to close 13 military bases across the country. She especially wanted to protect jobs in her own state.

REFFLEXIVE PRONOUNS end in -**self** or- **selves** and refer to the subject of the clause they are in, as

The football players sat by **themselves** in the corner of the cafeteria.
The graduating seniors threw **themselves** a party.

We recognize eight reflexive pronouns.

Singular Forms	**Plural Forms**
myself	ourselves
yourself	yourselves
himself, herself, itself	themselves

Reflexive pronouns can fill any noun slot except subject. When they are in the direct object slot of a sentence, you will not be able to turn the sentence into a passive in order to test for a transitive verb. You cannot, for instance, make

Hitchcock often put **himself** into his movies.

into

*****Himself** was often put by Hitchcock into his movies.

Reflexives can be confusing in one other way. Because reflexive pronouns always refer to the subject noun, students sometimes think that a reflexive pronoun following a transitive verb is a predicate noun and the verb a linking verb, particularly since they can't make a passive sentence with the verb. But in the Hitchcock sentence above, the pronoun **himself** functions as a direct object because **put** is transitive. In the next sentence, **himself** functions as the direct object of the Vc verb **crowned**.

Napoleon crowned **himself** emperor in 1804.

And in

My grandmother often hummed lullabies to **herself**.

the reflexive pronoun **herself** functions as the object of a preposition in a sentence with a Vg verb. It is the indirect object, with **to herself** functioning as an adverb of reception.

INDEFINITE PRONOUNS end in -**body**, -**thing**, or -**one**. Unlike the personal and reflexive pronouns, the indefinite pronouns don't refer to specific nouns. As the name suggests, the meaning of an INDEFINITE PRONOUN is indefinite or general. The most common indefinite pronouns are:

somebody	something	someone
anybody	anything	anyone
everybody	everything	everyone
nobody	nothing	no one

Chapter Summary: Function Words Can Expand Noun Phrases

We've looked at the nouns and pronouns and at the components of noun phrases, like determiners and genitive constructions. You can expand noun phrases with a variety of function words, most of which fall into the category "determiner." Genitive nouns, which are not determiners, come in two forms, phrasal and inflective. You can fill noun phrase slots with personal pronouns, reflexive pronouns, and indefinite pronouns.

Here are the main points in the chapter:

- This chapter looks at noun phrase components.
- We classify nouns as proper and common.
- Determiners are function words that include articles, demonstratives, numbers, possessive pronouns, and prearticles.
- Definite articles indicate shared information.
- Demonstratives point to things.
- Some possessive pronouns pattern with nouns; others fill noun phrase slots.
- Numbers that precede nouns are determiners.
- Prearticles include several closed-class categories.
- Postnoun modifiers follow nouns.
- Genitives occur both as -'**s** nouns and as -**of** phrases.

- "Genitive" is a more accurate term than "possessive."
- Personal, reflexive, and indefinite pronouns fill noun phrase slots.
- Personal pronouns occur in subject and object forms.
- Reflexive pronouns end in -**self** or -**selves**.
- Indefinite pronouns end in -**body**, -**thing**, or -**one**.
- You can expand noun phrases with a variety of function words.

EXERCISES

I. Identifying Noun Constituents and Analyzing Sentences

Identify the noun constituents in the following sentences and label the other constituents in the sentences, both their structures and functions. Identify the status of the MV constituents as well. Sentences with personal pronouns are presented in pairs or triplets in order to make them more natural; analyze the two or three sentences in the unit. Some noun phrases include adjectives or other structures that function as adjectives (like **hospital** in the example, a noun functioning as an adjective). It's not necessary to identify these yet. Simply label a constituent like **hospital unit** as a noun phrase; we'll discuss these structures later, in Chapter 7. Concentrate on the noun phrase and verb phrase constituents we've covered so far.

EXAMPLE

Tiger Woods will sign the kids' casts during his hospital visit.

Explanation: In this sentence, **will sign** is the main verb. **Will** is a modal in the present tense form. So the status of **will sign** is present conditional. **Tiger Woods** is a proper noun functioning as the subject of the sentence. **The kids' casts** is a noun phrase composed of the genitive noun **kids'** along with a common noun **casts** and then the definite article **the**. **During his hospital visit** is a prepositional phrase that functions as an adverb of duration. **His** is a possessive pronoun; **hospital** is a noun that functions as an adjective. Together with **visit**, they make a noun phrase, **his hospital visit**, that functions as the object of the preposition **during**.

Sentences
1. Bruce Wayne will turn eighty in 2019.
2. The torte recipe required a cup of almonds.
3. Kwanzaa celebrates the heritage of African Americans.

4. Cell phones outsell all other media now.
5. *The Cat in the Hat* uses a vocabulary of 225 words.
6. No comics craft ballets of abuse like the Three Stooges.
7. The oil industry's misjudgments have scarred Alaska deeply.
8. Stephen Jay Gould's books address the question of evolution.
9. Umpires must administer the rules of the game fairly.
10. My father's surgeon plopped herself into a plastic chair. She listened to dad's complaints.
11. Antismoking activists are dancing on the Marlboro Man's grave.
12. No one answered the phone at your house last night. I called four times.
13. John Kennedy was a magnetic politician. The media made him a shining knight.
14. The five Shiites found themselves on the wrong side of Kurdistan during the shelling.
15. Pep rallies serve several purposes. They give teams support. And they give students a sense of togetherness.
16. Pennsylvania's Longwood Gardens unfold in four miles of paths.
17. One Japanese honeysuckle may produce 30 feet of vine in a single year.
18. Helsinki is full of offbeat charm.
19. The Internet makes everyone equal.
20. Lisa Henson was the first woman president of the *Harvard Lampoon*.
21. The modern study of linguistics began with Noam Chomsky's *Syntactic Structures* in 1957.
22. Computers perpetuate a two-tiered system of education in our country.
23. Most of California was rain-free last month.
24. Lack of money fuels divorce.
25. Boredom is contagious. It can cause a chain reaction in a dorm.
26. Forty-two percent of the nation's entrepreneurs are women.
27. China's economic growth is outstripping its development of infrastructure.
28. A poem can change direction swiftly.
29. The beauty of a taco lies in the eyes of the beholder.
30. Ireland kept European culture alive during the Dark Ages.
31. A beef brisket can be the star of a Passover meal.
32. The Watergate investigation motivated President Nixon's resignation.
33. The display of the Confederate flag outrages many Americans.

34. John Amos transforms himself into a parade of characters in *Halley's Comet.*

35. The manufacture of U.S. weapons is in the hands of a few giant corporations.

36. Today's circuses preserve the excitement of the Big Top.

37. Teachers often label hyperactive children troublemakers.

38. Edgar Allan Poe's work inspired Stephen King.

39. Pam Tillis left country music at 19. She returned at 35.

40. Charleston puts on a pretty face for its visitors.

41. Judy Blume's *Tales of a Fourth Grade Nothing* is a comic novel of sibling rivalry.

42. Men's fashions are returning to an elegant look.

43. "Dark Star" was the Grateful Dead's signature song for 25 years.

44. Ted Turner built a family billboard company into an entertainment colossus.

45. Ad agencies call Nike's Winged Victory symbol "THE SWOOSH."

46. Michael Tilson Thomas became the music director of the San Francisco Symphony in 1995. The city wanted a charismatic orchestra director. Thomas is that. He is also fiercely intelligent.

47. Goya ranks behind Picasso as Spain's greatest artist.

48. Weight-related illnesses kill 300,000 Americans every year.

49. The federal government is reconsidering the economic decisions of the last five decades.

50. Serena Williams put on a display of mature tennis during the U.S. Open.

CHAPTER 5

Rearranging and Compounding

Changing Core Sentences

We have identified all the basic grammatical components—the nouns, verbs, adjectives, and adverbs. We've constructed the six core sentences with their intransitive and transitive verbs, their Vg and Vc verbs, their linking verbs and parts of BE. We've expanded noun phrases and verb phrases. We've considered subject, predicate, and complement relationships, direct object and indirect object relationships.

From this point on, we'll use the core sentences as building blocks. In this chapter, we'll change the shape of the blocks by rearranging constituents, and we'll put the blocks together into larger structures by compounding. By rearranging, we'll make negative sentences, two kinds of question sentences, passive sentences, existential-there sentences, and imperative sentences. We'll conjoin constituents within sentences, and we'll conjoin sentences to make compound sentences. We'll see how punctuation can create various effects within and between sentences. And we'll look at how conjunctive adverbs, like conjunctions, connect clauses.

Making Negative Sentences

One way to rearrange a core sentence is to change it from positive to negative. All the sentences so far have been positive. You make positive sentences negative by inserting the NEGATIVE WORD **not** after the first word of the main verb, unless the first word is a verb. If the status of the main verb is conditional, you insert **not** after the modal.

Many high school students can locate Australia on a map.

↓

Many high school students can**not** locate Australia on a map.

The next diagram shows that **not** and the modal together make an auxiliary (**Aux**) constituent. Of course, you can contract the **not** with the modal to make **cannot** into **can't**:

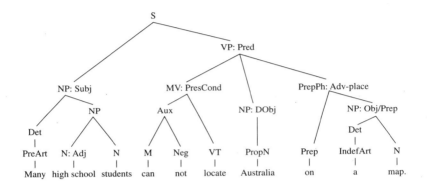

Many high school students **can't** locate Australia on a map.

If the status of the main verb is progressive aspect or perfective aspect, then you make the sentence negative by inserting **not** after the auxiliary HAVE or the auxiliary BE. Just as it does with modal, **not** makes an Aux constituent with HAVE or BE. Here are some examples, with diagrams.

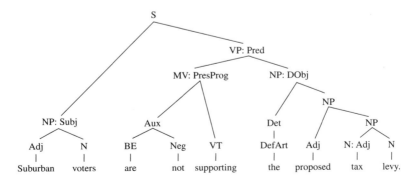

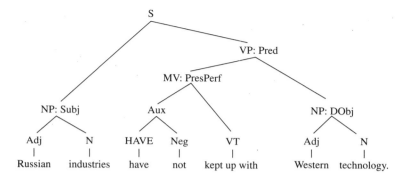

Suburban voters are supporting the proposed tax levy.

↓

Suburban voters are **not** supporting the proposed tax levy.

OR

Suburban voters **aren't** supporting the proposed tax levy.

Russian industries have kept up with Western technology.

↓

Russian industries have **not** kept up with Western technology.

OR

Russian industries **haven't** kept up with Western technology.

When the main verb of the sentence is the verb BE, you make the sentence negative by placing **not** after the BE. In this case, the **not** does not become part of Aux but part of the MV, along with BE.

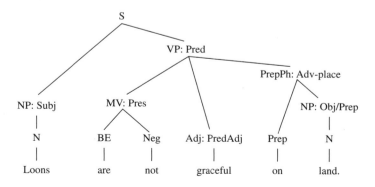

Loons are graceful on land.

↓

Loons are **not** graceful on land.

OR

Loons aren't graceful on land.

If the main verb of the sentence is a verb other than BE, you make the sentence negative by inserting **DO** along with **not** into the Aux constituent. Insert the Aux then DO beneath it on the diagram. Notice that DO will always indicate the same tense as the verb of the original sentence and that the verb itself will be in its base (nonfinite) form. The DO acts like a modal, and the verb acts just as it would if it followed a modal; the DO holds tense, and the verb is nonfinite. Neg and DO form an Aux constituent.

The senate approved the president's cabinet appointment.

↓

The senate **did not** approve the president's cabinet appointment.

OR

The senate **didn't** approve the president's cabinet appointment.

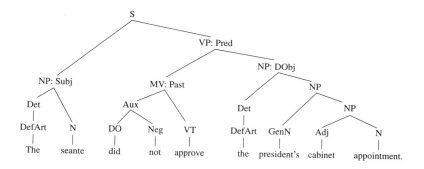

Changing Statements into Yes/No Questions

The core sentences are all STATEMENTS; they make assertions. But you can change statements into questions. The two most common question sentences are called yes/no questions and WH-questions.

YES/NO QUESTIONS are questions that you can answer with yes or no, like "Did Mary go to the movies last night?" or "Can the new pitcher throw a curveball?" To turn a core sentence into a yes/no question, you move the first word of the main verb to the front of the sentence, unless the first word is a verb. That is, the same constituents are involved in making yes/no questions as in making negative sentences. If the main verb contains a modal, HAVE, or BE, then you move the modal, HAVE, or BE. It does not matter whether the BE comes originally from the Aux, as in "Toxic wastes **are** threatening animal populations," or whether it is the verb BE, as in "Bill Gates' brainstorm **was** MS-DOS." Here are several statements turned into yes/no questions.

Nightmares **can** reveal psychotic states.

↓

Can nightmares reveal psychotic states?

Social problems **have** made police work difficult.

↓

Have social problems made police work difficult?

Toxic wastes **are** threatening animal populations.

↓

Are toxic wastes threatening animal populations?

Bill Gates' brainstorm **was** MS-DOS.

↓

Was Bill Gates' brainstorm MS-DOS?

The next diagram indicates that you disjoin part of the MV when you make a yes/no question: you move the first word of Aux.

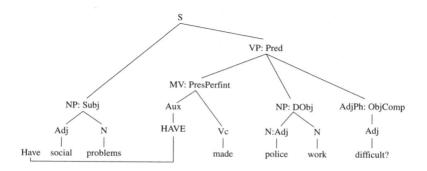

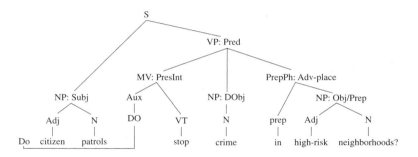

You also add **Int** to the status of the main verb, to indicate that the sentence is a question: it is in the interrogative mood. Notice that this disjunction (the movement of HAVE to the front of the sentence) does not change any functional relationships. The subject, the predicate, the direct object, and the object complement remain in exactly the same relationships. Even the main verb is still **HAVE ... made**, with the ellipsis indicating the fact that HAVE has been moved around the subject noun phrase. You do exactly the same for a modal or the auxiliary BE (**can ... reveal**, **are ... threatening**). The constituents in a yes/no question sentence keep their core relationships.

If the MV contains a verb other than BE and if it does not exhibit aspect or the conditional mood (if it has no modal, HAVE, or BE), then, just as you add DO to make a negative sentence, you add DO to make a yes/no question.

Citizen patrols stop crime in high-risk neighborhoods.
↓
Do citizen patrols stop crime in high-risk neighborhoods?

The DO acts like a modal. That is, it takes the tense form and becomes an Aux, as it does in a negative sentence. The verb shifts to its base form. And the main verb is the disjoined **Do ... stop**. The relationship between DO and the verb is easier to see when the verb is in past tense form and when it is irregular, as in:

The police department **bought** six Toyota hybrids
↓
Did the police department **buy** six Toyota hybrids?

Wh-Question Sentences

Wh-question sentences query a content phrase, generally a noun phrase or an adverb phrase. Sometimes they query determiners alone. To make a core sentence into a Wh-question, you replace a noun phrase with an INTERROGATIVE PRONOUN (**what, who, whom**), an adverb phrase with an INTERROGATIVE PROADVERB (**where, when, why, how, how often**), or a determiner with an INTERROGATIVE PRODETERMINER (**whose, which, what**). The interrogated phrase has to wind up at the front of the sentence. Here is an example of a core sentence changed into a Wh-question when its subject noun phrase is replaced by **who**:

> who
> ~~The GOP front-runner~~ joked with the reporters during
>   yesterday's press conference.
>   ↓
> **Who** joked with the reporters during yesterday's press conference?

Since the noun phrase replaced by **who** is the subject of the sentence, it is already at the front. If the phrase you're questioning is not the subject, you have to move it to the front of the sentence. Moving a phrase to make a Wh-question sentence also demands that you move a modal, HAVE, or BE, or that you add DO, because in a Wh-question, a finite constituent must sit next to the WH word. Here is a sentence with an adverb of manner questioned:

> how
> Business leaders can stimulate school reform ~~by investing in education~~.
>   ↓
> **How** can business leaders stimulate school reform?

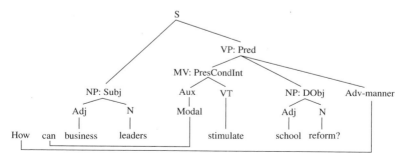

Just as the relationships between constituents remain the same when you disjoin them to make a yes/no question, the relationships between the constituents remain the same when you disjoin them to make a Wh-question. In the preceding example, the main verb remains **can ... stimulate**; the interrogative proadverb **how** functions as an adverb of manner. In the next example, the direct object noun phrase, **the Afghan troop movements**, is replaced by **what** and moved to the front of the sentence. But **what** remains the direct object of the sentence. **Had** is moved out of the normal Aux position, but **had ... worried about** is still the MV, just as **worried about** is still a two-word transitive verb, though its object has been moved to the front of the sentence:

what

The U.N. officers **had** worried about ~~the Afghan troop movements~~.

↓

What had the U.N. officers worried about?

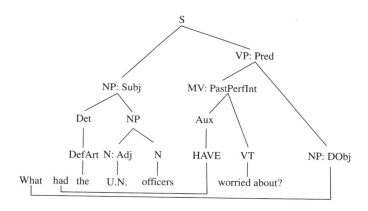

If the core sentence contains no auxiliary element, then you may have to add the auxiliary DO to the sentence in order to make it into a Wh-question. Here is a sentence with the verb **provided** as the only component of the main verb.

The satellite pictures of Venus provided the scientists new geological information.

Since the core MV has no auxiliary word, you have to add DO to Aux to complete the question sentence. Notice that, as with negative or yes/no question sentences in which you add DO, the DO takes on the tense form and the verb changes to the infinitive form. The relationships between the constituents remain the same. **Provide** is a Vg verb. **What** replaces the direct object noun phrase. **The scientists** is the indirect object. And **did . . . provide** is the MV.

what
The satellite pictures of Venus provided the scientists ~~**new geological information**~~.

↓

What did the satellite pictures of Venus **provide** the scientists?

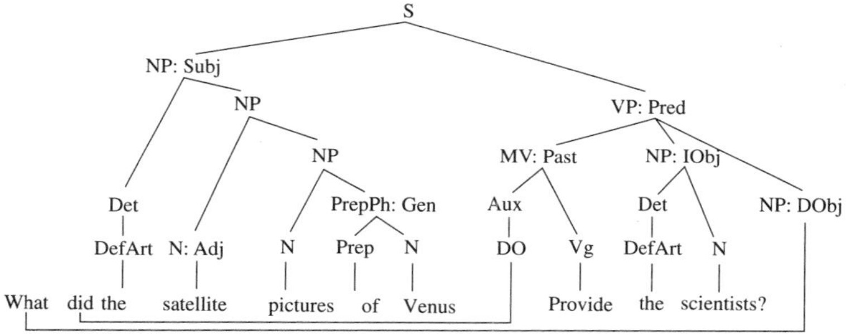

When you question a determiner or a genitive noun in a noun phrase, you move the whole noun phrase to the front of the sentence, not simply the determiner or genitive noun.

whose
The vandals trashed ~~**Sally's**~~ **car** last night.

↓

Whose car did the vandals trash last night?

which
The House Democrats voted ~~**this**~~ **way** on the education bill.

↓

Which way did the House Democrats vote on the education bill?

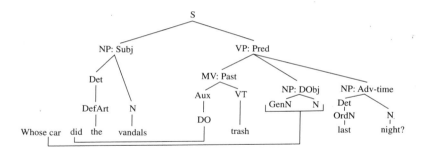

Passive Sentences

The most common rearranged sentence pattern is called a PASSIVE. The rearrangement into a passive sentence demands that you introduce BE into the auxiliary, add a prepositional phrase, change the verb into its past participial form, and move both the subject and object noun phrase constituents. Here is a core sentence rearranged as a passive:

Congress funded the cleanup.

↓

The cleanup was funded by Congress.

Passives can only be made from sentences with transitive verbs, one-place or two-place transitives (VT, Vg, or Vc). The passive is closely linked with transitive verbs; as you remember, the passive was originally introduced to test whether a verb was transitive. You make a sentence passive by taking the core object and moving it to the front of the verb; then you put the core subject into a prepositional phrase headed by the preposition **by**; finally, you change the core verb into its past participial form and add **BE**—either **is, was,** or **were**—to the Aux constituent. Here is another passive, with the movements shown in schematic form:

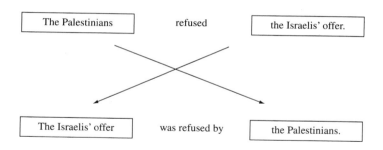

Since the core object noun phrase (**the Israelis' offer**) sits in the slot before the verb in the passive, it is called a GRAMMATICAL SUBJECT (the original object noun phrase occupies the grammatical space before a verb, the space that a subject normally occupies); the core subject (**the Palestinians**), now the object of a preposition (by the **Palestinians**), is called a LOGICAL SUBJECT (semantically, the core subject still does what a subject normally does: it performs an action). At the same time that it functions as the logical subject, the noun phrase you've moved into the prepositional phrase also functions as the object of a preposition. The **by**-prepositional phrase itself functions as an adverb of agency. Agency in this sense refers to "performing the action," what the subject of a transitive verb normally does. So, calling the prepositional phrase an adverb of agency is just another way of saying that the noun phrase object of the preposition relates to the verb just as a subject noun phrase normally relates to a transitive verb, as an agent or performer of the action. Since the object of the preposition is the original subject, you would expect it to retain this role as performer of the action.

Look closely at the main verb in the example. It is passive because it contains an auxiliary BE followed by a past participle (**was refused**): the passive is the only construction in English that contains BE followed by a past participle. The status of the main verb is past passive because the auxiliary BE is in its past tense form. Remember from Chapter 3 that tense occurs only once in a main verb and that it always changes the form of the first word in the main verb.

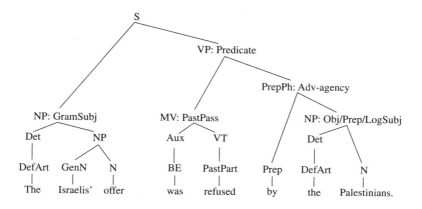

Here is a passive sentence with an irregular verb, **write**. It is easier to see the change from past to past participle with the verb **write**, since the past participle of an irregular verb is different from its past tense form.

Thomas Jefferson **wrote** the Declaration of Independence.

↓

The Declaration of Independence **was written** by Thomas Jefferson.

Deleting "By" from a Passive

Under certain circumstances, you may delete the **by**-phrase from passive sentences. You may delete it if the information in the **by**-phrase is available from other sources in the general context, like a previous sentence in the paragraph; or you may delete the **by**-phrase if the information in the **by**-phrase is general knowledge. If, for example, you were writing a story about police and gangs in Los Angeles, you might have already written that it is the new gangs in town that are challenging the police. So you wouldn't have to repeat **by the new gangs** in the following sentence:

The police are challenged **by the new gangs** in several neighborhoods.

↓

The police are challenged in several neighborhoods.

Or if you were writing an article for a gardening magazine, you might assume that the readers understand it is gardeners who grow hostas for their foliage. So you wouldn't have to include the phrase **by gardeners** in the following sentence:

Hostas are grown **by gardeners** for their handsome foliage.

↓

Hostas are grown for their handsome foliage.

With or without the **by**-phrase, a sentence is passive as long as its main verb contains an auxiliary BE followed by a past participle.

Core Arrangement of Passive Constituents

Where have all the constituents gone? They haven't exactly gone to graveyards, as the old Peter, Paul and Mary song said about the flowers.

But they have moved around in passive sentences. So sometimes their functions seem buried under six feet of earth. The best way to clarify for yourself what the sentence constituents are and what their functions are is to put the constituents back into their core arrangement. Let's look at a few examples. In the passive sentence

> The Russian royal family was executed in June 1917,

the agent phrase has been deleted. It would be something like **by Soviet soldiers** or simply **by someone**. So if you are unclear about relationships in the passive and want to rebuild the core sentence, you have to put the **by**-phrase back into the passive. Then you can reconstruct the active sentence by reversing the passive rearrangement:

> The Russian royal family was executed **by Soviet soldiers** in
> June 1917.
>
> ↓
>
> **Soviet soldiers** executed the Russian royal family in June 1917.

With the passive and active forms back to back, you should be able to see clearly what is going on in the passive. The verb is the transitive verb **executed**. It is transitive in the core sentence; it is transitive in the passive sentence, though its object noun phrase, **the Russian royal family**, has been moved to the grammatical subject position and its subject, **Soviet soldiers**, was moved into a **by**-phrase and then deleted. It's important to remember that only a transitive verb (VT, Vc, or Vg) can be made into a passive and that the verb remains transitive, even after it is made passive. Here's a bit more complicated example to make into an active sentence:

> The GOP's tax plan was considered divisive.

You have to reconstruct a deleted agent before you make the sentence active. **By reporters** seems reasonable; **by someone** would work. So, here is the rebuilt sentence:

> The GOP's tax plan was considered divisive **by reporters**.
>
> ↓
>
> **Reporters** considered the GOP's tax plan divisive.

The Vc verb **considered** is the main verb of the reconstructed active sentence. **The GOP's tax plan** functions as a direct object, and **divisive** is an adjective that functions as the object complement. Nothing new here. Having established the original relationships, you can determine the relationships in the passive sentence because they're the same. The main verb of the passive is **was considered**, with **considered** the head. **Considered** is a Vc verb in the active; it's a Vc in the passive. **Divisive** is an adjective functioning as an object complement in the active; it's an adjective functioning as an object complement in the passive. **The GOP's tax plan** is a direct object in the active; in the passive it's called a grammatical subject because it was moved into the slot before the main verb.

Past Participles and Adjectives

There is a problem you'll face when you have to identify a passive with a deleted **by**-phrase. A passive with a deleted agent can look like a core sentence that has BE as the main verb followed by a predicate adjective. This is because past participles and adjectives can look alike. Sometimes the difference between past participles and adjectives is obvious because of a sentence's meaning, as in

> The characters in the *M*A*S*H* episode were drunk. (Verb BE + adjective)
> The martinis were drunk by the characters on the *M*A*S*H* episode. (Aux BE + past participle)

In the first example, **drunk** is clearly an adjective because no one would dream of **drunk** as the past participle of a verb in this context (you can't **drink** characters). In the second example, **drunk** is clearly the past participle of the verb **drink** because martinis can't be **drunk** unless someone **drinks** them. At other times the meaning of a sentence does not clearly differentiate an adjective from a past participle:

> Lois is frustrated.

Lois may be frustrated **by Clark** (from *Clark frustrated Lois*), in which case the example sentence is passive (auxiliary BE plus a past participle). Or Lois may be in a state of frustration (verb BE plus an adjective). If you are given a sentence like the last example to analyze, with no contextual clues to help you decide whether **frustrated** is a past participle or an adjective, the best you can do is to indicate that you are aware of both possible analyses.

"Get" as a Passive Auxiliary

Passive sentences normally imply that the logical subject (the core subject) caused something to happen to the grammatical subject (the core object). But passive sentences can also suggest a sense of "becoming." **Get** seems to suggest this sense of becoming more strongly than **BE**. So sometimes you'll find **get** as the auxiliary in a passive sentence rather than **BE**, especially in informal language, in order to emphasize the sense of becoming, as in

The paper's TV critic panned the World Series telecasts.

↓

The World Series telecasts **were** panned by the paper's TV critic.

OR

The World Series telecasts **got** panned by the paper's TV critic.

Dad chewed out my little brother.

↓

My little brother **was** chewed out by Dad.

OR

My little brother **got** chewed out by Dad.

Rearranging a Passive Sentence

Once you turn a sentence into a passive, you can make it negative or change it into a question, just as if it were a core sentence with an auxiliary BE. Simply place the negative marker **not** after the BE in order to make a negative sentence. Move BE to the front of the sentence to make it a yes/no question, or move both BE and a Wh-word to make a Wh-question.

The communications satellite was recovered by the shuttle crew.

↓

The communications satellite was **not** recovered by the shuttle crew.

Billy the Kid **was** shot by Pat Garrett.

↓

Was Billie the Kid shot by Pat Garrett?

who

The state's prison-reform movement was initiated by ~~a political action committee.~~

↓

Who was the state's prison-reform movement initiated by?

The morinda citrifolia plant is treasured by Polynesians **for its medicinal value.**

why
↓

Why is the morinda citrifolia plant treasured by Polynesians?

Status and Passive

When you identify the status of the main verb of a passive sentence, you normally state that it is passive as the final comment. Here are some variations on a single sentence, with the status identified for each:

The protesting students **were protected** by a police contingent (Past Passive)

The protesting students **may be protected** by a police contingent. (Present conditional passive)

The protesting students **are being protected** by a police contingent. (Present progressive passive)

The protesting students **had been protected** by a police contingent. (Past perfect passive)

The protesting students **might have been protected** by a police contingent. (Past perfect conditional passive)

Existential-There Sentences

When a core sentence contains the verb BE followed by an adverb of place, you can sometimes add **there** and rearrange the constituents to produce a new sentence called an EXISTENTIAL-THERE SENTENCE. The name may sound imposing and difficult, but the rearrangement is straightforward. And the outcome is a common sentence type. Here are two examples:

Millions of drug dealers are in the United States.
↓
There are millions of drug dealers in the United States.

Several first-class restaurants are in the new mall.
↓
There are several first-class restaurants in the new mall.

To create the existential-there sentence, you move the original subject noun phrase around the verb BE and place **there** into the now empty core subject slot. As in a passive sentence, the constituent in the original subject position (the **there**) is called the grammatical subject, while the original core subject, which has been moved to the right of the verb, is called the logical subject. The following diagram shows the relationships in the first example sentence. The original subject noun phrase, **millions of drug dealers**, follows the verb BE as the logical subject; **there** fills the core subject slot as the grammatical subject (see the next diagram).

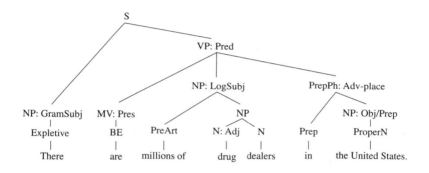

Some existential-there sentences don't seem to be rearrangements of core sentences; nonetheless, they have the other characteristics of rearranged sentences, including **there** as the grammatical subject, sitting to the left of the verb BE, and a noun phrase functioning as the logical subject, following the verb, as in

There may be a labor shortage in a few years.

For such a sentence, there does not seem to be a core-sentence source like **A labor shortage may be in a few years*.

Expletives

The **there** that functions as the grammatical subject in an existential-there sentence is called an expletive. An EXPLETIVE is a word that has a grammatical function in a sentence but has no meaning of its own. In the case of existential-there sentences, **there** replaces a noun and functions as a grammatical subject: it fills a noun phrase slot. But it is not a noun itself; nor is it a pronoun.

There are two other expletives in English: **DO** and **it** in certain circumstances can be expletives. The **DO** which occurs in the Aux of negative or question sentences to hold tense is an expletive. It has no other role but to show the tense form; it's sort of like a dummy modal. The **it** in the subject position of existential sentences like

>**It** is raining.
>AND
>**It's** hot today.

is also an expletive. The word **it** in such sentences is not a pronoun; it does not refer to a previous noun, as a pronoun would. The expletive **it** does perform a noun job, though. It functions as the subject of the sentence and fills a noun phrase slot. In Chapter 8, we'll look at rear-ranged sentences like

>**It** seems that the Orlando Magic will win the playoffs.
>AND
>**It** occurred to Andy that Barney needed help at the jail.

In these sentences, expletives function as grammatical subjects.

Imperative Sentences

IMPERATIVE SENTENCES are commands or instructions. They tell you to do something: clean your room, take the dog out, erase the blackboard. Parents and teachers use a lot of imperative sentences. So do writers of cookbooks and other how-to books. Here are a few examples of imperative structure:

>Mix the herbs with the spices.
>Stir the garnish into the soup.
>Don't wear black to the dance.
>Turn off your cell phone.
>Insert tab A into flange B before assembling base.

Deleting "You" and "Will" from Imperative Sentences

You've probably learned that imperative sentences have an "understood you" as subject. That is, you can understand **you** to be the subject of a sentence like **Stir the garnish into the soup**, though the word **you** does not occur in the sentence. It does seem to be the case that, in order to make a core sentence into an imperative form, you have to delete the pronoun **you** from the subject noun phrase. But it also seems to be the case that you have to delete a modal **will** along with the pronoun **you**. To demonstrate why this is so, we'll have to look first at how you make tag questions.

TAG QUESTIONS repeat the subject and auxiliary of a sentence in an added tag phrase. So, to make a tag phrase, you take the first word in AUX, make it negative (if it is positive), and add the subject of the sentence; if the subject is a personal pronoun, simply copy the pronoun. Otherwise, turn the noun phrase subject into a pronoun:

> Congress will pass the new tax bill.
>
> ↓
>
> Congress will pass the new tax bill, **won't it?**

> We have put too much money into the chemical weapons
>   program.
>
> ↓
>
> We have put too much money into the chemical weapons
>   program, **haven't we?**

Making tag questions is pretty straightforward. Now let's take a look at imperative sentences in relation to tags. If you were given an imperative sentence like

> Turn in the paper before class.

you would make the following tag:

> Turn in the paper before class, **won't you?**

As this example shows, when you make tags for imperative sentences, you invariably use both the pronoun **you** and modal **will**. Most grammarians take this fact to be proof that both **will** and **you** exist in the underlying (core) structure of imperative sentences. In other words, both **you** and **will** are "understood."

Diagraming Imperative Sentences

When you diagram imperative sentences, don't include the underlying constituents. Leave out the subject and modal, showing the verb phrase as the single constituent of S and the verb as the only constituent of MV, as in the diagram on the next page.

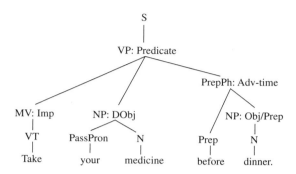

Imperative Sentences Lack Tense

Imperative is a mood, like indicative, interrogative, or conditional. You indicate that fact when you label the status of the main verb. The status is simply **imperative** or **imperative mood**, if you wish. The main verb of an imperative has no tense. Since you delete the modal **will** from an imperative sentence, you delete tense as well. The verb of an imperative is always in the infinitive form. An imperative is the only English sentence whose main verb is an infinitive.

The Negative Form of Imperatives

The negative form of imperatives contains a **DO not**, just like the negative of a sentence without an auxiliary constituent. Since imperatives delete **you** and **will**, it follows that to make an imperative into a negative, you insert an expletive **DO** in order to introduce the **not**. Otherwise, imperative sentences would sound like *Not wear black to the dance. But of course they don't. Here is how to derive a negative imperative:

You will wear black to the dance.

↓

Not wear black to the dance.

↓

Don't wear black to the dance.

Compounding Structures

The most common way to make sentences longer is to compound structures within them (the term "compound" is used interchangeably with "conjoin" or "coordinate"). When you COMPOUND structures, you put them together into a single constituent, usually with connective words and phrases called CONJUNCTIONS. If you compound more than two constituents, you usually need commas as well. You can compound any level of constituent—words, phrases, or clauses. Here are three nouns compounded:

Edison suffered from dyslexia.
Einstein suffered from dyslexia.
Michelangelo suffered from dyslexia.
↓
Edison, Einstein, and Michelangelo suffered from dyslexia.

On a diagram, you show compound words or phrases first as single constituents, along with their unitary function, then you break the units down into their separate constituents. In the next diagram, the constituent **Edison, Einstein, and Michelangelo** is first shown as a noun phrase, then the individual nouns are shown as separate noun phrases joined with the conjunction **and**.

The three noun phrases put together this way make a single compound noun phrase constituent that functions as the subject of the sentence. Compound words and phrases together make constituents that can function wherever and however single words or phrases can function. Here are compound noun phrases functioning as direct objects:

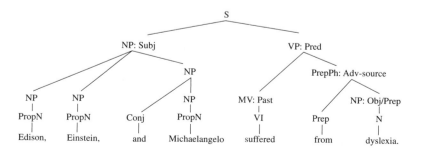

Lorenzo steals Shylock's daughter and a pile of Shylock's money.
Columbus didn't find **India or Japan**.

Here are examples of different kinds of compound words and phrases:

Vito Corleone became the Godfather and entered movie
mythology. (VP:Pred)
Soviet leaders usually left office **in a coffin or in disgrace**.
(PrepPh:Adv-manner)
Elephants are endangered **by poachers and by complacent
governments**. (Prep Ph:Adv-agency)
The new Macs were **unpacked and networked** on our office
router. (V)
Zeppelins and dirigibles evolved from balloons. (NP:Subj)

Here are conjoined sentences. Together they make one compound
sentence:

Hanna-Barbera introduced *The Flintstones,* and Disney gave us
The Lion King.

Coordinate and Correlative Conjunctions

There are two types of conjunction: coordinate and correlative. The
COORDINATE CONJUNCTIONS are the single words **and, but**, and
or. The CORRELATIVE CONJUNCTIONS are pairs of words—**both** . . .
and, either . . . **or, neither** . . . **nor,** and **not only** . . . **but also**. Correlative
conjunctions are more emphatic than coordinate conjunctions, because the
first of the pair demands that you anticipate the coordinated word or
phrase. Note the difference between the first example with the coordinate
conjunction **or** and the second version with a correlative conjunction
either . . . **or**:

Those prehistoric idols supposedly produced fecundity in the
marriage bed **or** the farm field.
Those prehistoric idols supposedly produced fecundity in
either the marriage bed **or** the farm field.

As you know, it's difficult to diagram disjoined constituents like correlative
conjunctions. In the diagram, the correlative conjunction **either** . . . **or** is
shown as two words linked together into one disjoined constituent. In this
reading, the conjunction is **either** . . . **or,** and the word **either** is moved to
the left of the compound noun phrase **the marriage bed** . . . **the farm field**.

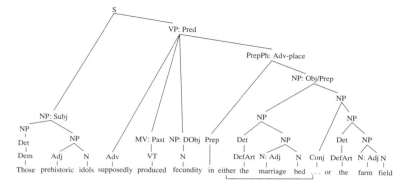

Conjoining and Commas

Normally when you conjoin only two words or phrases, you do not punctuate the compound:

> We celebrate the sesquicentennial of the Tootsie Roll and Cracker Jack in 2046.

When you conjoin more than two words or phrases, you generally put a conjunction before the final item in the compound and commas between the items:

> We celebrate the sesquicentennial of the Tootsie Roll, Cracker Jack, and Michelob in 2046.

When you use conjunctions to link sentences, you have several punctuation options. You can put a comma before the conjunction:

> The French love Charlie Chaplin's subtle clowning, **but** they revere Jerry Lewis' brash antics.

You can put a semicolon before the conjunction:

> The French love Charlie Chaplin's subtle clowning; **but** they revere Jerry Lewis' brash antics.

Or you can end the first sentence with a period and begin the next with a capital:

> The French love Charlie Chaplin's subtle clowning. **But** they revere Jerry Lewis' brash antics.

When you need to produce a special effect with compounds, you can change the normal punctuation. In the following example, for instance, the adverb of frequency **again** is repeated with conjunctions and no punctuation in order to emphasize the way the children rode the carousel:

The preschoolers rode the carousel **again and again and again**.

There are also times when you might want to use commas but no conjunctions:

Our office copier staples, stacks, collates.

Without conjunctions, the series jumps from one verb to another, almost mimicking the jerky movement of the copy machine. Notice how much smoother the movement is with a conjunction:

Our office copier staples, stacks, and collates.

In some cases—if they are brief—you can even connect sentences as you would phrases, either with commas alone, with commas and conjunctions, or with conjunctions only:

Winds howled, waves crashed, decks swayed.
OR
Winds howled, waves crashed, and decks swayed.
OR
Winds howled and waves crashed and decks swayed.

One other option would separate the sentences with periods:

Winds howled. Waves crashed. And decks swayed.

But separating this series of sentences with periods would lose some of the sense of the turbulence of the storm.

So the way you punctuate coordinate structures can change the effect sentences have on readers. Be careful, though, to break standard punctuation practice only when it is important to make a special point. Otherwise hold to the standard practice. It's what readers expect. And readers aren't normally happy to have their expectations go unmet unless they see good reason for it.

Attaching Conjunctions

One final issue with compounds is where and how to attach conjunctions. A conjunction always attaches to the constituent to its right. In the following sentence, **and** attaches to the noun phrase **Desi Arnaz:**

Lucille Ball **and Desi Arnaz** were the biggest sitcom stars of the 1950s.

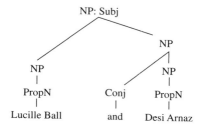

On a diagram, you show a conjunction attached to a noun phrase as in the following diagram. A conjunction introduces a phrase or clause it's attached to. It attaches to the constituent, but it doesn't quite become a part of it. You can think of a conjunction's relationship to the constituent it is attached to like that of a magnet attached to a refrigerator. The magnet attaches to the refrigerator, but everyone knows it's simply added on, not quite a component of the refrigerator. "Take the refrigerator," you might say to the repair man, "but let me keep my magnet."

Conjunctive Adverbs

Closely related to conjunctions are CONJUNCTIVE ADVERBS. They connect sentences, but they give a different kind of information about the relations between sentences than conjunctions do. Some grammarians call conjunctive adverbs DISCOURSE MARKERS. The reason is that conjunctive adverbs are in some sense the writer's or speaker's comments about how she wants her text read or understood; in that way, conjunctive adverbs mark the discourse. It's as if the writer is saying, "Now I'm going **to sum up**" or "Now I want you to understand what is happening **in the meantime**." The most common conjunctive adverbs are words and phrases like **besides, furthermore, first, for, finally, however, in the first place, in the meantime, likewise, moreover, nonetheless, notwithstanding, on the other hand, rather,** and **then**. They typically show comparison, contrast, cause/effect, and sequence. When you connect sentence with them, you punctuate with periods or semicolons.

Brand-name cereals are expensive. **Nonetheless**, they appeal to kids.

Semicolons show a closer relationship between the sentences.

Brand-name cereals are expensive; **nonetheless**, they appeal to kids.

Conjunctive adverbs do not have to introduce the second clause. You can generally move them to the middle or end of a clause:

Brand-name cereals are expensive; they **nonetheless** appeal to kids.
Brand-name cereals are expensive. They appeal to kids **nonetheless**.

Chapter Summary: Rearranging and Compounding Core Sentences

In this chapter, we've looked both at how to change the shape of our building blocks (the core sentences) to make them negatives or questions or passives or imperatives and how to put the blocks together into new, larger structures by compounding. This is the first chapter in which we've worked with the original core sentences as building blocks. In later chapters, we'll look at other ways to put the core sentences together in order to form larger, more complex sentences. Here are the main points in the chapter:

- Core sentences are building blocks.
- To make a sentence negative, insert **not** after the first auxiliary word or insert an expletive **DO** in it.
- To make a yes/no question, move the first auxiliary word of the main verb to the front of the sentence.
- Wh-question sentences query a noun phrase, adverb phrase, or determiner.
- Passives can only be made from sentences with transitive verbs.
- You may delete the **by**-phrase from passive sentences.
- To clarify the constituents and functions, put them back into their core arrangement.
- Past participles and adjectives can look alike.

- Sometimes **get** is the auxiliary in a passive sentence.
- You can make a passive sentence negative or change it into a question.
- When you identify status, passive is the final comment.
- To produce an existential-there sentence, move the subject and add **there**.
- An expletive has a grammatical function but no meaning of its own.
- Imperative sentences have no visible subject.
- Delete **you** and **will** to make an imperative sentence.
- When you diagram imperative sentences, leave out the subject and modal.
- The main verb of an imperative sentence has no tense.
- The negative form of imperatives contains **DO not**.
- When you compound structures, you put them together into a single constituent.
- There are two types of conjunction, coordinate and correlative.
- To conjoin more than two constituents, put conjunctions and commas between them.
- A conjunction attaches to the constituent to its right.
- Conjunctive adverbs connect sentences as discourse markers.
- We've rearranged the core sentences and compounded them into larger structures.

EXERCISES

I. Rearranging and Compounding Sentences

Change the following core sentences into the patterns indicated in parentheses.

EXAMPLE

Potato fields had been on Long Island before World War II. (There)

↓

There had been potato fields on Long Island before World War II.

1. Alfred Hitchcock directed *Psycho.* (Passive)
2. You will go to your room. (Imperative)
3. The Mafia is ripping off the government. (Yes/no question)

4. A kid can read something. (Wh-question with the object questioned)
5. No Saabs are in the school lot. (There)
6. The hospital threw out razor blades in safe ways. The hospital threw out hypodermic needles in safe ways. (Negative and compound noun phrases)
7. Hispanics have gained political clout during the last decade. Women have gained political clout during the last decade. African Americans have gained political clout during the last decade. (Use noun phrases from all three sentences to make one sentence with compound noun phrases; experiment with different ways of compounding and punctuating)
8. Hondas give you peace of mind. Hondas give you pride of ownership. (Compound with **not only ... too**)
9. Whole wheat flour can turn your brownies into nutritional treats. Whole wheat flour can turn your cakes into nutritional treats. Whole wheat flour can turn your cookies into nutritional treats. (Compound noun phrases; experiment with different ways of compounding and punctuating)
10. Police officers have the highest suicide rate. Miners have the highest job-fatality rate. (Conjoin the sentences with either a conjunction or a conjunctive adverb)

II. Analyzing Sentences

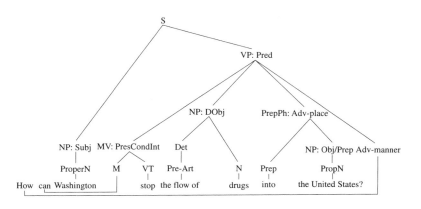

Analyze the following sentences, identifying the structures and their functions, as far as you are able. If the constituents are rearranged from their core positions, be sure to note whether the subjects and objects are logical and grammatical subjects. Be careful, also, to indicate whether any of the constituents are compounds; if they are, indicate how they are compounded—with conjunctions or conjunctive adverbs, or with punctuation alone. Feel free to diagram if you find that diagraming helps your analyses.

EXAMPLE

How can Washington stop the flow of drugs into the United States?

Explanation: **How can Washington stop the flow of drugs into the United States?** is a Wh-question sentence. It is derived from the statement **Washington can stop the flow of drugs into the United States in some way**. The modal **can** is moved to the front of the sentence; then the adverb of manner, the prepositional phrase **in some way**, is changed to the proadverb **how** and moved before the modal. The subject of the sentence is the proper noun **Washington**. The main verb is **can ... stop**; its status is present conditional interrogative. The transitive verb **stop** is followed by the object noun phrase **the flow of drugs**. The noun phrase object is composed of the prearticle **the flow of** and the noun **drugs**. The prepositional phrase **into the United States**, which functions as an adverb of place, is composed of the preposition **into** and the noun phrase **the United States** (see diagram on next page).

Sentences

1. Marco Polo might not have reached China on his Asia trip.
2. There are several Democratic candidates at this point.
3. Why do school buildings sit empty most of the day?
4. The Sox couldn't put together a rally in the fifth.
5. Fingernails are scrutinized by nutritionists for vitamin deficiencies.
6. The Marx Brothers were funny and progressive and creative.
7. Dutch New Amsterdam became English New York. But Dutch Breukelen remained.
8. Homer and Marge Simpson and their three kids put the fun in dysfunctional.

9. One third of American households sort their garbage now. So 40 million tons of garbage is recycled yearly.
10. The tarot cards were set out by the fortune-teller.
11. Homeowners shouldn't keep firewood close to the house.
12. There are thousands of Harry Potter fans throughout the world.
13. What influenced Dr. King's dream?
14. Could the pioneers and the Native Americans have coexisted without violence?
15. Julia Child's first TV show was called *The French Chef.* But she was neither French nor a chef.
16. Why didn't George Washington free his slaves after the Revolution?
17. How often has genocide reared its ugly head since the Holocaust?
18. Bake the mixture in the oven for 20 minutes.
19. Trinidad's mud volcanoes don't spew lava. They belch mud.
20. Some Southern states honor both Robert E. Lee and Martin Luther King Jr. on Martin Luther King Day.
21. Macbeth is consumed by ambition, deceit, and remorse.
22. Gunfire could be heard throughout Jerusalem.
23. Diet and exercise can lower cholesterol.
24. Boys don't read Nancy Drew.
25. Churchill, Stalin, and Roosevelt created modern Europe at Yalta in 1945.
26. Alzheimer's strips away mind and ideas.
27. There was no warning before the quake.
28. Did the Druids build Stonehenge for Celtic rites?
29. Help the hungry in your community.
30. Can the wilderness heal an oil spill?
31. Martin Luther King Jr. called for liberty and justice.
32. There are raspberries and blackberries in the tart.
33. Whose birthdays do we celebrate in February?
34. The century's first decade turned into a decade of terrorism and economic collapse.
35. Where can you escape from crowds, cell phones, and fax machines?
36. Rap rhythms and gospel messages make Christian hip-hop a strange musical blend.
37. How do you teach kids respect and tolerance?
38. Modern poetry can be ironic, ambiguous, and complex.

39. There are many superb burgundies in California.
40. Why can't America afford good nursing care?
41. Americans love golf. But it is a cruel, inscrutable game.
42. There's big money in burger franchises.
43. The Balkan countries can't escape their bellicose history.
44. White teenage girls define beauty in terms of physical perfection. In contrast, black teenage girls define it in terms of the right attitude.
45. There are four outdoor concerts at the riverfront park this summer.
46. Pop spotted the overturned van and stopped our car.
47. Marine recruits are taught the values of the Corps by their D.I.s.
48. The women's movement won't fade away.
49. Walt Whitman's poetry was not appreciated in his day. Nonetheless, *Leaves of Grass* sings out fresh and vibrant today.
50. Dr. Seuss won fame with sweetly screwball drawings and catchy rhymes.

CHAPTER 6

Constructing Relative Clauses

Dependent Clauses

Clauses are either independent or dependent. All the clauses we've looked at so far are sentences, INDEPENDENT CLAUSES. Independent clauses are not included within other clauses. DEPENDENT CLAUSES (also called SUBORDINATE CLAUSES) are included within larger clauses; the grammatical term for included within is EMBEDDED.

Subordinate constructions, phrases or clauses, are embedded as either nouns, adverbs, or adjectives. In this chapter, we'll look at clauses called RESTRICTIVE RELATIVE CLAUSES. Because they are always embedded within noun phrases and become attributes of head nouns, restrictive relative clauses are also called ADJECTIVE CLAUSES.

Whether they are dependent or independent, all clauses contain a noun phrase subject and a finite verb phrase predicate. So the subordinate clauses we'll meet in this and later chapters are structurally the same as the independent clauses we've looked at and analyzed in the previous chapters. They all have the same parts. Subordinate clauses just occur in different places than independent clauses: they are embedded within larger clauses.

Little Sentences Combine to Make Big Sentences

When we embed a clause as a dependent clause, we take one sentence and combine it into another. In essence, we combine little sentences to make big sentences.

We create dependent clauses in our speech and writing with ease. We can as easily learn to recognize and parse them. The dependent clauses we'll look at in this chapter are called relative clauses. More specifically, they are restrictive relative clauses.

Why We Combine Clauses

Why do we combine clauses within larger structures when we speak and write? We don't have to, of course. We could simply string independent clauses together with **ands**, as small children frequently do. It wouldn't be unusual for a child to tell you about her trip to the store in this way: "I went to the store, and I bought some peanut butter, and I took it home, and I was gonna make a sandwich." But stringing clauses together is an inefficient way to speak or write. As we grow older, we learn to combine clauses in order both to specify relationships between our ideas and to save words. So we'd probably make the child's sentence into something like, "When I went to the store, I bought some peanut butter, which I took home to make a sandwich." The new sentence is much more efficient; it contains fewer words and states more clearly the relationships between the events. If you read the original string of clauses and then the combined sentence aloud, you'll see how much more adult the combined sentence sounds. When the clauses are simply conjoined, you can almost hear a child's breathless outburst.

A Relative Clause Embeds into a Noun Phrase

Building sentences by embedding clauses into one another is natural. If you were assigned a paper about labor relations at a factory in your town, you might write the following two statements:

> The labor arbitrators examined the problems.
> The problems had caused the strike.

Since both sentences contain the noun phrase **the problems**, you can combine the two sentences into one, making the second into the relative clause **that had caused the strike**.

> The labor arbitrators examined the problems.
>   **that**
> ~~The problems~~ had caused the strike.
>   ↓
> The labor arbitrators examined the problems **that had caused the strike**.

When you combine clauses, you follow the design that the language allows. You embed a relative clause into a noun phrase, nesting a constituent within a constituent to create a new, larger constituent. Chapter 2 indicates that the hierarchy is the basic structural principle of language and that all constituents are structured as hierarchies, boxes nested within boxes. When you embed a relative clause into the noun phrase of a larger clause, you follow that same principle: you nest it within a hierarchy. The next tree diagram illustrates the relationship between the dependent clause and the sentence in this example about labor arbitrators and strikes.

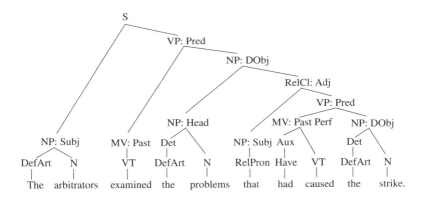

The relative clause is embedded within the larger clause; the "larger clause" in the example happens to be a sentence. Like all restrictive relative clauses, the relative clause in our example is embedded within a noun phrase constituent, in this case the object noun phrase of the sentence. So the original direct object noun phrase, **the problems**, and the embedded clause, **that had caused the strike**, combine to make a new noun phrase constituent, **the problems that had caused the strike**. The expanded noun phrase, like the original one, **the problems**, is the direct object of the verb **examined**. This is an important point to understand. It's worth repeating: the original noun phrase and the embedded clause make a new noun phrase constituent. The new noun phrase is a single noun phrase constituent, and it functions as the direct object of the verb **examined**. You can't separate the parts and say that **the problems** functions as the direct object. It is the whole new constituent, as a unit, that functions as the direct object.

Look again at the noun phrase **the problems that had caused the strike**. The original noun phrase **the problems** functions as the head of the new phrase. The relative clause functions as an adjective within the larger noun phrase. **The problems that had caused the strike** is a new constituent. It is a noun phrase, and it can be used anywhere that the original noun phrase could be used.

These two points are crucial to understanding what happens when clauses are embedded as restrictive relative clauses: (1) the relative clause and the noun phrase it is embedded into form a new noun phrase constituent, a single unit, and (2) the relative clause becomes an attribute of that noun phrase and thus is called an adjective clause.

Because they make a single noun phrase constituent with a noun phrase head, we don't punctuate restrictive relative clauses. In Chapter 9, we'll look at nonrestrictive relative clauses, which do need punctuation.

The Way It Was Is the Way It Is

Before we study the structure of relative clauses, let's look at a story that might help you remember the overall lesson. A TV commercial for the Bob Evans restaurant chain a few years ago depicted customers enjoying their food in a relaxed, old-fashioned atmosphere; the visual message was that the restaurants brought back the friendly service and the hearty food of bygone days. The voiceover, spoken by a resonant male voice, emphasized the visual message with the statement, "The way it was is the way it is." It's a good theme for a restaurant chain that wants to make its customers feel comfortable in familiar surroundings; and it could be the theme for every chapter on rearranging and combining sentences. It's certainly the theme for this section on the structure of relative clauses. You should feel comfortable parsing relative clauses because there's something familiar and comfortable about them. The way it was is the way it is.

Relative Clauses and Sentences

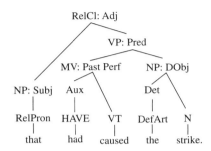

Now we can look more closely at relative clauses. The relative clause **that had caused the strike** has the same structure you've come to expect in a clause. The diagram shows the relative clause constituent separated from the rest of the diagram. The relative clause has exactly the structure it had when it was a separate sentence, except that the relative pronoun **that** has replaced **the problems** as the subject noun phrase. **Had caused the strike** is the verb phrase that functions as the predicate of the clause. The verb **cause** is a transitive verb; **the strike** is a noun phrase that functions as its object. The status of the main verb **had caused** is past perfect. The major difference between this clause and the independent clauses you've already learned to parse is that it doesn't stand alone: it is embedded within another clause.

Not only can you embed a core sentence as a relative clause, but you can also embed a clause that has been rearranged or compounded. In the next sentence, the relative clause **that can be made easily with common ingredients** is a passive.

Methamphetamine is a drug that can be made easily with common ingredients.

When you take the relative clause out and rebuild it into a sentence, you have

The drug can be made easily with common ingredients.

The noun phrase that becomes the relative pronoun, **the drug**, is the grammatical subject. But still, there's nothing new here. Grammar constantly recycles old parts.

Everything you know about the structure of independent clauses remains the same for relative clauses (or any other dependent clause). There are still six basic verb types. You can expand both the main verb constituents and the noun phrase constituents. You can rearrange and conjoin constituents as well. In Bob Evans restaurants or in dependent clauses, you're in familiar surroundings: the way it was *is* the way it is.

Restrictive Relative Clauses as Adjectives

Dependent clauses are not combined haphazardly into matrix clauses but are placed into specific constituents. A restrictive relative clause, for instance, is embedded within a noun phrase of a matrix clause. It may be embedded within any noun phrase in a matrix clause—a subject, a direct object, an oblique object, an object complement, a predicate noun.

Relative clauses that are embedded within noun phrases—the restrictive relative clauses we look at in this chapter—function as adjectives, which simply means they are embedded into noun phrases as attributes. Here's a relative clause embedded within the subject noun phrase of its matrix clause:

The senator *who co-sponsored the abortion bill* didn't attend the president's reception.

The subject noun phrase of the matrix is **the senator** *who co-sponsored the abortion bill*. That noun phrase is composed of two constituents, a head noun phrase **the senator** and a relative clause *who co-sponsored the abortion bill*. The next diagram shows the complete sentence, with the noun phrase subject highlighted by a rectangle. It's important to remember that the noun phrase subject is composed of a head noun phrase and a relative clause and that the two constituents together, the head and the attribute, make one single noun phrase constituent. Like all the relative clauses in this chapter, *who co-sponsored the abortion bill* is embedded in a noun phrase and functions as an adjective, an attribute.

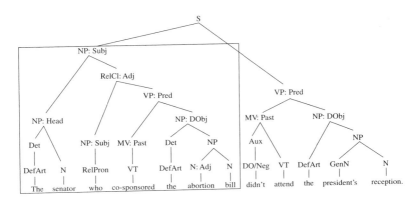

Making a Relative Clause

To construct relative clauses, take a sentence and change one of its noun phrases into a relative pronoun. In the following sentence, the subject noun phrase **computers** is replaced by the relative pronoun **that:**

> **that**
> ~~Computers~~ think like humans.
> ↓
> **that** think like humans

Relative pronouns must occur at the front of their own clauses. So if you make the subject noun phrase into a relative pronoun, as in the example, that's all you have to do to complete the relative clause; the subject noun phrase is already at the front of the relative clause. If you make any other noun phrase into a relative, you must also move the relative pronoun into the initial position—as in the next example, where the direct object **the program** is replaced by the relative pronoun **which;** then the relative pronoun is moved to the front of the clause.

> **which**
> The Defense Department presented **the program** to Congress.
> ↓
> **which** the Defense Department presented to Congress

After you create a relative clause, you embed it into a noun phrase in a matrix clause, as in the next example, where the relative clause is embedded into the matrix noun phrase **the program:**

> The program will increase naval firepower dramatically.
> **which**
> The Defense Department presented **the program** to Congress.
> ↓
> The program **which the Defense Department presented to Congress** will increase naval firepower dramatically.

Here are some more examples. Notice how the second sentence in each example is made into a relative clause and then combined into a noun phrase in the first sentence to make a new, larger sentence.

> We arrived in Denver after a breathtaking flight.
> **that**
> ~~The flight~~ ended in a smooth touchdown.
> ↓
> We arrived in Denver after a breathtaking flight **that ended in a smooth touchdown**.

> Dieters are culinary terrorists.
> **who**
> ~~Culinary terrorists~~ bring fear into your kitchen.
> ↓
> Dieters are culinary terrorists who bring fear into your kitchen.

> The bill bans aid to the rebel government.
> that
> Congress passed **the bill** yesterday.
> ↓
> The bill **that congress passed yesterday** bans aid to the rebel government.

Relative Pronouns Replace Noun Phrases

The RELATIVE PRONOUNS are **who, whom, which,** and **that.** The four relative pronouns replace different kinds of noun phrases in relative clauses. Both **who** and **whom** replace noun phrases that refer to humans; **who** replaces human noun phrases functioning as subjects, while **whom** replaces human noun phrases functioning as objects, either direct objects or oblique objects. For example, if you make

The terrorist had threatened some female hostages.

into a relative clause, you can replace the subject noun phrase **the terrorist** with **who**, to produce:

Police psychologists calmed the terrorist.
     who
~~The terrorist~~ had threatened some female hostages.
          ↓
Police psychologists calmed the terrorist **who had threatened some female hostages**.

Or you can replace the object noun phrase **some female hostages** with **whom**, to produce:

Some female hostages escaped before the shootout.

⌐————————————————————————————— **whom**
⌊The terroris had threateneed ~~some female hostages~~.
               ↓
Some female hostages **whom the terrorist had threatened** escaped before the shortcut.

Which replaces noun phrases that do not refer to humans, whether those noun phrases function as subjects or objects. So you can make

Those grains can clear cholesterol from the blood.

into a relative clause by replacing the subject noun phrase **those grains** with **which**, as in

Barley is one of those grains.
     which
~~Those grains~~ can clear cholesterol from the blood.
          ↓
Barley is one of those grains which can clear cholesterol from the blood.

Or you can make

The gang committed the violence in Central Park.

into a relative clause by replacing the object noun phrase **the violence** with **which**, as in

New Yorkers were shocked by the violence.

> **which**
> ↓ The gang committed **the violence** in Central Park

↓

New Yorkers were shocked by the violence **which the gang committed in Central Park**.

Remember that you must move a noun phrase to the front of a relative clause unless the noun phrase is the subject and thus already at the front of the clause. In effect, this means that you must move direct objects, predicate nouns, object complements, indirect objects, or objects of prepositions.

That is the most versatile and probably the most frequently used of the relative pronouns. You can use it instead of **who, whom**, or **which**. **That** can replace any noun phrase in a relative clause, whether it's human or nonhuman, whether it functions as a subject, direct object, oblique object, predicate noun, indirect object, or object complement. Here are some example clauses with **that** as the relative pronoun:

Antonia Fraser's *Warrior Queens* concerns women **who** massacred their rivals.

OR

Antonia Fraser's *Warrior Queens* concerns women **that** massacred their rivals.

The Chilean crash survivors buried the dead pilot **whom** they had planned to eat.

OR

The Chilean crash survivors buried the dead pilot **that** they had planned to eat.

Oliver Sacks writes about schools **which** have harmed the deaf by teaching them only sign language.

OR

Oliver Sacks writes about schools **that** have harmed the deaf by teaching them only sign language.

That is easy to use; it reduces the number of decisions you have to make when you construct a relative clause. So it has become the relative pronoun of choice. Many writers replace **who**, **whom**, and **which** with **that** whenever possible.

"Whose" Replaces a Possessive Pronoun or a Genitive Noun

The relative pronouns together with **whose** make the RELATIVES. **Whose** (sometimes called a RELATIVE DETERMINER) is different from the other relatives. Rather than replace a whole noun phrase, **whose** replaces only a possessive pronoun or a genitive noun, as in the following example:

> Stewed okra is a dish.
> **whose**
> ~~The dish's~~ **charms are seldom appreciated.**
> ↓
> Stewed okra is a dish **whose** charms are seldom appreciated.

In the example, **whose** replaces a genitive (**the dish's**) **in the subject noun phrase of the relative clause. If you replace the possessive pronoun or genitive noun in an object noun phrase with** whose, **you have to move the whole noun phrase, not simply the possessive, to the front of the relative clause. Here is an example with** whose **in an object noun phrase:**

> Native Americans are asking for their land to be returned.
> _____**whose**
> ⌐The government "appropriated" **their** territory in the
>   nineteenth century.
>
>   ↓
> Native Americans **whose territory the government appro-priated in the nineteenth century** are asking for their land to be returned.

Relative Pronouns in Prepositional Phrases

When you replace the object of a preposition with a relative pronoun, you may move the whole prepositional phrase to the front of the clause, or you may move just the relative pronoun, stranding the preposition at the end of the clause. The next example shows the different choices:

The park is scheduled to become a parking lot.

which

The neighborhood kids play baseball in ~~the park~~.

↓

The park **in which the neighborhood kids play baseball** is scheduled to become a parking lot.

OR

The park **which the neighborhood kids play baseball in** is scheduled to become a parking lot.

The second choice, with the preposition left at the end of the clause, sounds more natural. So we often construct clauses that way when we're speaking or when we're writing. But some writers and teachers prefer to front the whole prepositional phrase, especially in more formal writing.

The Functions of Fronted Relatives

Since the principle is so important, it's probably worth repeating the Bob Evans restaurant rule here: the way it was is the way it is. Here's how the rule relates to relative clauses. When you move a noun phrase to the front of a relative clause, it retains the relationship it had before it was moved: an object remains an object; a predicate noun remains a predicate noun; an object complement remains an object complement; an indirect object remains an indirect object; an object of a preposition remains an object of a preposition. Here's a sentence that has a relative clause with a direct object brought to the front. The next diagram illustrates that the fronted noun phrase, the relative pronoun **that**, remains the direct object of the clause.

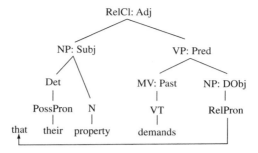

Condominium owners share the upkeep expenses.

Condominium owners share the upkeep expenses **that their property demands**.

Though the relative pronoun is disjoined from the normal object position following the verb, it retains the direct object relationship. The noun phrase subject of the relative clause is **their property**; **demands [that]** is the predicate; **that** is the object of the transitive verb **demands**. It remains the object, though it no longer follows the verb.

Find the Constituents of the Relative Clause

Students who have a difficult time parsing embedded clauses often find it easier if they pull the clause out of the sentence they're analyzing. If you take the relative clause out, you can reconstruct it as a sentence and easily identify its constituents. Here's an example:

The *Scientific Daily* report tells about seniors for **whom cognitive training works**.

The relative clause is **for** whom cognitive training works. You know that a relative pronoun is moved to the front of its clause and that when a relative is the noun phrase object of a prepositional phrase, the prepositional phrase is often moved as a unit to the front. In this case, you can move the prepositional phrase back to its original position to produce

cognitive training works **for them**

You also know that a relative pronoun replaces a noun phrase that is the same as the head of the matrix noun phrase which the clause is embedded in. By this logic, **whom** in the example must have replaced the noun phrase **seniors**. With that insight, you can rebuild the independent clause:

Cognitive training works for seniors.

It's generally that simple to reconstruct a relative clause as an independent clause and to be back into territory you should know well by now.

Remember the principles that underlie our grammatical system. The core sentences are building blocks. You add subordinate clauses by combining sentences. If you can combine sentences, you can take them apart. And finally, the way it was is the way it is.

Deleting Object Noun Phrases from Relative Clauses

Normally, you move object noun phrases to the front of their clauses after you make the phrases into relatives. But you can also delete object noun phrases from relative clauses. Speakers and writers often delete object noun phrases because it's an efficient way to create clauses and because it saves having to decide whether to use **who, whom, that,** or **which.** The object noun phrases have been deleted from the relative clauses in the second of each of the following output sentences. Though they no longer contain relative pronouns, the dependent clauses are still relative clauses.

The administration denied all the requests.
                          that
The students made ~~the requests~~.

↓

The administration denied all the requests **that the students made.**

OR

The administration denied all the requests **the students made.**

I left the expressway to get a look at the tower.
              which
I had seen ~~the tower~~ rising above the tree line.

↓

I left the expressway to get a look at the tower **which I had seen rising above the tree line.**

OR

I left the expressway to get a look at the tower **I had seen rising above the tree line.**

The substitute teachers seemed not to like us children.
                                whom
We taunted those substitute teachers.

                          ↓

The substitute teachers **whom we taunted** seemed not to like us children.

                          OR

The substitute teachers we taunted seemed not to like us children.

Even when you delete an object noun phrase from it, a relative clause remains a relative clause, and the verb in the relative clause remains transitive. A clause is a clause because it has a noun phrase subject and a finite verb phrase. A verb is transitive because it has an object noun phrase or because it had an object noun phrase when its clause was a core sentence.

Embedding Relative Clauses into Subordinate Clauses

The matrix clauses we've looked at so far have been sentences, independent clauses. But a matrix clause may itself be embedded within another clause, as you've known since you were a little kid, when you embedded one relative clause after another to tell about the house that Jack built:

This is the man who married the woman who owned the dog that chased the cat that killed the rat that stole the cheese that lived in the house that Jack built.

You wouldn't expect to find sentences as extreme as this, but embedding constituents in embedded constituents is common practice. It's one way we make sentences longer and more complex. Here's a less extreme example, with one relative clause (**who retired from the NBA**) embedded in another relative clause (**that include former stars**).

The Globetrotters may play teams **that include former stars who retired from the NBA.**

Together, they make a single relative clause constituent. The next diagram indicates all the relationships in the sentence. The Globetrotters sentence is a good example of the principle that big sentences are composed of little sentences, often several little sentences. Boxes nested within boxes. Here are the underlying clauses and their derivation:

The Globetrotters may play teams.
that
~~The teams~~ include former stars.

↓

The Globetrotters may play teams **that include former stars**.
who
~~The former stars~~ retired from the NBA.

↓

The Globetrotters may play teams **that include former stars who retired from the NBA**.

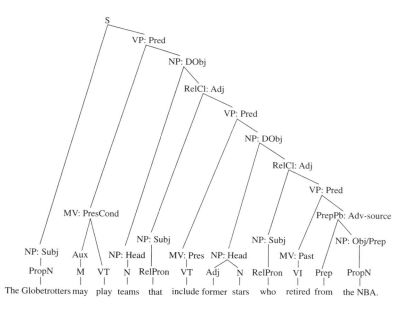

Chapter Summary: Constituents in Independent or Dependent Clauses

To sum up this chapter, whether they are independent or dependent, clauses have the same basic constituents: a noun phrase subject and a finite verb phrase predicate. Independent clauses stand alone as sentences; dependent clauses are embedded within larger, matrix clauses as nouns, adjectives, or adverbs. The dependent clauses discussed in this chapter are restrictive relative clauses embedded within matrix noun phrases as adjectives (attributes).

You make a clause into a relative clause by replacing one of its noun phrases with a relative pronoun and, if necessary, moving the pronoun to the front of the relative clause; if the relative replaces a genitive pronoun or occurs in a prepositional phrase, then you move the whole phrase which the relative is in. After moving the relative, you embed the relative clause within a noun phrase in a matrix clause.

The relatives are **who, whom, that, which,** and **whose**. The most common relative is **that:** to use it, you don't have to differentiate either subjects from objects, as you do between **who** and **whom**, or human from nonhuman, as you do between **which** and **who** or **whom**. **Whose** replaces possessive pronouns or genitive nouns.

When you're analyzing sentences, it sometimes helps to see relationships if you take the relative clauses out of their matrix clauses and change them back into complete sentences. It's important to remember that the relationships within a relative clause do not change from their core-sentence relationships, no matter where you move constituents.

The principle behind building grammatical units is simple: take structures you already have available and use them again and again. Use a noun phrase as a subject, a direct object, a predicate noun, or an object complement; a noun phrase is a noun phrase wherever it occurs in a clause. Use a clause as a sentence, or combine it into another clause as an adjective, noun, or adverb; a clause is a clause whether it is independent or dependent.

You don't combine constituents helter-skelter. You build constituents into hierarchies, because the hierarchy is the basic design of all grammatical constituents—phrases or clauses. Boxes nest within boxes.

Here are the main points in the chapter:

- Little sentences combine to make big sentences.
- All clauses contain noun phrase subjects and finite verb phrase predicates.
- We combine clauses for efficiency.

- A relative clause embedded into a noun phrase makes a noun phrase constituent—one constituent.
- The way it was is the way it is.
- A relative clause has exactly the structure it had when it was a separate sentence.
- Restrictive relative clauses are embedded within noun phrases as adjectives.
- To make a relative clause, replace a noun phrase with a relative pronoun, then front the pronoun.
- The four relative pronouns replace different kinds of noun phrases.
- **Whose** replaces a possessive pronoun or a genitive noun.
- For a relative in a prepositional phrase, move the prepositional phrase or the relative pronoun alone.
- Fronted relatives retain their original functions.
- Separate the relative clause from the matrix clause to find its constituents .
- You can delete object noun phrases from relative clauses.
- You can embed relative clauses into subordinate clauses.
- Independent or dependent clauses have the same constituents.

EXERCISES

I. Combining Sentences

Combine the following pairs of sentences. Make the second sentence of each pair into a relative clause, and then embed it into the first.

EXAMPLE

The first graders played "go fish" with cards.
The cards had pictures of animals on them.

↓

The first graders played "go fish" with cards **that had pictures of animals on them**.

1. The comet appears every 20 years.
   Dr. Okada discovered the comet.
2. Everyone respected the quarterback.
   The quarterback refused to give up.
3. The most valuable experiences were small ones.
   I had the experiences on my trip to Europe.

4. Children will probably become abusers of drugs or alcohol. Children's parents abuse alcohol.

5. Many nations are restricting emissions of noxious gases. The noxious gases threaten the atmosphere.

II. Breaking Out Underlying Sentences

Identify the matrix clause and the relative clause in each of the following sentences. Then write out the complete sentences from which the matrix and relative clauses are derived.

EXAMPLE

Honeydew is a sweet libation that can enhance a summer brunch.

↓

Honeydew is a sweet libation. (Matrix clause)
The sweet libation can enhance a summer brunch. (Relative clause)

1. Gloria Steinem wrote about the campaign in which Geraldine Ferraro ran for vice president.

2. The Sherpa guides who led us through the mountains became our steadfast friends.

3. The recent terrorist attacks should change the way you think about national resistance movements.

4. Midway was a battle that shaped naval strategy during World War II.

5. There are historical insights in the *Encyclopedia of Southern Culture* every American should be aware of.

III. Analyzing Sentences

Analyze the following sentences, identifying the structures and their functions, as far as you are able. It may help you to write out the underlying sentences from which the relative clauses are derived or to diagram the sentences.

EXAMPLE

Norman Rockwell's paintings suggest a stroll during which you experience dramatic scenes.

Explanation: The sentence is composed of the subject noun phrase **Norman Rockwell's paintings** and the verb phrase predicate **suggest a stroll during which you experience dramatic scenes**. The main verb of the matrix clause is the transitive verb **suggest**, which is in the present indicative form. **A stroll during which you experience dramatic scenes** is the noun phrase functioning as the direct object of the matrix clause. This noun phrase is composed of the head noun phrase **a stroll** and the relative clause **during which you experience dramatic scenes**. Since the relative pronoun **which** is the object of the preposition **during**, the prepositional phrase **during which** was brought to the front of the relative clause. The prepositional phrase functions as an adverb of time within the relative clause. The subject of the relative clause is **you** and the predicate is

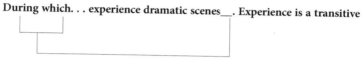

During which. . . experience dramatic scenes___. Experience is a transitive

Experience is a transitive verb in the present indicative form. The noun phrase **dramatic scenes** functions as the object of the verb **experience**. It is composed of the adjective **dramatic** and the head noun **scenes**. If you broke out the main clause, it would be **Norman Rockwell's paintings suggest a stroll**. If you broke out the relative clause, you would make **You experience dramatic scenes during the stroll**.

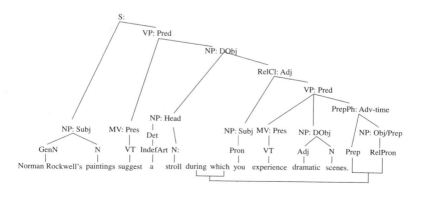

Sentences

1. My folks don't like the guy I'm dating now.
2. Lucille Ball was a glamour girl who became a clown.
3. The drug epidemic is a cancer which threatens the nation's survival.
4. Countries whose energy consumption does not decrease will suffer during the next decade.
5. Dad wanted the subwoofer system which Mom considered overpriced.
6. Elephants are complex social animals that can feel compassion.
7. The American soldiers met Afghan children who had overcome the squalor that surrounded them.
8. The cows that were stolen from Colorado ranches wound up in Utah.
9. The university dismissed the coach whose recruiting practices the NCAA questioned.
10. The joyous Cubs fan rang a bell that rivaled Big Ben.
11. The best fiction comes from writers who have a sensitive vision of the world.
12. The warden opened the gray steel door that connects death row to the execution chamber.
13. Jerry Springer interviewed parents whose authority had been questioned by their children.
14. Mercer Sullivan is an anthropologist who studies youth crime on the streets of Brooklyn.
15. The new mall established a climate in which high-class stores could thrive.
16. Woody Allen is the vulnerable artist who takes things personally.
17. Senior citizens who have suffered strokes come to the clinic for speech therapy.
18. We rode white-water rapids that battered our raft perilously.
19. Special-education teachers succeed with students for whom there has been no hope.
20. Our Zagreb trip was complicated by a taxi driver who spoke no known language.
21. There are several ornamental grasses that will flourish in partial shade.
22. Ginger Rogers and Fred Astaire tapped and shimmied through ten movies that define Hollywood's romantic heyday.

23. Mountain bikers race on courses that screech up rock-strewn passes and scream down log-infested trails.
24. The new tech school provides classrooms in which every student has a computer.
25. Gospel singer Fontella Bass' voice bursts with a spirit that seems to come from a different world.
26. The social pressures that encourage women to starve themselves include men's expectations and media representations of lithe models.
27. The light that gets through your dirty windows will be noticed by your guests.
28. The "killer brownie" I bought at the snack bar was sinfully rich.
29. The foods your mother prepared can keep you healthy.
30. Sue Miller's books explore the underground passages that connect family members.
31. Wisconsin boasts a dairy industry that flourishes because of lush pastures.
32. African Americans have won political influence that was denied them for centuries.
33. The prevalence of family violence has spawned a shelter network that offers women refuge.
34. Nintendo is a madness that strikes adolescent boys.
35. Laptop computers you can slip into a backpack are replacing blue books at college exams.
36. The demand that greeted his Kindle novel surprised Stephen King.
37. Barbie emanates an attraction that keeps young girls hooked.
38. Apple gave us a computer anyone can use.
39. Neighborhood crime-watch groups are organizations through which police can build civilian support.
40. John Kennedy was a magnetic politician whom the media made a shining knight of Camelot.
41. Pectinase dissolves the white material that sticks to orange peel.
42. The FDA monitors the food we buy.
43. Satellites read the infrared emissions that reveal the ocean's temperature.
44. Grizzly bears have eaten people who have ventured into their domains.
45. The pancreas is a gland that produces insulin.

46. Vince Lombardi embodied the ruthless values the nation accepted in the '50s and '60s.

47. How did the engineers discover the design flaw that caused the crash of the 747?

48. Eleanor Roosevelt rewrote the script which had prescribed a First Lady's role.

49. Seahorses are the only fish who practice steadfast monogamy.

50. F. Scott Fitzgerald lived like the characters he wrote about.

....

CHAPTER 7

Reducing Relative Clauses to Phrases

Deriving Prepositional and Participial Phrases

This chapter shows you how to reduce relative clauses to prepositional or participial phrases that you embed as adjectives (attributes) within noun phrases. Phrases like **in the back room** or **eating the pizza** or **hired by the summer camp**, phrases which are embedded in noun phrases like *the boys* **in the back room** or *the boys* **eating the pizza** or *the boys* **hired by the summer camp** derive from relative clauses (~~who are~~ **in the back room** or ~~who are~~ **eating the pizza** or ~~who were~~ **hired by the summer camp**) and function just as restrictive relative clauses would. This deletion of constituents from embedded clauses to produce embedded phrases is another case of the grammatical system making optimum use of a few basic constituents from which to derive a great many structures.

Reducing Clauses

In the last chapter, we saw how to embed relative clauses into matrix clauses to function as adjectives, as in

The students assembled on the steps of the administration building.
> **who**
> ~~The students~~ were protesting the new dorm rules.

↓

The students **who were protesting the new dorm rules** assembled on the steps of the administration building.

Now let's look at how you can reduce relative clauses to phrases. In the preceding example, you make the relative clause **who were protesting the new dorm rules** into a present participial phrase **protesting the new dorm rules** by deleting the subject pronoun **who** and the auxiliary **were**.

> The students ~~who were~~ **protesting the new dorm rules** assembled on the steps of the administration building.
>
> ↓
>
> The students **protesting the new dorm rules** assembled on the steps of the administration building.

By deleting a subject relative pronoun and BE, you reduce relative clauses to present participial phrases, past participial phrases, or prepositional phrases.

Embedding Phrases

A PRESENT PARTICIPIAL PHRASE is a phrase headed by a present participle. When you embed a participial phrase into a matrix noun phrase, it becomes a single constituent with that noun phrase, just as a restrictive relative clause does. So **the students protesting the new dorm rules** is a noun phrase composed of a noun phrase head, **the students**, and a present participial phrase, **protesting the new dorm rules**. Also like a relative clause embedded in a noun phrase, the present participial phrase functions as an adjective, as you can see in the diagram of the noun phrase.

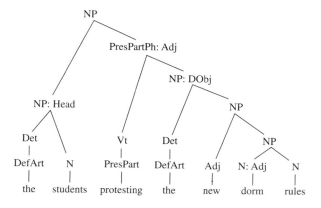

Participial Phrases Are Verb Phrases

Participial phrases are verb phrases (they're what's left of the predicate of a relative clause). So they retain all the internal characteristics associated with verb phrases: they contain the same six kinds of verbs as the core sentences. The participial phrase in the diagram, **protesting the new dorm rules,** is composed of the transitive verb **protesting** followed by a noun phrase, **the new dorm rules,** which functions as the object of **protesting.** Here are several examples of present participial phrases constructed with different types of verbs.

Group therapy can help people **fighting drug addiction.**

I played soldier among the apple trees **growing in my grandpa's orchard.**

The hurricane **bearing down on Haiti** frightened the island residents.

The police officer **returning the victim's effects to her family** didn't reveal the gory details of the crime.

In the first example, **fighting** is transitive, with **drug addiction** functioning as a direct object. In the second example, **growing** is intransitive, followed by a prepositional phrase, **in my grandpa's orchard. Bearing down** is a two-word intransitive. And **returning** is a Vg verb followed by a direct object, **the victim's effects,** and a prepositional phrase functioning as an adverb of reception, **to her family.**

Here is the participial phrase from the third example diagramed to illustrate its internal structure.

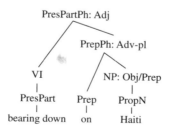

Present participial phrases are nonfinite verb phrases; you delete tense when you delete BE from the main verb. Because they are nonfinite, participial phrases have no status. But they are headed by the same six types of verbs as other verb phrases, and they retain the structure of verb phrases that we learned in the first two chapters. The way it was is still the way it is.

Making Some Verbs into Present Participles

One exception to the rule about deleting a relative pronoun and BE concerns verbs that cannot be made progressive; we call these STATIVE VERBS. When you change a relative clause with such a verb into a participial phrase, you have to make the verb into a present participle, not simply delete BE and the noun phrase. For instance, in the following example,

> The "screwball comedies" which featured Cary Grant defined urbane humor in the 1930s.

the verb **feature** doesn't allow a progressive form with BE (there is no *which were featuring Cary Grant). Nonetheless, you can make **feature** into a present participle:

> The "screwball comedies" **which featured Cary Grant** defined urbane humor in the 1930s.
> ↓
> The "screwball comedies" **featuring Cary Grant** defined urbane humor in the 1930s.

Deriving Past Participial Phrases

Just as you can delete BE and the subject pronoun from a relative clause to create a present participial phrase, you can also delete BE and a grammatical subject from a relative clause to create a PAST PARTICIPIAL PHRASE. Here is a sentence with an embedded past participial phrase.

> Students who are taught phonics by their primary teachers can sound out unfamiliar words.
> ↓
> Students **taught phonics by their primary teachers** can sound out unfamiliar words.

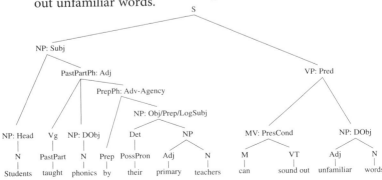

A clause from which you derive a past participial phrase will always be passive, since that's the only construction in which a past participle follows BE. The relative clause underlying the phrase **taught phonics by their primary teachers** is passive. Here is the derivation of the past participial phrase, beginning with the passive sentence:

> who
> ~~Students~~ are taught phonics by their primary teachers.
> ↓
> ~~who are~~ taught phonics by their primary teachers
> ↓
> taught phonics by their primary teachers

The verb of a past participial phrase will always be transitive, either VT, Vg, or Vc. The verb **taught** in the example is a two-place transitive Vg.

Since the relative clause from which you derive a past participial phrase is passive, you can delete its **by**-phrase, just as you can delete the **by**-phrase from an independent clause that is passive.

> A tiny pump **~~which is~~ implanted beneath a diabetic's skin by a doctor** can regulate insulin dosage better than injections.
> ↓
> A tiny pump **implanted beneath a diabetic's skin ~~by a doctor~~** can regulate insulin dosage better than injections.
> ↓
> A tiny pump **implanted beneath a diabetic's skin** can regulate insulin dosage better than injections.

The constituent you have left when you delete the **by**-phrase is still a past participial phrase.

Embedded Prepositional Phrases

Another structure you can derive from a relative clause by deleting BE and the subject noun phrase is a prepositional phrase. When you derive participial phrases, you delete the subject noun phrase and an auxiliary BE. When you derive a prepositional phrase to embed in a noun phrase, you always delete the subject noun phrase and the verb BE, as in:

> The refrigerator ~~which is~~ **in the center of the nursery** is filled with baby formula for early-morning feeding.
>
> ↓
>
> The refrigerator **in the center of the nursery** is filled with baby formula for early-morning feeding.
>
> The art critic considered the paintings ~~which were~~ **from Renaissance Florence** the best in the exhibition.
>
> ↓
>
> The art critic considered the paintings **from Renaissance Florence** the best in the exhibition.

Constituency: Adjective or Adverbs

Prepositional phrases embedded in noun phrases function as adjectives, just like the past and present participial phrases you embed in the same way. Prepositional phrases that occur within verb phrases, on the other hand, function as adverbs. Constituency determines whether a prepositional phrase functions as an adjective or an adverb. Take a close look at the next example.

> The mill in Oak Brook, Illinois, was a shelter for slaves traveling on the Underground Railroad.

This sentence contains three prepositional phrases: **in Oak Brook, Illinois**; **for slaves traveling on the Underground Railroad**; and **on the Underground Railroad**. The prepositional phrase **for slaves traveling on the Underground Railroad** functions as an adjective because it is embedded in the noun phrase **a shelter for slaves traveling on the Underground Railroad**; in the same way, **in Oak Brook, Illinois** functions as an adjective because it is embedded in the noun phrase **the mill in Oak Brook, Illinois**. But the prepositional phrase **on the Underground Railroad** functions as an adverb since it occurs in a participial phrase, **traveling on the Underground Railroad**. It is not embedded directly in a noun phrase; it exists within a verb phrase. The next diagram illustrates this point.

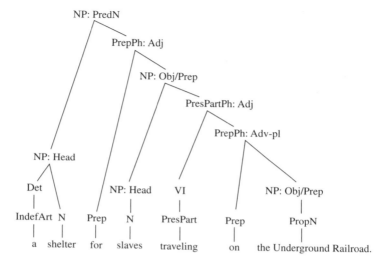

How the Components of an Embedded Phrase Function

It is important to understand constituency within embedded phrases. Here is the main point: although the whole phrase embedded within a noun phrase functions as an adjective, the components of the embedded phrase function within the phrase just as they do when the phrase is not embedded.

Since a present participial phrase is a verb phrase, the relationships within it will be governed by the verb that functions as its head. A transitive verb will be followed immediately by a noun phrase direct object (**fighting** *drug addiction*); an intransitive verb may be followed by an adverb—e.g., **growing** *in my grandpa's orchard* (in this case it is a prepositional phrase functioning as an adverb of place). In a past participial phrase, the verb may be followed by a prepositional phrase functioning as an adverb of agency, or the agent phrase may be deleted (**implanted** *beneath a diabetic's skin by a doctor,* or **implanted** *beneath a diabetic's skin*). Since a prepositional phrase is composed of a preposition followed by a noun phrase that functions as its object, an embedded prepositional phrase will have the same two components (*in the center of the nursery*). If you have trouble seeing the relationships within an embedded phrase, you may find it useful to break the embedded phrase out of the matrix and rebuild the clause that underlies the phrase:

~~who were~~ fighting drug addiction
~~that were~~ growing in my grandpa's back yard
~~which is~~ implanted beneath a diabetic's skin by a doctor
~~which is~~ in the center of the nursery

The relationships within the predicate or prepositional phrase of the rebuilt clause will be the relationships within the embedded participial or prepositional phrase. The embedded phrase itself, the whole phrase, functions as an adjective within the matrix noun phrase into which it is embedded. The constituents of the embedded phrase, though, are just that: constituents of the embedded phrase. The issue is one of constituency. The whole embedded phrase is a constituent of its matrix noun phrase; the components of the embedded phrase are constituents of the embedded phrase—whether that embedded phrase is a present participial, past participial, or prepositional phrase.

Prepositional Phrases Headed by "With"

Embedded prepositional phrases headed by **with** are difficult to derive. They seem to come from underlying phrases with **have** rather than **is**. For instance, in the sentence

A house with a computer and a flat-screen TV announces the
    sophistication of its occupants.

the prepositional phrase

with a computer and a flat-screen TV

seems to derive from

which has a computer and a flat-screen TV

It is likely that there is an intermediate step which turns **has** into **is with**. We won't worry about how such an intermediate step occurs. For our purposes, it is enough to say that the phrase **with a computer and a flat-screen TV** derives from

which is with a computer and a flat-screen TV

And we should note that a clause which contains **is with** occurs only as a structure underlying derived prepositional phrases headed by **with**. It never occurs as a separate clause on its own.

We Won't Derive One-Word Modifiers

To be consistent, we could derive single-word modifiers in the same way we derive multiple-word phrases. But we'll simplify the grammar and assume that such one-word structures occur before nouns, as we have been doing to this point. Otherwise, we'd have to go through the whole derivation process and then rearrange the constituents to move such structures to the front of their head nouns, as with these participles:

> The Empire State Building achieved fame **that was enduring** in *King Kong.*
>
> ↓
>
> The Empire State Building achieved fame **enduring** in *King Kong.*
>
> ↓
>
> The Empire State Building achieved **enduring** fame in *King Kong.*

> The captain from our intelligence unit interrogated the guerrillas **who were captured**.
>
> ↓
>
> The captain from our intelligence unit interrogated the guerrillas **captured**.
>
> ↓
>
> The captain from our intelligence unit interrogated the **captured** guerrillas.

Or these adjectives:

> The relievers have given the Reds pitching **which is consistent**.
>
> ↓
>
> The relievers have given the Reds pitching consistent.
>
> ↓
>
> The relievers have given the Reds **consistent** pitching.

With one-word adverbs that function as adjectives in a noun phrase, we'd also have to decide whether to leave them after their head nouns or move them before the nouns.

> Harry longed for the blonde who lived in the apartment ~~which was~~ upstairs.
>
> ↓

Harry longed for the blonde who lived in the apartment
upstairs.

$$\downarrow$$

Harry longed for the blonde who lived in the **upstairs**
apartment.

To save time and energy, we'll forego consistency for simplicity and not
derive such one-word structures. You should keep in mind, though, that
one-word constituents that function as adjectives are closely related to
the multiple-word phrases we are deriving.

Embedded Phrases and Commas

Like the relative clauses from which they derive, the phrases discussed in
this chapter are restrictive: they are bound within noun phrases and
function as adjectives. Because they are restrictive, the phrases are not
set off by commas. In Chapter 9, we'll examine nonrestrictive modifiers,
modifiers that are set off by commas.

Making Long Sentences from Just a Few Kinds of Phrases and Clauses

Building sentences and taking sentences apart leads to several meta-
phors that might help you to understand grammatical structure and
parsing. We've mentioned some in earlier chapters. The second chapter
notes that the relationships among the structures in long sentences are
like nested boxes, boxes that fit within one another. In another chapter,
we constantly repeat that "the way it was is the way it is."

Because phrases and clauses fit within one another, you can make
long, complex sentences from just a few kinds of phrases and clauses.
Look at the following sentence about meals which begin with spicy foods
and end with exquisite desserts:

Dinners that begin with "fireworks" should end with fantasies
like hazelnut eclairs.

A sentence such as this, with several embedded structures, may look
daunting to parse. But if you remember that even the longest, most
complicated sentence is composed of smaller constituents nested within
it, you can take the sentence apart piece by familiar piece.

This insight on nesting leads to the second point: parsing is basically a matter of identifying those familiar constituent pieces. In the 1992 presidential campaign, Bill Clinton's staff hung a sign at their campaign headquarters that read, "It's the economy, Stupid." They wanted the campaign to keep focused on what they saw as the central issue of that election. During that campaign year, some of my students made copies of a sign that read

It's Constituency, Stupid.

They said they put the signs over their desks to remind themselves that constituency is always the central issue in grammatical analysis. That '92 election is long over, but the sign about the economy helped the Clinton campaign focus on the election's central issue, and win. Through the years, similar signs about constituency have helped many of my students focus on the central issue in parsing. Let's parse the hazelnut-eclair sentence to see how constituents nest within constituents. Here is the sentence again:

Dinners that begin with "fireworks" should end with fantasies like hazelnut eclairs.

The predicate in the sentence contains the following constituents that nest within one another. The smaller constituents embed into the larger constituents one at a time. First, the noun **hazelnut** (functioning as an adjective) is embedded into the noun phrase **hazelnut eclairs.**

Then the noun phrase becomes the object of the preposition **like** in the prepositional phrase **like hazelnut eclairs**.

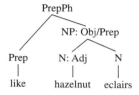

In turn, the prepositional phrase is embedded into the noun phrase **fantasies like hazelnut eclairs**, where it functions as an adjective.

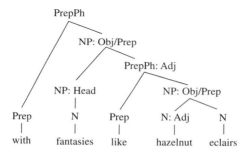

This noun phrase is the object of yet another prepositional phrase, **with fantasies like hazelnut eclairs.**

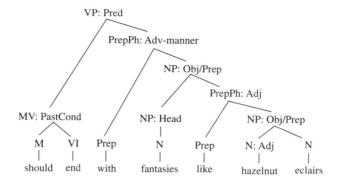

And this prepositional phrase functions as an adverb of manner within the verb phrase predicate **should end with fantasies like hazelnut eclairs.**

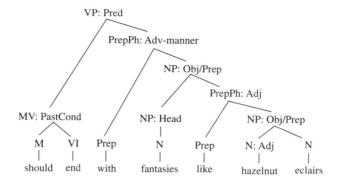

The noun phrase subject is built the same way, with constituents folding into one another to make larger constituents. First, the noun "**fireworks**" becomes the object of the preposition **with**; the prepositional phrase **with "fireworks"** functions as an adverb of manner within the verb phrase **begin with "fireworks"**; the verb phrase **begin with "fireworks"** functions as the predicate of the relative clause **that begin with "fireworks"**; and the relative clause functions as an adjective within the noun phrase **dinners that begin with "fireworks."**

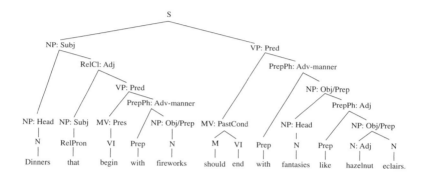

Here's another metaphor for parsing. In class, I've sometimes compared parsing sentences to peeling onions, taking off one layer at a time. When you peel off one onion layer, the one beneath it looks similar; you peel layer from layer until you reach the innermost layer. A student stopped me one day to remark that parsing is more like "existential onion peeling, beginning with the innermost layer and working your way out." She was right. It's probably best to think of parsing as identifying one constituent at a time and "working your way out" from the center of the onion.

The Clauses That Underlie a Sentence's Constituents

You can also look at a sentence in terms of the clauses that underlie it and the processes that combine the underlying constituents. At the core of the hazelnut-eclair sentence is a main clause:

Dinners should end with fantasies.

Two clauses underlie the structures embedded within the main clause:

Dinners begin with fireworks.
The fantasies are like eclairs.

The first becomes a relative clause embedded into the subject noun phrase of the main clause:

that
~~Dinners~~ begin with fireworks.
↓
that begin with fireworks

The second becomes a prepositional phrase embedded into the matrix noun phrase **the fantasies**:

~~The fantasies are~~ like hazelnut eclairs.
↓
like hazelnut eclairs

The independent clause and the two embedded constituents produce

Dinners that begin with "fireworks" should end with fantasies like hazelnut eclairs.

Either way you look at the sentence, you can see that the constituents that enfold within one another and the processes that create the embedded structures are familiar. You've seen them all before in earlier chapters. It's important to understand how to take sentences apart into their building blocks and combine them into their completed forms.

One final metaphor for how to take sentences apart. Grammar is the ultimate recycler; it wastes neither parts nor processes. It uses both over and over again. Several years ago, a witty student called this view of grammatical construction "Morenberg's first law of thermogrammatics": grammatical constituents are neither created nor destroyed, just changed in form. Well, if it works for you. . . .

Grammatical Ambiguity

Even when you understand the principle of how clauses are combined into larger structures and how constituents fit within other constituents, you sometimes face difficult decisions when you try to identify certain sentence components and their relationships. Sometimes a sentence is ambiguous. That is, it may be understood in more than one way. Here is an ambiguous sentence:

Jerry Spinelli wrote the book in our living room.

The sentence may mean either that Jerry Spinelli wrote the book while he was in our living room or simply that our living room contains a book that Jerry Spinelli wrote, wherever he might have written it.

Ambiguity can be caused by many factors—sound or meaning or grammar. The ambiguity of the example sentence is grammatical; it's caused by a constituency problem: the sentence is ambiguous because the prepositional phrase **in our living room** may function in two different ways. In one, it functions as an adverb of place, forming a constituent with the verb phrase **wrote the book in our living room**, as in the next diagram.

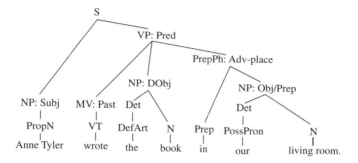

Alternatively, it may function as an adjective phrase, forming a constituent with the object noun phrase **the book in our living room**, as in the next diagram.

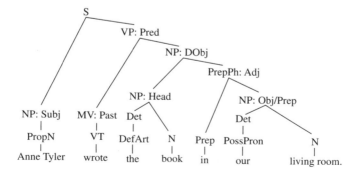

When you come upon a sentence like this with two possible constituent analyses, you may not be able to decide which analysis is correct, unless you have more information than a single sentence can give you. In speech or writing, you can usually tell which is the correct interpretation, because the context provides more information. But when you get such a sentence as an individual item in a grammar book, probably the best thing to do is to indicate that you understand both possible analyses.

Chapter Summary: Phrases Derived from Relative Clauses

You derive each of the structures discussed in this chapter—present participial phrases, past participial phrases, and prepositional phrases—from relative clauses by deleting subject noun phrases and BE. When you delete BE, you delete finiteness as well. The structures you derive in this way are used to expand noun phrases, and, though they belong to different grammatical classes, they function as adjectives, just like the relative clauses from which they derive.

Grammar takes old parts and combines them in various ways to make new, larger constituents. This ability to use parts over and over again in different constructions is a basic principle of grammar. It is the reason you can construct a multitude of complex phrases and clauses with just a small number of structures. Parts fit within parts as hierarchies to make new constituents.

When you parse sentences, you should look for constituents and how they nest within one another so that you can take them apart piece by piece.

Here are the main points of the chapter:

- Some relative clauses can be reduced to phrases.
- Delete a subject pronoun and BE from a relative clause to produce present or past participial or prepositional phrases.
- An embedded phrase and its matrix noun phrase become one constituent—a noun phrase.
- Participial phrases are verb phrases.
- You have to make stative verbs into present participles.
- Past participial phrases are derived from passive clauses.
- The source of an embedded prepositional phrase is a clause with the verb BE.
- Constituency determines whether a prepositional phrase functions as an adjective or an adverb.
- The components of an embedded phrase function within the phrase just as within a clause.

- Prepositional phrases headed by **with** come from underlying phrases with **have**.
- We won't derive one-word modifiers.
- Because they are restrictive, embedded phrases are not set off by commas.
- You make long, complex sentences from just a few kinds of phrases and clauses.
- Parsing is a matter of identifying constituents.
- You can look at a sentence in terms of the clauses that underlie its embedded constituents.
- Sentences may be grammatically ambiguous.
- The structures discussed in this chapter are derived from relative clauses.

EXERCISES

I. Breaking Out Underlying Sentences

Identify the main clauses and embedded phrases in each of the following sentences. Then write out the complete sentences from which the main clause and embedded phrases are derived. Don't derive single-word adjectives or nouns that precede head nouns, like **British** in the example.

EXAMPLE

The British sloop sailed across waters haunted by pirate ships.

↓

The British sloop sailed across waters. (Main clause)
The waters were haunted by pirate ships.

1. The possums in the neighborhood foraged among the rubbish.
2. Our motorboat passed tiny shacks built on palm-wood stilts.
3. Two native women carrying buckets of water from the well walked by our Land Rover.
4. A British botanist named William Burchell invented the African safari.
5. The rainbows arching over Iguacu Falls link Brazil and Argentina in a colorful bond.

II. Combining Sentences

Combine the following pairs of sentences to make the structures indicated in parentheses.

EXAMPLE
>The antipasto features tender squid.
>The antipasto is displayed in the glass case. (Past participial phrase)
>
>↓
>
>The antipasto displayed in the glass case features tender squid.

1. Overcast skies ruined our weekend.
    The overcast skies were punctuated by thunderstorms. (Past participial phrase)
2. The debate vexes federal lawmakers.
    The debate is about taxes (Prepositional phrase)
3. The hotel guests listened to musicians.
    The musicians were playing Tahitian songs. (Present participial phrase)
4. The bank robbers shot at the police helicopter.
    The police helicopter was hovering above their car. (Present participial phrase)
5. The region is a tourist mecca.
    The region is below Mexico City. (Prepositional phrase)

III. Analyzing Sentences

Analyze the following sentences. Draw diagrams if that helps you to identify constituents and relationships. You may also want to write out the underlying clauses, though don't derive single-word adjectives and nouns that precede head nouns. And you may find it helpful to work from "the inside out," identifying constituents and then deciding whether those constituents fit within or next to other constituents.

EXAMPLE
>The mother fox caring for the pups threatened the human intruders.
>*Underlying clauses:*
>The mother fox threatened the human intruders.
>~~The mother fox~~ was caring for the pups.

Explanation: **The mother fox caring for the pups** is the noun phrase subject of the sentence; **threatened the human intruders** is the verb phrase predicate. The main verb is the transitive verb **threatened**; its status is past indicative. The object of **threaten** is **the human intruders**. The noun phrase subject of the clause is composed of the head noun phrase **the mother fox** and the present participial phrase **caring for the pups**, which functions as an adjective.

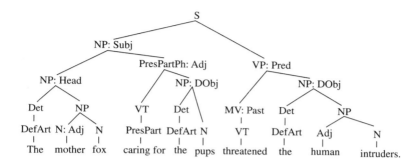

Sentences

1. Foreigners traveling in Russia should drink bottled water.
2. Most of the doctors trained in Ohio practice in other states.
3. George Harrison posed as a monk in prayer.
4. Our national frustration with welfare is exploited by some politicians.
5. The books sold at this sleazy newsstand are not available in the city library.
6. Wall Street traders investing in foreign markets have earned 6 percent interest this year.
7. The restaurant served shrimp boiled in a special Creole sauce.
8. Astronomers have identified a new class of gamma rays coming from a mysterious source.
9. Rural communities across America lack physicians.
10. The police scattered the young men loitering outside the convenience store.
11. Bighorn Canyon National Park contains multilayered canyons blanketed by juniper woodlands and rolling prairies.
12. The New York Philharmonic aims at lucid performances filled with orchestral detail polished to a high sheen.
13. There are no quick fixes for broken children.
14. Dr. Putman's cosmetic dentistry will give you a face with a great smile.

15. Hungarian cooks serve a garlicky cucumber salad called *uborka salata.*

16. Salvador Dali made the world beyond the rational seem real in his paintings.

17. NASA draws upon knowledge accumulated over decades.

18. Children are unnerved by parents suffering job distress.

19. The first city destroyed by an atomic bomb was Hiroshima.

20. The land around this church was the first property blacks owned in our town after the Civil War.

21. There are several Vietnamese dishes on the restaurant's menu.

22. I ate cold pizza under the watchful gaze of the Malibu Barbie sitting on my date's dining room table.

23. Companies advertising in *Vogue* aim toward women in their thirties.

24. The three teenage girls admitted to the hospital yesterday had attempted suicide.

25. Major dance companies throughout the world still perform Balanchine's ballets.

26. Penguins in Antarctica can't avoid the throngs of human tourists.

27. Iowa is the state with the first presidential primary caucus.

28. The peak covered with new snow attracted most of the skiers.

29. The Druid ritual begins with a sudden shout that surprises the audience.

30. Vietnam was the first war brought to American homes by television.

31. The physicians in the rehab program treat compulsive behavior patterns.

32. Kids selling crack on the streets have become common sights in our big cities.

33. Throngs crowding the Anchorage streets cheered the dogsled teams starting the Iditarod race.

34. The apiary at Miami University is surrounded by a wall that protects the bees from onlookers. (**From onlookers** functions as a goal adverb; the goal [intent] of the wall is to keep onlookers away.)

35. Pop singers like Linda Ronstadt often cross over and record country tunes. (**Often** is an adverb of frequency that introduces the predicate.)

36. Chaka Khan's private foundation helps children in trouble.

37. Your Cadillac dealer can provide details about the rebate.

38. The two Egyptian statues carved in granite completed the Louvre's Middle Kingdom exhibit.

39. The vet sedated the zoo's tiger with a tranquilizer made for house cats.

40. Hideo Nomo was the first major league player from Japan since the sixties.

41. Patti LaBelle achieves a stage presence blending regal poise and down-home ease.

42. Parents who overprotect their children may be abusing them with love.

43. The first hookless fasteners produced in 1893 snagged and tore clothes. But zippers have improved and become commonplace on clothes, camping gear, and luggage.

44. Jerry Garcia would play a phrase, repeat it, and toy with it like a cat toying with a mouse.

45. Humphrey Bogart's character in *Casablanca* is tough but softhearted.

46. Winterset, Iowa, has become a mythical place in the hearts of middle-aged Americans entranced by the romantic power of *The Bridges of Madison County.*

47. Elvis' leather outfit is one of the gems displayed at the Rock and Roll Hall of Fame and Museum in Cleveland.

48. The AARP is the most powerful lobbying group in Washington.

49. Television has made Olympic gymnasts like Mary Lou Retton and Nadia Comaneci into household names.

50. Home runs flying into deserted stands enunciate the problem of major league baseball.

CHAPTER 8

Making Noun Clauses, Gerunds, and Infinitives

Noun Clauses, Gerunds, and Infinitives Fill Noun Phrase Slots

The clauses, gerunds, and infinitives introduced in this chapter are nouns because they fill noun phrase slots. Here, for instance are a subordinate clause, a gerund, and an infinitive. They all fill direct object slots. You can tell they fill noun phrase slots because you can substitute pronouns for them, usually **this** or **something:**

> The Hubble confirmed that every large galaxy has a black hole
>   at its center.
>
>   ↓
> The Hubble confirmed **this/something**.
> The dieters started walking briskly for exercise.
>
>   ↓
> The dieters started **this/something** for exercise.
>
> Lincoln attempted to keep the union together.
>
>   ↓
> Lincoln attempted **this/something**.

That-Clauses

As we learned with relative clauses, a clause must have a noun phrase subject and a finite verb phrase, whether it is dependent or independent.

When it is dependent, it functions either as a noun, adjective, or adverb according to where it is embedded in a matrix construction and what it does. The only clauses we'll look at in this chapter are noun clauses.

The first noun clauses we'll examine are called THAT-CLAUSES because they are usually introduced by the word **that**. That-clauses can occur in almost any noun slot in a sentence—as subject, direct object, object complement, or predicate noun. Here is a noun clause functioning as a direct object of the verb **claim**:

Chinese cooks claim that snake meat keeps you warm in winter.

To demonstrate that the subordinate clause **that snake meat keeps you warm in winter** functions as a direct object, you can turn the matrix sentence into a passive, making the clause into a grammatical subject, as any object noun phrase would become in a passive sentence.

That snake meat keeps you warm in winter is claimed by
   Chinese cooks.

Since the subordinate clause fills a noun phrase slot, it is a noun clause. You can think of the sentence **Chinese cooks claim that snake meat keeps you warm in winter** as composed of two underlying clauses, with the second becoming a noun clause and replacing **this** in the matrix.

Chinese cooks claim **this**.
Snake meat keeps you warm in winter.
   ↓
Chinese cooks claim that snake meat keeps you warm in winter.

The word **that** which introduces noun clauses is called a SUBORDINATE CONJUNCTION or a SUBORDINATOR. It is not a pronoun: it does not replace a noun phrase within the noun clause as a relative pronoun does within a relative clause. The subordinator **that** marks the subordinate clause: it indicates that the clause is a noun clause. The subordinator attaches to the noun clause, though it does not become a constituent of the clause. The diagram of the Chinese cook sentence shows how to handle the relationship between the subordinator **that** and the clause. It pictures a noun clause within a noun clause. The outer clause contains the subordinator and remains one level above the clause nucleus. This device of a clause within a clause is an attempt to indicate that the subordinator is attached to the clause but that it does not become a constituent of it.

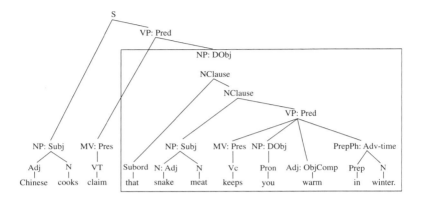

This explanation of how the subordinator **that** attaches to the noun clause is just like the explanation in Chapter 5 that a conjunction attaches to a constituent much like a magnet attaches to a refrigerator: "The magnet attaches to the refrigerator, but everyone knows it's simply added on, not quite a component of the refrigerator." The subordinator **that** attaches to the noun clause and forms a new noun clause with it, though **that** has no function in the clause except to introduce it. The subordinator is not a constituent within the clause.

Here are two more sentences to illustrate that-clauses in different noun phrase positions; the first noun clause functions as a subject, the next as a predicate noun

> **This** worries the president's economic advisors.
> High interest rates are slowing home sales.
> ↓
> That high interest rates are slowing home sales worries the
>   president's economic advisors.
>
> The problem is **this**.
> Children watch far too much TV.
> ↓
> The problem is that children watch far too much TV.

The subordinator **that** does not have to appear when a noun clause functions as a direct object or as a predicate noun. You may say either

> The Federal Aviation Administration conceded **that** the UFO sighting had occurred.
>
> OR
>
> The Federal Aviation Administration conceded the UFO sighting had occurred.

But **that** has to appear when the that-clause functions as the subject of a sentence. You may not say

> *Industrial plants will cut thousands of jobs this year worries Labor Department officials.

You must introduce a subject that-clause with **that**. You have to say

> **That** industrial plants will cut thousands of jobs this year worries Labor Department officials.

Noun Clauses Fill Noun Phrase Slots

Since that-clauses look like relative clauses, you'll have to be careful not to confuse the two. The major difference between relative clauses and noun clauses is that relative clauses are embedded into noun phrases following noun phrase heads and function as adjectives. Noun clauses fill whole noun phrase slots; they replace noun phrases and function like nouns. Here is the sentence with the noun clause about snake meat again, followed by a sentence with a similar relative clause.

> Chinese cooks claim that snake meat keeps you warm in winter. (NC)
>
> Chinese cooks prepare snake-meat dishes **that keep you warm in winter**. (RC)

The noun clause fills a noun phrase slot; it functions as the direct object of the verb **claim,** as we proved when we made the sentence passive. The clause follows the transitive verb **claim** and is a constituent of the verb phrase, as any direct object noun phrase would be. The subordinator **that** introduces the noun clause but has no function within it. In the second example, the clause **that keep you warm in winter** sits next to the noun phrase **snake-meat dishes**, which functions as the head of the noun phrase **snake-meat dishes that keep you warm in winter**. The relative clause is a constituent of the noun phrase. In addition, the relative pronoun **that** functions as the subject within the relative clause; it does not simply introduce the relative clause. As with most questions about grammatical analysis, the answer as to whether a clause is a noun clause or a relative clause lies in constituency. Remember the sign that students posted over their computers?

It's Constituency, Stupid!

You should never forget constituency.

Extraposing That-Clauses

Sometimes when a that-clause functions as a subject, you can move it to the end of the sentence and fill the subject position with an expletive **it**, as in the following example.

That the 747s crashed into the World Trade Center astonished Americans.

$$\downarrow$$

It astonished Americans that the 747s crashed into the World Trade Center.

This movement from the subject position is called EXTRAPOSITION. When you extrapose a clause and fill its subject position with an expletive **it**, the clause functions as the logical subject and the expletive as the grammatical subject. Some grammarians focus only on the surface form of sentences and claim that an extraposed clause functions as a complement to the noun phrase object; they call it a COMPLEMENT TO A NOUN PHRASE or a NOUN PHRASE COMPLEMENT. In the same way, they would claim that, in the next example, the extraposed noun clause functions as a complement to the predicate adjective **remarkable**; they call it a COMPLEMENT TO AN ADJECTIVE. You should be aware that you can look at extraposed clauses in both ways—in terms of their surface relationships (complement to a noun or adjective) or in terms of their underlying relationship (logical subject). The next diagram shows both relationships.

That Barbie has sold well for decades is remarkable.

↓

It is remarkable that Barbie has sold well for decades.

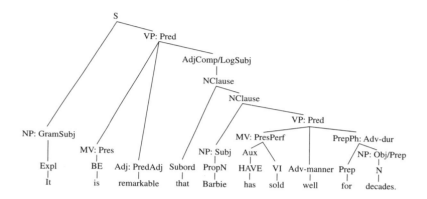

Extraposition is purely stylistic for English speakers. We extrapose clauses because sentences with long predicates and short subjects sound better to us than do sentences with long subjects and short predicates. If you read back through the example sentences, you can hear how ungainly the sentences with short predicates and long subjects are.

Some Sentences with Expletives and Noun Clauses Don't Seem to Be Derived

Some sentences with expletives in the grammatical subject position and noun clauses at the end don't seem to be derived from extraposed clauses, since their "underlying" sentences sound odd when spoken. Nonetheless, for consistency, we'll consider sentences like

That nations apologize is seldom.

which probably never occur, as underlying sources for sentences like

It is seldom that nations apologize.

This way, we can call the expletives grammatical subjects and the noun clauses complements, or even logical subjects. And that does seem to be the correct analysis for them.

Wh-Subordinators Act as Content Words within Noun Clauses

WH-CLAUSES are the second kind of noun clauses we'll examine. Wh-clauses are named for the words that introduce them, the subordinators **who**, **when**, **where**, **how**, **how often**, **why**, and **whether**. Wh-clauses can function as subjects, objects, predicate nouns, complements, and objects of prepositions. Here is an example of a Wh-clause functioning as the subject of a sentence.

> **What software manufacturers pray for** is a hot-selling product like Quicken.

Wh-subordinators are different from the subordinator **that**. Wh-subordinators not only introduce noun clauses, but they are also content words. In the example sentence, for instance, the subordinator **what** both introduces the noun clause **what software manufacturers pray for is a hot selling product like Quicken** and functions within the noun clause as the object of the two-word transitive verb **pray for**. **What** is both a subordinator and a noun. In the derivation of the last example, this can be shown by replacing the indefinite pronoun **something** with **what** and then moving **what** to the front of the clause.

```
                                          ──what
  Software manufacturers pray for something.
```
This is a hot-selling product like Quicken.
↓

> **What software manufacturers pray for** is a hot-selling product like Quicken.

Producing Wh-noun clauses is similar to producing relative clauses or Wh-questions. In each, you replace a noun phrase or adverb phrase with a pronoun or proadverb and move the pro-form to the front of the clause; the pro-form you move retains its original function within its own clause—if it started out as a direct object, it remains a direct object; if it started out as an adverb of time, it remains an adverb of time. With Wh-noun clauses, though, the pro-forms are subordinators as well. In the example sentence, **what** is both a pronoun that functions as the object of the two-word transitive verb **pray for** and a subordinator that introduces the noun clause. The next diagram, with the noun clause highlighted by a rectangle, shows this.

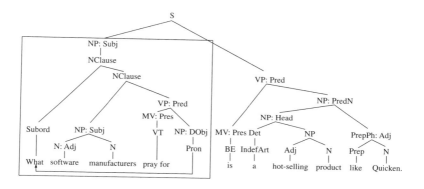

Wh-words in noun clauses are the same words as interrogative pronouns and proadverbs. **Who, whom,** and **what** replace nouns. **Who** and **whom** replace human nouns; **what** replaces nouns other than humans. **When, where, how often,** and **why** replace adverbs of time, place, frequency, and reason, respectively. In the derivations we illustrate, the Wh-pronouns substitute for indefinite pronouns in underlying clauses, while the Wh-proadverbs substitute for such indefinite adverbs as **sometime, somewhere, somehow,** or **for some reason.**

It might seem odd that noun clauses can be introduced by proadverbs; it is a fact nonetheless. These subordinate clauses are noun clauses not because of what introduces them but because of how they function and where they are embedded in matrix clauses. This is the central point to remember about all the noun substitutes in this chapter. In the following example, the subordinate clause **how rock music fills a spiritual void in our society** replaces **this** in the matrix; it fills a noun phrase slot and functions as the object of the transitive verb **explain.**

Bloom's book explains **this.**

⌐—————————————————————————**how**
ˎRock music fills a spiritual void in our society **somehow.**

↓

Bloom's book explains how rock music fills a spiritual void in our society.

The next diagram illustrates the point that the clause **how rock music fills a spiritual void in our society** functions as an object within the matrix and is therefore a noun clause.

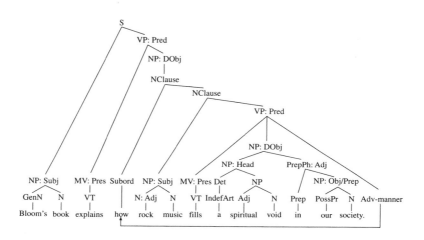

Like that-clauses, Wh-noun clauses can fill almost any noun phrase position in a matrix sentence. Here are Wh-noun clauses filling different noun phrase slots. The first functions as the object of a preposition; the second functions as a direct object following a Vg verb.

The Depression-era photographs remind us of **this**.

┌────────────────**who**
↓ We are ~~some people~~.

↓

The Depression-era photographs remind us of **who we are**.

The school superintendents told the governor **this**.

┌──────────────────────────────**how**
↓ Her tax proposals would affect educational spending **somehow**.

↓

The school superintendents told the governor how her tax proposals would affect educational spending.

Wh-Clauses Are Related to Question Sentences

The point is that you can turn an independent clause into a noun clause by "Wh-ing" (double-u aich-ing) a noun or adverb and then embedding the clause into a noun phrase slot in a matrix sentence. Noun clauses with Wh-words are called INDIRECT QUESTIONS because they seem to be related to Wh-question sentences. The Wh-word is moved to the front of the clause, just like the Wh-word in a Wh-question sentence is moved to the beginning of the sentence. This is true of all the Wh-words we've looked at so far, those that question nouns or adverbs.

But one Wh-subordinator is different: **whether**. **Whether** has neither a noun nor adverb function within its own clause; it is not a pronoun or a proadverb: it is only a subordinator, a word added to the noun clause to introduce it. **Whether** seems to make indirect question sentences into something more like yes/no questions than Wh-questions. Take a look at the next example, for instance, where the noun clause functions as the object of **asking**.

> Police officials are asking whether the war against drug traffickers will succeed.

The sentence can be paraphrased as a matrix clause followed by a yes/no question.

> Police officials are asking, "Will the war against drug traffickers succeed?"

Not only can whether-clauses be paraphrased by yes/no questions, but they can also function as predicate nouns in sentences that indicate the clauses are Wh-questions.

> The question is whether the president is a tough negotiator.

In addition, clauses with **whether** can be paraphrased with **whether or not**, in the same way that you can add **or not** to a yes/no question:

> Will the war against drug traffickers succeed **or not?**
> Police officials are asking whether or not the war against drug traffickers will succeed.
>
> OR
>
> Police officials are asking whether the war against drug traffickers will succeed or not.

All of these characteristics seem to emphasize the relationship of whether-clauses to yes/no questions.

One other fact about clauses with **whether**. Contemporary writers and editors use **if** more and more as a subordinator in place of **whether**, though some teachers and editors still consider **whether** more correct as a subordinator to introduce noun clauses. Thus, you can always say

Historians can't decide **whether** J. Edgar Hoover was a brilliant administrator or simply a skilled manipulator of public opinion.

You can sometimes say,

Historians can't decide **if** J. Edgar Hoover was a brilliant administrator or simply a skilled manipulator of public opinion.

The next diagram illustrates the major structural and functional points about clauses with **whether:** that they are noun clauses and that **whether** is neither a pronoun nor a proadverb but simply a subordinator that introduces a particular kind of noun clause.

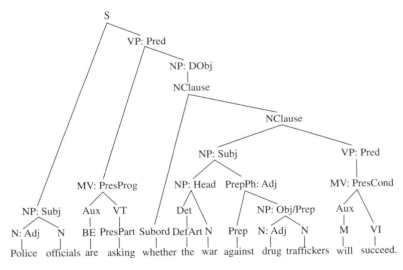

Reducing Clauses to Infinitive Phrases

Some noun clauses can be reduced to INFINITIVE PHRASE. Remember from Chapter 2 that an infinitive is the base form of a verb, a principal part that is nonfinite, tenseless. In the following example, the underlying clause **they should avoid fatty foods** can be made into a noun clause, or it can be reduced to an infinitive phrase **to avoid fatty foods.**

Dieters know **this**.
They should avoid fatty foods.

↓

Dieters know that they should avoid fatty foods.

OR

Dieters know to avoid fatty foods.

In the example, the infinitive phrase, like the noun clause, functions as the object of the matrix verb **know**.

An infinitive phrase is a verb phrase. In the example, **should avoid fatty foods** becomes **to avoid fatty foods**. Since an infinitive is a verb, the structures within the infinitive phrase remain in the same relationships with the verb as they were when the phrase was a predicate in the underlying clause. The way it was *is* the way it is! So **fatty foods** is a noun phrase that functions as the object of the transitive verb **avoid**. The next diagram illustrates both points: (1) that the infinitive phrase fills a noun phrase slot as the object of the matrix verb, and (2) that the infinitive phrase remains a verb phrase constituent, with all its internal relationships intact. The diagram indicates that the verb **avoid** is the head of the infinitive phrase.

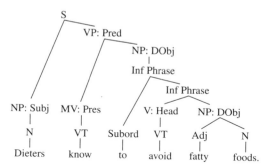

Here are two situations that may cause you problems. The first is that you cannot always make a clause into both an infinitive phrase and a noun clause, but only into one or the other. You can combine the next two sentences, for instance, into a single sentence with an infinitive phrase.

The prince's main job is **this**
The prince attends ceremonial dinners.

↓

The prince's main job is to attend ceremonial dinners.

But you cannot combine them into a single sentence with a noun clause. There is no

> *The prince's main job is that he attends ceremonial dinners.

The second problematic situation is that you'll sometimes have to decide whether an infinitive functions as the head of an infinitive phrase that fills a noun phrase object slot or whether it is the head of the main verb constituent. Another way to look at this second situation is to consider the constituency of the word **to**. In the sentence

> Judge Judy asked **to see the evidence.**

the infinitive phrase **to see the evidence** functions as the object of the transitive verb **asked**. **To** is a subordinator introducing the infinitive phrase. But in

> Judge Judy **wanted to see** the evidence.

wanted to see is a main verb; **wanted to** is a semimodal; **to** forms a constituent with want. **See** is the head of the main verb, and **the evidence** functions as the direct object of **see**. You might want to look back at the discussion of modals and semimodals in Chapter 3.

Infinitives without "To"

The word **to** often introduces infinitives. Some grammarians say that **to** replaces the tense of the verb. Whether or not **to** actually replaces tense, **to** does function in relation to an infinitive phrase much like **that** functions in relation to a noun clause—as a subordinator. And just as **that** does not always have to occur with a noun clause, **to** does not always have to occur with an infinitive phrase. Here are two examples. **To** introduces the infinitive phrase in the first sentence but not in the second.

> The Peace Corps allows Americans **to teach survival skills.**
> The Peace Corps lets Americans **teach survival skills.**

Since the verbs **allow** and **let** are Vc verbs, the infinitive phrases **to teach survival skills** and **teach survival skills** both function as object complements.

Infinitive Phrases Introduced by "For . . . To"

Some infinitive phrases are introduced by the subordinator **for . . . to**. The disjoined **for** and **to** work together as a single subordinator, as in:

IRS identifies laundered drug money.
This is tough.

↓

For IRS to identify laundered drug money is tough.

Notice that the subject of the underlying clause, **IRS**, becomes part of the infinitive phrase, surrounded by **for . . . to**. The noun phrase that sits between the **for** and **to** is called the subject of the infinitive phrase. In the example, **IRS** functions as the subject of the infinitive phrase **for IRS to identify laundered drug money**. If the subject of an infinitive phrase is a pronoun, the pronoun will be in the object form:

For **him** to win the election demanded Obama relate his message to middle-class voters.

Him is the object form of the personal pronoun. The verb phrase constituent of an infinitive phrase introduced by **for . . . to** is called a PARTIAL PREDICATE, to differentiate it from a predicate, which must show tense.

Though they have a subject, infinitive phrases introduced by **for . . . to** remain phrases because they lack finiteness. Remember that, except for an imperative, a clause must contain BOTH a noun phrase subject and a finite verb phrase predicate, a verb phrase with tense. Without a finite verb phrase, a construction is a phrase. Without finiteness a verb phrase has no main verb constituent and no status. Study the diagram of the IRS sentence.

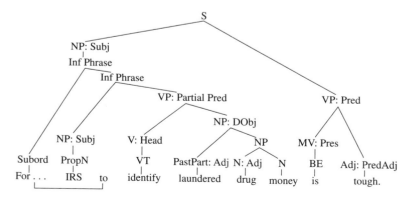

Like noun clauses, infinitive phrases can sometimes be extraposed. In the following example, the infinitive phrase **to look like an** *Elle* **model** functions as the subject of the sentence.

To look like an *Elle* **model** is the goal of many teenage girls.

You can move the infinitive phrase to the end of the sentence if you insert an expletive **it** in the subject position:

It is the goal of many teenage girls **to look like an** *Elle* **model**.

The expletive **it** is the grammatical subject; the extraposed infinitive phrase is the logical subject as well as the complement to the noun phrase **the goal of many teenage girls**.

Infinitive phrases introduced by **for . . . to** can be extraposed also. Here is a sentence with an extraposed **for . . . to** infinitive phrase:

For terrorists to poison a city's water supply would be easy.
↓
It would be easy for terrorists to poison a city's water supply.

In this case, the extraposed infinitive phrase functions both as the complement to the predicate adjective **easy** and as the logical subject, while the expletive **it** functions as the grammatical subject of the sentence.

Some Infinitives Function as Adverbs

Some infinitives function as adverbs, not as nouns. ADVERBIAL INFINITIVES are often introduced by the subordinator **in order to**. In the following sentence, the infinitive phrase **in order to keep its economy in gear** functions as an adverb of reason; it tells why Japan must overcome serious obstacles:

Japan must overcome serious obstacles **in order to keep its
economy in gear**.

This sentence is diagramed below. The three-word subordinator **in order to** can often be reduced to the single word **to**, as in the following:

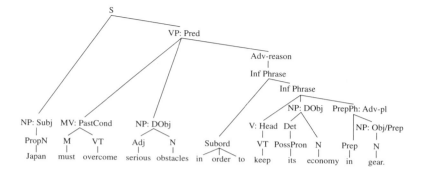

Physicists study the structure of atoms **in order to find out how the world works**.

↓

Physicists study the structure of atoms **to find out how the world works**.

The subordinator **in order to** is one key to identifying adverbial infinitives. An infinitive phrase introduced by **in order to** functions as an adverb. No doubt about that. When an infinitive is introduced by **to**, you can identify it as an adverbial infinitive if you can change the **to** into **in order to**. Whether it is introduced by **to** or **in order to**, an adverbial infinitive always functions as an adverb of reason. The other key is that adverbial infinitives never fill a noun phrase slot. Adverbial infinitives, by the way, are always adverbs of reason.

Gerunds are "-ing" Verb Forms

Like infinitives, gerunds are nonfinite verbs; GERUNDS are -**ing** verb forms that fill noun phrase slots. **Becoming a Hollywood playboy** is a gerund phrase which fills the direct object slot in the next example:

Nick Nolte resisted this.
Nick Nolte became a Hollywood playboy.

↓

Nick Nolte resisted becoming a Hollywood playboy.

Gerunds are derived from clauses. In this case, the gerund phrase **becoming a Hollywood playboy** originates from the predicate of the clause **Nick Nolte became a Hollywood playboy**. Gerund phrases, like infinitive phrases, retain their internal structure as verb phrases. In the original clause, **became** is a linking verb followed by a predicate noun, **a Hollywood playboy**. In the gerund phrase, the gerund **becoming** remains a linking verb followed by a predicate noun, **a Hollywood playboy**. One last point to note about the structure of gerunds: the -**ing** of a gerund phrase is a subordinator, like the **to** of an infinitive phrase. The next diagram illustrates the relationships.

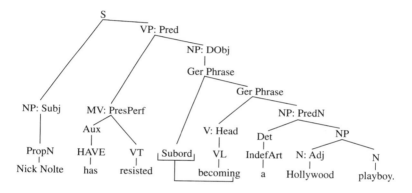

Gerunds can occur in several different noun positions. The next example shows a gerund phrase functioning as the subject of a sentence:

This is difficult for rural towns.
Rural towns recruit doctors.
↓
Recruiting doctors is difficult for rural towns.

And here is a gerund phrase functioning as the object of a preposition:

Merrill Lynch sells partnerships for **this**.
The partnerships invest in real estate.
↓
Merrill Lynch sells partnerships for **investing in real estate**.

As you've probably anticipated, you have to learn to differentiate gerunds from present participles. Gerunds, like present participles, are **-ing** verb forms. But that is their only similarity. Present participial phrases always derive from underlying structures that contain **be** plus -ing. Gerunds never do. Present participial phrases never fill noun phrase slots. Gerund phrases always fill noun phrase slots; a gerund is a verbal noun and only a verbal noun. All a gerund can do is fill a noun phrase slot. The **-ing** of present participles is an inherent feature of verbs; a present participle is one principal part of a verb. The **-ing** of a gerund is actually a subordinator, like the **to** of infinitives; that's why a gerund is not listed as a principal part.

Gerund Phrases May Contain a Subject in the Genitive Form

Most gerund phrases begin with the -ing verb. But there is a gerund phrase that contains its own subject. Such a gerund phrase is called a GERUND WITH GENITIVE because the subject of a gerund is always in the genitive form. Here is an example with an inflective genitive:

Woody Guthrie sings.
This still enthralls listeners.

↓

Woody Guthrie's singing still enthralls listeners.

We could call the 's inflection a component of the subordinator along with the **-ing**, but we'll continue to call only the **-ing** the subordinator.

The next diagram illustrates a few basic points. **Woody Guthrie's singing** is a gerund-with-genitive phrase (a gerund phrase which carries its own subject, **Woody Guthrie's**, and in which the gerund, **singing**, functions as a partial predicate). The gerund-with- genitive phrase functions as the subject of the Woody Guthrie sentence. The **-ing** is a subordinator.

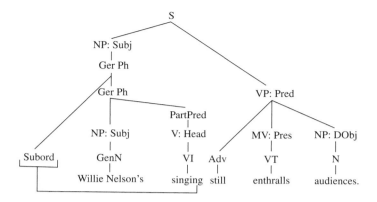

Here is a sentence with a gerund phrase whose subject is the possessive pronoun **her:**

> The ballerina improved this as a martial arts student.
> The ballerina dances.
>
> ↓
>
> The ballerina improved her dancing as a martial arts student.

The main points to remember about gerunds are that (1) a gerund is an **-ing** verb which fills a noun phrase slot, a verbal noun; (2) some gerund phrases may include subjects, which are either inflective genitives or possessive pronouns; and (3) a gerund phrase remains a verb phrase.

Studying Grammar Is Cumulative

Through the years, I've found that when some students do the exercises, they look for only those structures and processes in sentences that a particular chapter is about. If the chapter is on noun clauses and related structures, they look for noun clauses, infinitives, and gerunds. A sentence in the exercises that contains a relative clause instead of a noun substitute can throw them for a loop. Yet only in a grammar book chapter do you find sets of sentences put together with just a few related structures and processes. When we write and speak, we are likely to combine many structures into single sentences and use many processes within individual sentences.

From the point of view of a grammar course or a grammar book, grammar is cumulative. What you learn in the first week (or the first chapter) will still be important in the fifteenth week (or the tenth chapter). Here, for instance, is a sentence that includes a long gerund phrase (**gathering friends together to share the dishes that make Southern food unique**) functioning as the object of the preposition **by:**

> Kentuckians celebrate the Derby by gathering friends together to share the dishes that make Southern food unique.

Within the gerund phrase is an adverbial infinitive phrase, **to share the dishes that make southern food unique.** And within that is a restrictive relative clause, **that make southern food unique.** The main verb of the independent clause, **celebrate,** is a transitive verb in the present tense. The main verb of the relative clause, **make,** is a Vc.

Understanding the second chapter of this book depends on your understanding the first. Understanding the tenth chapter will depend on your understanding the first through the ninth. To be successful at grammatical analysis, then, you have to remember that you might find almost any combination of structures and processes within an individual sentence.

Chapter Summary: Embedded Structures That Fill Noun Phrase Slots in Matrix Clauses

Independent clauses can be formed into clauses and phrases—noun clauses, infinitive phrases, and gerund phrases—that fill noun phrase slots in matrix clauses. That's the main theme of this chapter. There are two kinds of noun clauses: that-clauses and Wh-clauses. Noun clauses can fill almost any noun phrase slot. **That** and the Wh-words which introduce noun clauses are subordinators; the Wh-words—except for **whether**—are also nouns or adverbs within their own clauses.

Both infinitive and gerund phrases are verb phrases that can fill noun slots. They sometimes occur with their own subjects. Infinitive phrases that can be introduced with **in order to** function as adverbs of reason.

Here are the main points of Chapter 8:

- Noun clauses, gerunds, and infinitives fill noun phrase slots.
- That-clauses can fill almost any noun phrase slot.
- You can often extrapose that-clauses from subject positions.
- Some sentences with expletives and noun clauses don't seem to be derived.
- Wh-subordinators act as content words within noun clauses.
- Wh-clauses are related to question sentences.
- You can reduce clauses to infinitive phrases.
- Infinitives can occur with or without the subordinator **to**.
- Infinitive phrases introduced by **for . . . to** contain subjects and partial predicates.
- Some infinitives function as adverbs.
- Gerunds are **-ing** verb forms that fill noun phrase slots.
- Gerund phrases may contain a subject in the genitive form.
- Studying grammar is cumulative.
- Independent clauses can be formed into clauses and phrases that fill noun phrase slots in matrix clauses.

EXERCISES

I. Breaking Out Underlying Sentences

Identify the main clauses and embedded phrases in each of the following sentences. Then write out the complete sentences from which the main clause and embedded phrases are derived.

Prius owners love what Toyota does for them.

↓

Prius owners love this.
Toyota does something for them.

EXAMPLE

1. Eliminating liquor and tobacco billboards may reduce substance abuse.
2. Scientists do not fully understand how superconductors work.
3. People join groups like Alcoholics Anonymous to control all sorts of addictions.

4. Japanese students in American business schools learn to understand Western business practices.

5. It is obvious that many city dwellers consider themselves environmentalists.

II. Combining Sentences

Combine the following pairs of sentences. Make the second of each pair into a noun clause, infinitive phrase, or gerund phrase, according to the instructions in parentheses.

EXAMPLE

The *Newsweek* article explains **this**.

Barack Obama became president in some way. (Wh-noun clause)

↓

The *Newsweek* article explains how Barack Obama became president.

1. Psychiatrists don't know **this**.
   Some people become compulsive for some reason. (Wh-clause)
2. **This** can be difficult for arthritics.
   Arthritics turn a doorknob. (Gerund)
3. A mother bird will attempt **this**.
   A mother bird distracts predators from her nest. (Infinitive phrase)
4. **This** occurred to the vice president.
   Some TV reporters are carnivorous. (Extraposed that-clause)
5. Researchers recorded the songs of whales.
   Researchers wanted to analyze their patterns. (Adverbial infinitive phrase)

III. Analyzing Sentences

Analyze the following sentences. Feel free to use diagrams if those help you to see and understand functions. You may find it helpful to break the exercise sentences down into their component sentences and to work from "the inside out," identifying constituents and then deciding whether those constituents fit within or next to other constituents. Notice that these exercise sentences may have constructions that have been discussed in other chapters, as well as gerunds, infinitives, and noun clauses.

EXAMPLE

> Eating in Japanese restaurants taught me that raw fish won't hurt you.

The example sentence derives from three underlying sentences.

> I eat in Japanese restaurants.
> This taught me this.
> Raw fish won't kill you.

Explanation: The example is a complicated sentence that contains both a gerund phrase and a noun clause. The gerund phrase, **eating in Japanese restaurants**, functions as the subject of the sentence. The head of the gerund phrase is the intransitive verb **eat** followed by a prepositional phrase, **in Japanese restaurants**, that functions as an adverb of place. The main verb of the sentence, **taught**, is a two-place transitive Vg. The personal pronoun **me** functions as an indirect object; the noun clause **that raw fish won't kill you** functions as the direct object.

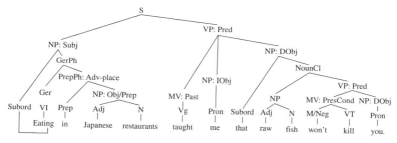

Sentences

1. Robert Kennedy said we need love, wisdom, and compassion in the U.S.
2. James Cagney is remembered for playing gangsters on the screen. But he considered himself a singer and dancer.
3. That the Raiders returned to Oakland angered LA football fans.
4. It angered LA football fans that the Raiders returned to Oakland.
5. The journalism class asked the visiting reporter why she prefers the police beat.
6. America cannot postpone confronting environmental problems.
7. Psychologists who study aphasia want to understand how memory works.

8. The defense attorney's probing displeased the judge.
9. Doctors know that certain hormones can intensify depression.
10. The basic rule in the White House is that debate should be internal.
11. The Nicaraguan refugee went to Los Angeles to join her sister.
12. Some book reviewers criticize Pat Conroy for retelling the story of his dysfunctional family in each of his novels.
13. It doesn't take long for Crystal Gayle's audience to understand that she is Loretta Lynn's sister.
14. Psychiatrists have not shown why Freudian therapy works.
15. The British revere Winston Churchill for rallying their country against Nazi aggression.
16. Internet surfers use electronic bulletin boards to swap software.
17. The Israeli press chided the Syrians for what they called unfriendly activity.
18. Helping fat children lose weight means walking an emotional tightrope.
19. Computer companies haven't shown teachers how they can use technology in the classroom.
20. It takes skill and luck for a gambler to win at blackjack.
21. Thomas Edison became famous for inventing the light bulb.
22. Scientists take wondering as a course of action.
23. Calling a Texan a liar will usually provoke a fight.
24. Twenty percent of Americans don't believe that murderers should be executed by the state.
25. Martin Luther King Jr. wondered whether the United States was a just country.
26. Holocaust survivors want to prevent genocide by preserving the memory of the atrocities visited upon them.
27. It may surprise parents that infant seats don't protect children in serious crashes.
28. The barren diner in Edward Hopper's "Nighthawks" suggests that urban America is lonely and sad.
29. It takes a solid pitching staff for a team to win a pennant.
30. A survey by a cooking magazine found that Americans eat leaner food now.
31. President Truman decided to use the atomic bomb.
32. It is Russian policy to control oil production around the Black Sea.
33. The Middle East combatants resist making a meaningful peace.

34. The experiment will determine whether the new radium therapy can cure leukemia.
35. My new GPS makes finding my way around Florida a breeze.
36. Neuroscientists have found differences in how men and women use their brains.
37. Modeling is an industry that abuses its young and masks the carnage in layers of hairspray.
38. Entomologists believe that termite flatulence causes 20 percent of the world's methane.
39. That the continent's ice shelves are cracking indicates that Antarctica is warming.
40. Thomas Jefferson claimed to abhor slavery, but he owned slaves all his life.
41. Lionel Dahmer's *A Father's Story* explores how the innocent boy he remembers became a vicious killer.
42. Julia Roberts admits it's hard for her to listen to former hubby Lyle Lovett's music.
43. Painting the Sistine Chapel's ceiling was Michelangelo's greatest achievement.
44. Jane Bryant Quinn makes money make sense.
45. The B-29 veered sharply after dropping its deadly load on Hiroshima.
46. Oceanographers know that reefs play a crucial role in an ocean's ecosystem.
47. It is clear that the South has become a Republican dominion.
48. Playing one parent against the other is a fundamental skill of adolescents.
49. Bones found in a quarry near Shanghai encourage some biologists to believe that primates originated in Asia.
50. It is difficult for teens to be honest with their parents.

CHAPTER 9

....

Adding Modifiers to Sentences

Nonrestrictive Modifiers

In previous chapters, you've seen how sentences are expanded by clauses or phrases that are embedded as adjectives or nouns. The relative clauses, noun clauses, gerund phrases, participial phrases, and other structures described in those earlier chapters are bound into phrases within matrix clauses. The relative clauses, participial phrases, and other structures described in this chapter are not bound within phrases but are added to clauses parenthetically. These added constituents are called NONRESTRICTIVE MODIFIERS. Because they are not bound within phrases, nonrestrictive modifiers are set off from the core sentence constituents by punctuation marks that indicate their parenthetical nature: commas, dashes, colons, or parentheses.

Nonrestrictive Modifiers Are Not Bound within Phrases

Some grammarians refer to nonrestrictive modifiers as FREE MODIFIERS or SENTENCE MODIFIERS; these three names are interchangeable. Because they are not bound within phrases, non-restrictive modifiers can often be moved to different locations in a sentence: they can be placed at the end or beginning of a main

189

clause or sometimes even within the main clause, separating the subject from the predicate. Here is a nonrestrictive prepositional phrase placed first at the beginning of a sentence, then between the subject and the predicate, and finally at the end of the sentence:

> **Except for fools and lunatics**, everyone knows nuclear war would be catastrophic.
>
> Everyone, **except for fools and lunatics**, knows nuclear war would be catastrophic.
>
> Everyone knows nuclear war would be catastrophic—**except for fools and lunatics**.

Whether you are able to move a particular modifier to the beginning or end of an independent clause or to use it to interrupt the subject and predicate generally depends on the meaning relationship between the modifier and the clause it is added to. This is an important point. Since they are not bound within phrases, nonrestrictive modifiers are generally considered sentence modifiers, additions to independent clauses. As sentence modifiers, they do not function as adjectives but as sentence adverbs.

The structures that can occur as nonrestrictive modifiers are not new to you, though. Most of the structures that occur as nonrestrictive modifiers also occur as restrictive modifiers. The nonrestrictive modifiers we'll look at are relative clauses, participial phrases, infinitive phrases, prepositional phrases, noun phrases, and adjective phrases. The only structures we study in this chapter that we haven't looked at before are absolute phrases and adverb clauses.

Nonrestrictive Relative Clauses Sit Next to Noun Phrases

We'll discuss the characteristics of nonrestrictive modifiers using relative clauses as our examples. In most ways, NONRESTRICTIVE RELATIVE CLAUSES are good examples of nonrestrictive modifiers in general, though they can't move around the main clauses they attach to. A nonrestrictive relative clause must sit next to a noun phrase:

No entertainer brought more joy to filmgoers than Fred
Astaire.

who

~~Fred Astaire~~ turned energy, dignity, and wit into pure dance.

↓

No entertainer brought more joy to filmgoers than Fred
Astaire, **who turned energy, dignity, and wit into pure
dance**.

Tiger Woods breaks golf records with regularity.

whom

↓The press enjoys writing about ~~Tiger Woods~~

↓

Tiger Woods, **whom the press enjoys writing about**, breaks
golf records with regularity.

Though nonrestrictive relative clauses share the same structure and
are derived in exactly the same way as restrictive relative clauses, by
replacing a noun phrase with a relative pronoun and moving it to the
front of its clause, nonrestrictive relative clauses do not function in the
same way, nor do they mean the same thing. Restrictive relative clauses
imply that there is a larger or different group from the one named in the
main clause. For instance, the next example, with a restrictive relative
clause, says that there is a group of biologists who study racial genetics.
But it implies that there is also a group of biologists who do not study
racial genetics, as the second sentence indicates:

Biologists **who study racial genetics** have been criticized by
groups on both ends of the political spectrum. But those who
study less controversial areas of life are generally untouched by
such criticism.

If you make the relative clause nonrestrictive, you change the meaning
of the sentence radically:

Biologists, who study racial genetics, have been criticized by
groups on both ends of the political spectrum.

The new sentence no longer implies that there is a group of
biologists who do not study racial genetics as well as one that does. It
makes two equivalent statements: that biologists have been criticized
by groups on both ends of the political spectrum and that biologists (all

of them) study racial genetics. Here's another pair of sentences to indicate how restrictive relative clauses imply larger groups while nonrestrictive ones do not.

> The town's cops keep a careful eye on the high school boys who hang out at the pool hall.
> The town's cops keep a careful eye on the high school boys, who hang out at the pool hall.

In the first example, the cops watch carefully only the boys who hang out at the pool hall; we must presume there is also a group of boys who do not hang out at the pool hall. In the second example, the cops keep a careful eye on the high school boys, all of whom, we are told, hang out at the pool hall.

Nonrestrictive Relative Clauses Make Added Comments

Nonrestrictive modifiers imply nothing about different groups. They make parenthetical comments that are in addition to those in the main clause and equivalent to the comments in the main clause. Nonrestrictive modifiers have characteristics of parenthetical comments and of compounded comments.

It's almost as if you introduced nonrestrictive modifiers with the phrase **and by the way** and made those and-by-the-way clauses parenthetical.

> Biologists (**and by the way**, biologists study racial genetics) have been criticized by groups on both ends of the political spectrum.
> The town's cops keep a careful eye on the high school boys (**and by the way**, the high school boys hang out at the pool hall).

This and-by-the-way feature underscores the notion that nonrestrictive modifiers are equivalent in meaning to the comments in independent clauses. If you wanted to make two equivalent statements about the Beatles, both that the band has become a cultural icon and that the four Beatles made British rock popular in the United States, you could construct two separate sentences joined by the conjunction **and**:

> The Beatles have become a cultural icon. And they made British rock popular in the United States.

Or you could say the same thing by making one of the statements into a nonrestrictive relative clause:

The Beatles, **who made British rock popular in the United States,** have become a cultural icon.

Since nonrestrictive modifiers relate differently to main clauses and attach to main clauses in a different way than do restrictive modifiers, they look different on diagrams as well. The diagram of the Beatles sentence illustrates how a nonrestrictive relative clause attaches to an independent clause.

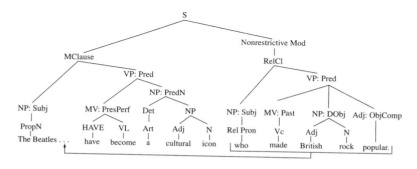

The diagram indicates that the nonrestrictive relative clause is not bound within a larger clause; the relative clause is shown as equivalent to the independent clause. It is moved between the subject and predicate, next to the noun phrase **the Beatles**, and separates that subject noun phrase from its predicate. In the surface form of the sentence, you must indicate the equivalence and the additive nature of the relationship between the nonrestrictive relative clause and the independent clause by separating the two constituents with punctuation marks—commas, dashes, or parentheses.

Nonrestrictive Participial Phrases

NONRESTRICTIVE PARTICIPIAL PHRASES look like restrictive participial phrases: they occur in both past and present participle forms. And they are derived exactly like restrictive participial phrases. You derive a nonrestrictive present participial phrase from a clause by deleting the noun phrase subject and BE of the underlying clause; you derive a past participial phrase by deleting the grammatical subject and BE from a passive underlying clause; sometimes you delete the agent phrase as well. But, since they are not bound within noun phrases, nonrestrictive participial phrases are movable. Here are examples of nonrestrictive participial phrases—both present and past—in various sentence positions:

Steinbeck produced *The Grapes of Wrath* in five months, **writing in longhand**.

OR

Steinbeck, **writing in longhand**, produced *The Grapes of Wrath* in five months.

OR

Writing in longhand, Steinbeck produced *The Grapes of Wrath* in five months.

Prodded by public opinion, three senators reversed their vote on the controversial tax bill.

OR

Three senators, **prodded by public opinion**, reversed their vote on the controversial tax bill.

OR

Three senators reversed their vote on the controversial tax bill, **prodded by public opinion**.

Nonrestrictive Participial Phrases Function as Adverbs

Since they are sentence modifiers, nonrestrictive participial phrases don't function as adjectives; they are not attributes of noun phrases. They function as adverbs. Notice that the present participial phrase of the example, **writing in longhand**, is not only an additional commentary, but its action also takes place at the same time as the action in the main clause. That is, the writing in longhand and the production of *The Grapes of Wrath* occurred at the same time. In this case, the participial phrase functions as an adverb of attendant circumstance. This is a fancy way of saying that the present participial phrase is an additional commentary whose action takes place at the same time as the action in the main clause. Nonrestrictive present participial phrases often function as adverbs of attendant circumstance.

Nonrestrictive past participial phrases often show cause or reason, as in the example where the senators reversed their vote because they were **prodded by public opinion**. The past participial phrase functions as an adverb of reason, an additional comment and a reason. We often place past participial phrases before the main clause, since we generally state causes before effects. The sentence is diagramed below.

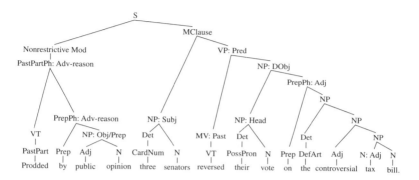

So, nonrestrictive participial phrases share the same structure as their restrictive kin. But they function differently because they are attached to matrix clauses differently.

Appositives Sit Next to Nouns

Noun phrases and adjective phrases that are used as nonrestrictive modifiers are called APPOSITIVES. Perhaps the most familiar non-restrictive modifiers are APPOSITIVE NOUN PHRASES. Appositive noun phrases occur next to other nouns and explain them, as in the following, where the noun phrase **the candidate's wife** tells us who Juliana is:

Next, the reporters questioned Juliana.
Juliana is the candidate's wife.

↓

Next, the reporters questioned Juliana, **the candidate's wife**.

Appositive noun phrases derive from predicate nouns following a BE verb, as in the example, where the subject noun phrase **Juliana is** is deleted in order to leave the predicate-noun phrase **the candidate's wife.** This noun phrase is then attached to the main clause as a nonrestrictive modifier, as the diagram below shows.

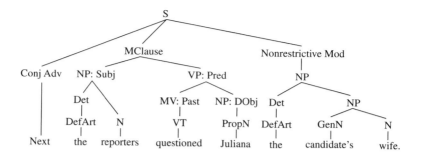

Appositive noun phrases can be complex, because noun phrases can be long and complicated—including within them other phrases or even clauses. In the following example, the noun phrase **a dazzling but destructive woman** contains a compound adjective:

> Daisy, **a dazzling but destructive woman**, is Fitzgerald's ideal "Southern belle."

OR

> **A dazzling but destructive woman**, Daisy is Fitzgerald's ideal "Southern belle."

Notice that the appositive noun phrase, **a dazzling but destructive woman**, can precede **Daisy**, the noun it is in apposition to. The next appositive noun phrase, **the males in the bee colony**, has a prepositional phrase (**in the bee colony**) functioning adjectivally within it.

> Drones, **the males in the bee colony**, exist solely to mate with the queen.

In the next example, the noun phrase **an old man whose stringy hair was tied back in a single braid** contains a restrictive relative clause, **whose stringy hair was tied back in a single braid**:

> The tourists retreated from the panhandler, **an old man whose stringy hair was tied back in a single braid**.

Though less often mentioned in grammar books, APPOSITIVE ADJECTIVES occur with some frequency, particularly in narrative writing. Like appositive nouns, they derive from sentences with the verb BE, and they serve to identify or define noun phrases they are juxtaposed to in the main clause. Appositive adjectives originate as predicate adjectives. Here are some examples:

> It is a large school building, **square and high**.
> Many adolescents see overeating as the perfect rebellion—**safe but obnoxious**.
> The Simpsons' life—**chaotic, absurd, and entirely banal**—has become the model for too many American families.
> OR
> **Chaotic, absurd, and entirely banal,** the Simpsons' life has become the model for too many American families.

Appositive adjectives attach to matrix clauses in exactly the same way as do appositive nouns.

Absolute Phrases

ABSOLUTE PHRASES, sometimes called NOMINATIVE ABSOLUTES, are different from the other nonrestrictive modifiers: they contain both a noun phrase subject and a partial predicate, a predicate lacking finiteness. They look enough like clauses that students sometimes confuse the two. But if you understand how to derive them from clauses, you should be able to identify absolute phrases without difficulty.

To construct an absolute, you generally delete BE from a clause, whether it is the verb BE or the auxiliary BE. In the next example, the verb BE is deleted from the clause **a razor blade was in her grip** in order to produce the absolute **a razor blade in her grip**:

> The detective looked at the young lady lying in the pool of blood.
> A razor blade ~~was~~ in her grip.
> ↓
> The detective looked at the young lady lying in the pool of blood, **a razor blade in her grip**.

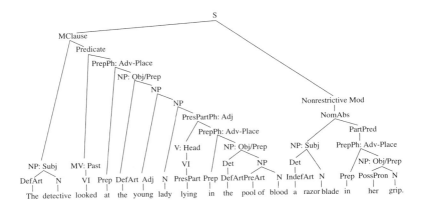

The diagram of the example sentence indicates the structure of the absolute and its relationship to the main clause.

In the previous example, we deleted the verb BE to produce the absolute. In the next example, we'll delete the auxiliary BE that precedes a present participle:

> The turkey hen brooded her downy poults during the storm.
> Her outstretched wings were providing shelter for the baby birds.
>
> ↓
>
> The turkey hen brooded her downy poults during the storm—
> **her outstretched wings providing shelter for the baby birds**.

Or you can delete the auxiliary BE that precedes a past participle in a passive clause:

> Buildings crumbled along San Francisco's Market Street.
> Their foundations were damaged by the quake.
>
> ↓
>
> Buildings crumbled along San Francisco's Market Street, **their foundations damaged by the quake**.

Absolute phrases are used in interesting ways. Absolute phrases are the only structures in English that allow you to narrow in on a scene as if you were using a zoom lens on a camera. You can draw a general scene in a main clause, like **the detective looked at the young lady lying in the pool of blood**. Then you can zoom in on the scene with an absolute, focusing specifically on the **razor blade in her grip**. You can zoom in on the outstretched wings of the turkey hen or note the damaged foundations of the buildings on Market Street after the quake.

Absolutes are sometimes mistaken for clauses because they contain a noun phrase subject and a partial predicate, what is left after you delete BE from a finite verb phrase. But after you delete BE, the verb phrase is not finite. So an absolute cannot be a clause; it has a subject but only a partial predicate. A clause must have both a noun phrase that functions as a subject and a verb phrase that functions as a predicate, a finite verb phrase. **A razor blade in her grip**, for instance, is an absolute phrase because it is composed of a noun phrase subject, **a razor blade**, and a prepositional phrase that functions as a partial predicate, **in her grip**. To make the absolute phrase into a clause, you'd have to insert **was** in order to create a complete predicate,

A razor blade **was** in her grip.

Since the action in an absolute generally occurs at the same time as the action in the main clause, absolutes are attendant circumstances. And they move with some freedom before or after the main clause, or between the subject and the predicate. Here are two example sentences, with absolute phrases in various positions; the second has a conjoined pair of absolutes:

The fullback charged into the end zone, **his legs pumping like the pistons of a fine-tuned engine**.

OR

His legs pumping like the pistons of a fine-tuned engine, the fullback charged into the end zone.

OR

The fullback—**his legs pumping like the pistons of a fine-tuned engine**—charged into the end zone.

The Range Rover sat near the water hole, **its lights off and its engine silent**.

OR

Its lights off and its engine silent, the Range Rover sat near the water hole.

OR

The Range Rover—**its lights off and its engine silent**—sat near the water hole.

Sometimes absolute phrases are introduced by the preposition **with**, as in:

With a twinkle in his eye, the old man said good-bye to his grandson.

The United States and Canada share the busiest border in the world—**with one hundred million people crossing every year**.

Our English teacher read "Stopping by Woods" as Robert Frost might have, **with the spoken lines taking on a life of their own**.

When it precedes an absolute phrase, **with** is an introductory word, like a subordinate conjunction. It is not a part of the absolute itself. So absolute phrases that are introduced by **with**, like **with a twinkle in his eye** or **with one hundred million people crossing every year**, are not prepositional phrases. They remain absolute phrases.

Adverb Clauses Share Some Characteristics of Nonrestrictive Modifiers

Though ADVERB CLAUSES are not in the strictest sense nonrestrictive modifiers, they do share two characteristics with nonrestrictive modifiers. They have similar freedom of movement around and within a main clause, and—when they precede or interrupt a main clause—they must be separated from the main clause with a comma or a dash. They differ from nonrestrictive modifiers because they derive within the predicate of a main clause, not as an additional comment separate from the main clause. They are, after all, adverbs. Adverb clauses are subordinate clauses that function in the full range of adverb roles, including manner, place, time, reason, and condition. Here are a few examples of adverb clauses:

Stephen King became a celebrity **after he published *Carrie*.**
(Adverb of time)

OR

After he published *Carrie*, Stephen King became a celebrity.

OR

Stephen King, **after he published *Carrie*,** became a celebrity.

Many night-blooming plants would die out **if bats did not disperse their seeds**. (Adverb of condition)

OR

If bats did not disperse their seeds, many night-blooming plants would die out.

OR

Many night-blooming plants—**if bats did not disperse their seeds**—would die out.

Americans will be able to weekend in Hong Kong or Australia **because aerospace planes will be so fast.** (Adverb of reason)

OR

Because aerospace planes will be so fast, Americans will be able to weekend in Hong Kong or Australia.

Midas was attracted to gold **just as moths are attracted to bright lights.** (Adverb of manner)

OR

Just as moths are attracted to bright lights, Midas was attracted to gold.

Civilian life was destroyed **where the German armies swept through Russia.** (Adverb of place)

OR

Where the German armies swept through Russia, civilian life was destroyed.

Adverb Clauses and Subordinate Conjunctions

The words that introduce adverb clauses, like **where, just as, because, if,** and **after,** are often the same as the prepositions that precede noun phrases to make prepositional phrases. But they are not called prepositions when they introduce adverb clauses. Like the words that introduce noun clauses, the words that introduce adverb clauses are called subordinate conjunctions or subordinators. These subordinators have no function within the adverb clauses they introduce; they do not replace any constituents within the clauses.

The following diagram of the second version of the Stephen King sentence illustrates the structure of adverb clauses and their relationship to main clauses. Since the adverb clause originates within the predicate, I've shown it beginning there, under **VP:Pred,** and moving to the front of the sentence, attached to **S.** This is an attempt to show that adverb clauses are not separate, additional structures, like nonrestrictive modifiers.

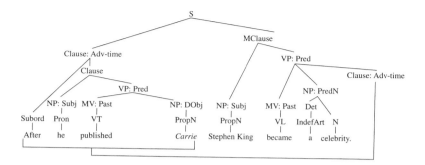

What the subordinators in adverb clauses do is establish specific adverb relationships like time, place, manner, and condition that link the content of adverb clauses to the content of main clauses. Notice how the relationships between the subordinate clause and main clause change when you switch from one subordinator to another:

If it rained on the beach, we retreated under the palm trees. (Condition)

Unless it rained on the beach, we retreated under the palm trees. (Negative condition)

Before it rained on the beach, we retreated under the palm trees. (Time)

Because it rained on the beach, we retreated under the palm trees. (Reason/cause)

As soon as it rained on the beach, we retreated under the palm trees. (Instancy)

Whenever it rained on the beach, we retreated under the palm trees. (Frequency)

While it rained on the beach, we retreated under the palm trees. (Duration)

Nonrestrictive Modifiers Change the Pace, Rhythm, and Movement of Sentences

Writers often put more than one nonrestrictive modifier into a sentence. Using sentence modifiers is one way a writer has of changing the pace, the rhythm, and the movement of her sentences. Here are a few examples of sentences with at least two free modifiers each. The first example has a present participial phrase and a nominative absolute. It begins with the present participial phrase to reflect the movement of the gymnast's twisting flip: **hurling herself into a full twisting flip.** The sentence moves through the main clause that compares her rotation to that of an artillery shell; then it concludes with an absolute phrase that focuses on the relation of the gymnast's head to the ground: **her head pointing improbably at the floor.**

> **Hurling herself into a full twisting flip,** the gymnast rotates like an artillery shell—**her head pointing improbably at the floor.**

The next sentence uses a nonrestrictive relative clause to interrupt the main clause. It concludes with a summarizing noun phrase appositive.

> Thomas Hart Benton, **whom Harry Truman called the best painter in America,** was a swaggering Hemingway-like character, **a "roughneck artist."**

Here's a sentence that opens with a prepositional phrase; following the main clause are a pair of present participial phrases compounded into a single phrase:

> **In the Old West,** marshals were the shock troops who enforced federal laws, **hunting fugitives or collecting taxes.**

In the next sentence, a pair of absolute phrases follows the main clause. The second absolute comments upon the first:

> The hunter stepped into the clearing—**his rifle in his left hand, barrel up.**

The final example has three appositive noun phrases following the main clause—one on how the house looks, one on how it feels, one on how it smells. By focusing on the individual parts of the house, the three appositives produce a sense that the writer has covered completely the subject of how the architect's design creates the home's enveloping warmth.

> Good design creates the enveloping warmth of architect Tanaka's house—**the sensuous curves of the ceiling, the texture of coarse concrete walls, the fragrance of heated tatami floors.**

A Grammar Course Should Prepare You to Analyze Real Sentences

Many grammar books present simple example sentences that exist only in grammar books. But one goal of a course in grammar must be to prepare students to analyze sentences they will run across in everyday life—real sentences from their own writing and that of their classmates; from novels, poems, and psychology texts; from magazines like *Reader's Digest, Newsweek,* and *The Smithsonian.* Here, for instance, is the opening sentence from a *National Geographic* article on Tibetan nomads. The sentence is long and complex, with restrictive and non-restrictive structures. It's also an interesting sentence, like many you'll run across in professional writing or in successful student writing. You should by now be able to analyze it successfully. Try your hand at taking it apart and naming the parts before you read the analysis that follows it. Try to reconstruct the underlying clauses that are combined into the larger sentence also. And don't forget that no matter how long or complex a sentence becomes, you simply peel off one familiar layer at a time to analyze it.

> Sitting beside a dung fire in his black yak-hair tent, aromatic smoke whirling around his head, Trinley, a 63 year-old Tibetan nomad, rhythmically pumped the fire with his goatskin bellows.

The base of this sentence is the main clause **Trinley . . . rhythmically pumped the fire with his goatskin bellows**, upon which several nonrestrictive structures are hung. The subject of the matrix is the proper noun **Trinley**; the predicate is **rhythmically pumped the fire with his goatskin bellows**. The predicate begins with **rhythmically**, an adverb of manner; the main verb is **pumped**, the past tense form of the transitive verb, which is followed by a direct object, **the fire**. The matrix is completed by a prepositional phrase, **with his goatskin bellows**, which functions as an instrumental adverb (it names the instrument used to pump the fire). Preceding the matrix are two nonrestrictive structures—a present participial phrase, **sitting beside a dung fire in his black yak-hair tent**, and a nominative absolute, **aromatic smoke whirling around his head**. Interrupting the subject and predicate of the main clause is the noun phrase appositive, **a 63-year old Tibetan nomad**.

Underlying the main clause and the modifiers are the following sentences:

> Trinley sat beside a dung fire in his black yak-hair coat.
> Aromatic smoke was whirling around his head.
> Trinley rhythmically pumped the fire with his goatskin bellows.
> Trinley is a 63-year old Tibetan nomad.

You should be able to combine the small sentences into the larger sentence, label all the constituents, and identify all the relationships. In the Chapter 10, we'll suggest reasons why writers construct sentences the way they do; for now, we'll restrict ourselves to analyzing the structures and their relationships.

Chapter Summary: Doing Grammar Is About Understanding the System That Generates Sentences

Many different structures can be nonrestrictive modifiers—including relative clauses, participial phrases, prepositional phrases, noun or adjective phrases, and nominative absolutes. Nonrestrictive modifiers are not bound within a matrix phrase; they are attached to and nearly equivalent with the main clause. Because they are not embedded within a phrase, they are generally set off from other constituents by commas, parentheses, colons, or dashes; nonrestrictive modifiers are parenthetical comments. Another consequence of not being embedded within phrases is that nonrestrictive modifiers have more freedom of movement within a sentence than restrictive modifiers. They can begin a sentence, end it, or interrupt the sentence by separating the subject from the predicate. Unlike restrictive modifiers, nonrestrictive modifiers do not imply a larger group but function as additional commentary, often as adverbs of attendant circumstance. Adverb clauses, though they are not strictly nonrestrictive, have the same freedom of movement as nonrestrictive modifiers.

Another important point in this chapter is that, with the grammar you have learned, you can analyze and discuss even complex sentences by student or professional writers. If you remember that every sentence, no matter how complex, can be broken down into underlying sentences, you can "peel away" the layers of complex structures until you reach the core and then systematically rebuild all the structures and relationships. Getting to the essence of sentences and understanding the system that produces them is what doing grammar is about.

Here are the main points of Chapter 9:

- Nonrestrictive modifiers are added to clauses and must be separated from them by internal punctuation: commas, colons, parentheses.
- Nonrestrictive relative clauses must sit next to noun phrases.
- Nonrestrictive relative clauses make additional comments (parenthetical comments).
- Nonrestrictive participial phrases occur in both past and present participle forms.
- Nonrestrictive participial phrases function as adverbs.
- Appositives sit next to nouns and identify or define them.
- Absolute phrases contain noun phrase subjects and partial predicates.
- Adverb clauses share some characteristics of nonrestrictive modifiers.
- Nonrestrictive modifiers change the pace, rhythm, and movement of sentences.
- A grammar course should prepare you to analyze real sentences.
- Doing grammar is about understanding the system that produces sentences.

EXERCISES

I. Breaking Out Underlying Sentences

Identify the main clause, the embedded constituents, and the non-restrictive constituents in each of the following sentences. Then write out the underlying sentences from which the final constituents are derived.

EXAMPLE
    I drove my pickup across Wyoming, the radio blaring
       country-western songs I sang along to.

↓

    I drove my pickup across Wyoming.
    The radio blared country-western songs.
    I sang along to country-western songs.

1. Route 27, which meanders through Florida's citrus and cattle country, takes you into the state's agricultural heartland.
2. Cliff Stoll's book on computer espionage, *The Cuckoo's Egg*, grabs you—its short sentences and terse paragraphs creating an exciting pace.
3. Where the plague appeared in the fourteenth century, death was sudden and terrifying.
4. The decor of her apartment, planned by a Japanese decorator, evokes Yoko's oriental heritage.
5. After you cross the Golden Gate Bridge, driving north from San Francisco, Highway 101 loses its city slickness, becoming a country road that winds through rolling hills.

II. Combining Sentences

Combine the following core sentences to make main clauses and the nonrestrictive structures indicated in parentheses.

EXAMPLE

Photography became a tool of journalism soon after its invention.

Photography traveled with the U.S. Army during the Mexican War in 1846. (Present participial phrase)

↓

Photography became a tool of journalism soon after its invention, traveling with the U.S. Army during the Mexican War in 1846.

1. William Faulkner read a great deal in his youth. (Adverb clause)
   William Faulkner disliked school.
2. Scientists have found the fossil of the oldest known vertebrate.
   The oldest known vertebrate is a jawless fish. (Appositive noun phrase)
3. The wind streamed past the schooner.
   The wind was whipping its mainsail. (Present participial phrase)
4. Young John Kennedy lived a happy youth.
   His leisure time was spent in play and study. (Nominative absolute)
5. The reporter said this.
   History is a record of battles. (Noun clause)
   He was ignoring human accomplishments. (Present participial phrase)

III. Analyzing Sentences

Analyze the following sentences, identifying the structures and functions. If you wish, you may use diagrams to show relationships. Remember to differentiate between restrictive and nonrestrictive modifiers.

EXAMPLE
  Julie bakes her mother's rhubarb pie, using safflower oil in the
    crust instead of Crisco.

Explanation: This sentence is composed of a main clause, **Julie bakes her mother's rhubarb pie,** and a nonrestrictive present participial phrase, **using safflower oil in the crust instead of Crisco.** The subject of the main clause is the proper noun **Julie**; the predicate is the verb phrase **bakes her mother's rhubarb pie,** which has a transitive verb **bakes** and a noun phrase direct object, **her mother's rhubarb pie.** The head of the participial phrase, **using**, is a transitive verb, followed by a noun phrase direct object, **safflower oil.** The participial phrase is completed by two prepositional phrases functioning adverbially; **in the crust** is an adverb of place, and **instead of Crisco** is an adverb of contrast. The diagram is below.

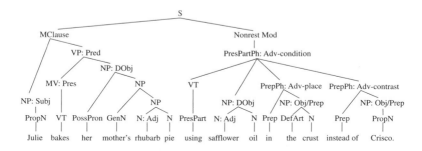

Sentences

  1. Romans believed the appearance of Sirius, known as the Dog Star, made the weather hotter.
  2. Many Bronx buildings have been abandoned and torched, leaving streets barren and empty.
  3. Buried in a remote Guatemalan rain forest, the ancient city of Tikal contains thousands of Mayan structures.

4. As I walk to my car, I can see the snow-filled mountains that brought me to Wyoming.

5. The *J.B. Ford*—the freighter I worked on as a teenager—steams no more.

6. Hoping to catch a last glimpse of their families, the children lingered for a moment before boarding the camp bus.

7. Bruce Springsteen, who exemplifies intelligent rock and roll, has become a political symbol.

8. Pelted by wind and rain, we struggled with the tent flaps in order to keep dry.

9. The camera-toting tourists swarmed from the monorail, joining Epcot's early morning rush.

10. When I think of my grandfather now, I see him on a tractor, tilling ground in wind that cuts a bitter day.

11. The lions rose, yawning and stretching, as they began their search for the day's first meal.

12. Several dozen boats sit on the dry bed of the Aral Sea—their anchors buried in the sand.

13. The Range Rover sat near the salt lick, lights off and engine silent, concealing three hunters and their equipment.

14. I stood for hours at Cincinnati's riverfront dock, awaiting the arrival of a Mississippi steamboat—a paddle-wheeler named the *Memphis Queen*.

15. The mother bear curled up beside a tree, while the cub grazed on grass, an important part of a young bear's diet.

16. The mayor of Djénné pointed to the town's masterpiece of Muslim architecture, the great mosque in the city square.

17. I hit the gas pedal instead of the brake, the policeman on the corner staring as I ran the red light.

18. Canyon Ranch—a former dude ranch converted into a fitness spa—is not a fat-farm for the rich.

19. It's easy to write about Cajun culture when you're living in that world—eating seafood gumbo, listening to swamp pop on the radio.

20. Harlem Renaissance writers were important for their own words and because they built an African American literary tradition.

21. Stately and erect, the United Artists Tower looms prominent along the skyline overlooking Nashville's Music Row.

22. As Caribbean cooking becomes popular, plantains—exotic bananas eaten as a starch—may replace potatoes at the American table.

23. To defend the government of South Vietnam, American forces tore the country apart.

24. One of the strangest comic book villains is Catwoman—whose heart belongs to crime and to Batman.

25. Barefoot and disheveled, my son stood shamefaced before me, as I had once stood before my father.

26. Keeshawna's birthday cake was like those baked by my Southern grandmother—moist, rich, and sticky.

27. Unlike my mother—who had to drop out of school at 16—I was heading for college.

28. When FDR's funeral train passed through towns, thousands turned out to say good-bye—heads bowed, openly weeping.

29. Some of the most memorable geographic places never existed: like Tolkien's Middle Earth and Swift's Lilliput.

30. As part of their palaces, the ancient Persian rulers built walled gardens, *pairidaezas*.

31. With the World Trade Center gone, the lower Manhattan skyline seems barren.

32. Large and dark, the bear raced across the forest floor, leaving the hunter alone in the clearing.

33. The night sky displays wondrous objects: giant galaxies that look like pinwheels, gauzy nebulae that drift through the Milky Way.

34. Like thousands of Honduran children, Wilmer Alvarado begs in the streets while his mother sells trinkets in the market.

35. Tangy and cool—gazpacho hits the spot when the weather turns hot and muggy.

36. Bears are solitary animals—loners accustomed to ranging over large areas.

37. The hurricane weakened rapidly as it moved onshore.

38. When Chubby Checker introduced the Twist in 1960, no-touch dancing replaced ballroom dancing.

39. Overcrowding—because it threatens the stability of the population—is a prison's greatest problem.

40. Cincinnati public radio's series of African American concerts was called *Karamu,* the Swahili word for celebration.

41. Jonas Salk, who perfected his vaccine in 1955, released parents and children from the great dread of summertime, paralytic polio.

42. *Citizen Kane,* despite critical acclaim, did not make a profit during its first release.

43. South Dakota's Black Hills are considered sacred by the Lakota Sioux, who believe humans and spirits meet in harmony among these ancient rocks.

44. It's hard to believe that Sam Cooke, who had a heavenly voice, came to a hellish end—shot by a clerk in a sleazy motel.

45. The chef of the new brewpub understands her mission—to turn out high-quality munch-chow.

46. Rachel Carson's *Silent Spring,* published in 1962, triggered an environmental revolution which protected animals and humans from poisonous pesticides.

47. To the Pilgrims, the American continent was sacred soil, a new promised land.

48. Yellowstone authorities allow buffalo herds to range freely, so that researchers can observe their natural migratory patterns.

49. Mickey Mantle ran the bases like a charging bull, his head down, his legs pumping furiously.

50. The federal government owns hundreds of tourist attractions—including the Grand Canyon, the White House, and Steamtown, a railroad theme park in Scranton, Pennsylvania.

CHAPTER 10

What Can You Do Now That You Can Do Grammar?

Reflecting on Writing and Reading

What #@!$% good is knowing how to do grammar? That's the question you're probably asking at this point. It's the right question to ask. And it deserves a thoughtful answer.

I hope to show in this chapter that the hard work you've put into the grammar lessons can help you become not only a better sentence analyzer but a more knowledgeable writer and a more perceptive student of literature as well—perhaps even a better teacher of writing and literature. The conscious knowledge of grammar you've gained by working through the first nine chapters should help you to reflect on what you read and write and to understand yourself as both a language maker and a language user. This conscious knowledge of grammar gives you the language to talk about and to question the stylistic components of literature and of your own writing. I hope you learn to see grammar as a language that enables you to think about, to talk about, and to use language.

If *analyzing* and *identifying* were key words in earlier chapters, *reflecting* is the key word in this chapter. Much of the reflection centers on the various ways the grammar of your language gives you to compose sentences. What the chapter asks you to do is reflect on those options and consider why you write sentences the way you do and how you react to the sentences other writers compose. After all, if every sentence can be composed in many different ways, the way you choose to write a sentence must change its effect. Part of effective writing is to match grammatical structure with meaning.

As Stephen King says in *On Writing*, "Grammar is not just a pain in the ass; it's the pole you grab to get your thoughts up on their feet and walking."

Style

When we reflect on language in the way I propose in this chapter, we move away from purely grammatical concerns into rhetorical concerns. Francis Christensen claimed that grammar tells you the structures and relationships that are possible in a language, while rhetoric tells you what structures and relationships are effective in a given context. Rhetoric is concerned with quality. Grammar is concerned with acceptability. But you must know grammar to understand rhetoric.

King and most other writers, professional and student, concern themselves with the structure of sentences and how structure and quality—grammar and rhetoric—relate.

In the Preface, I told a story about combining sentences. I'll repeat the story here as a precursor to the discussion of style. To introduce my linguistics students to the idea that the syntactic component of language is creative and can produce an unlimited number of sentences from a small core of structures, I gave them two sentences to combine into one sentence in as many different permutations as they could construct. I've sometimes used the two sentences **It surprised me** and **Jane arrived late** as the input. You're allowed to add "small words" (like conjunctions and articles) and change word forms (say, from an adjective to a noun, "late" to "lateness"), but you must keep the basic nouns, verbs, and adjectives in some form. Normally, students will come to the next class with 50 to 70 sentences. Some years ago, a math major determined he would set the all-time record; he did. He conducted a factor analysis on his output and produced 467 different sentences. He claimed he could have gone on, but grew weary of the task. Here are some of the 467 possibilities:

That Jane arrived late surprised me.
It surprised me that Jane arrived late.
I was surprised when Jane arrived late.
Jane's late arrival surprised me.

It was Jane's late arrival that surprised me.
It was surprising to me that Jane arrived late.
I was surprised by Jane's late arrival.
The lateness of Jane's arrival was surprising to me.
For Jane to arrive late surprised me.
Jane arrived late, surprising me.
Jane arrived late, and I was surprised.
The surprising thing to me was the lateness of Jane's arrival.
Jane arrived late; I was surprised.
Because Jane arrived late, I was surprised.
What a surprise it was to me when Jane arrived late.

You get the idea. The grammar of English allows each of these versions; all 15 are acceptable English sentences, along with at least 452 others. Grammar does not care that, in certain contexts, one or the other of these sentences would be more effective. Rhetoric does. Grammar is concerned with acceptability; rhetoric is concerned with quality. A writer has a number of options when she writes a sentence; her final choices are called her STYLE. Style is a concern of rhetoric. One characteristic of an effective writer is that her stylistic choices fit her content; they may even evoke the content: the way you say things affects what you say.

Let's look again at parsing. In the last chapter, I presented a sentence about a Tibetan nomad. I used the sentence there to make the point that you should be able to parse even long, complex sentences that contain several nonrestrictive modifiers. Here's the sentence again.

Sitting beside a dung fire in his black yak-hair tent, aromatic smoke whirling around his head, Trinley, a 63-year-old Tibetan nomad, rhythmically pumped the fire with his goatskin bellows.

The author could have written the same ideas without resorting to nonrestrictive modifiers:

Trinley was a 63-year-old Tibetan nomad. He sat beside a dung fire in his black yak-hair tent. Aromatic smoke was whirling around his head. He rhythmically pumped the fire with his goatskin bellows.

But she did use nonrestrictive modifiers. So you have to ask yourself why she chose to begin her sentence with a present participial phrase, pair it with a nominative absolute, and interrupt the main clause with an appositive noun phrase. My three-sentence revision is just as acceptable from a grammatical standpoint. But my three sentences don't capture the strangeness of the scene with anywhere near the effectiveness of the original sentence. By juxtaposing a present participial phrase with an absolute phrase (when you might expect parallel phrases), and by interrupting the strange setting described in the main clause with a matter-of-fact detail, the writer shows just how odd the scene seemed. She wants to capture that oddness for the reader, who's probably sitting on a comfortable sofa in a climate-controlled house in an American suburb. The Tibetan scene is foreign to the writer and to the reader. The structure of the sentence emphasizes that point.

Here's a brief example from an Ernest Hemingway novel. In the first chapter of *The Sun Also Rises,* Hemingway introduces Robert Cohn, a character who acts as a foil to the protagonist and narrator, Jake Barnes. Jake is decisive and—most of all—realistic. Robert is indecisive and unrealistic. Cohn is used by other people, especially women. So Jake often talks about him in passive constructions, in order to emphasize the fact that Cohn seldom acts on his own but is acted upon. Here are several sentences about Cohn from the first chapter of the novel. The first and last examples are gerund phrases derived from passive clauses.

> . . . [Cohn] learned [boxing] painfully and thoroughly to counteract the feeling of inferiority and shyness he had felt on **being treated as a Jew at Princeton.**
>
> He . . . **was married by the first girl who was nice to him.**
>
> **[Cohn's] divorce was arranged.** . . .
>
> **[Cohn] had been regarded purely as an angel.** . . .
>
> **He had been taken in hand by a lady who hoped to rise with the magazine.**
>
> . . . Cohn never had a chance of **not being taken in hand.**

Hemingway could easily have made each of these constructions active. Cohn could have married the first girl, or arranged his own divorce, or acted as an angel, for instance. You have to believe that Hemingway chose the passive versions to emphasize grammatically the point he was trying to make about Cohn's dependence on others for guidance. After all, Hemingway didn't introduce any other character in the same way.

Here's another example. Tom Romano is known by English teachers for several books about teaching writing in high school, including

Clearing the Way and *Blending Genre, Altering Style.* Tom has written but not yet published an adolescent novel titled *Blindside.* The first chapter of *Blindside* introduces the main character, Nick, and his girl-friend, Julie. When the novel opens, Nick is in Julie's bedroom. Her parents come home unexpectedly, and Nick has to scramble for his clothes and escape through the front door just as her parents open the door from the garage into the kitchen. He runs through the neighbor-hood to get as far away as quickly as possible. The following paragraph describes Nick's run:

> Nick took long strides, pumping his arms, running with more purpose than he ever had on a football field. He shot through the subdivision that quiet October morning, keeping aslant the windows of Julie's house. He rocketed through backyards, vaulting low fences, ducking clothes lines, rousing dogs to clamorous barking, staying away from the street should Mr. Kelly decide to leave the house as unexpectedly as he'd arrived.

Tom could have written that paragraph in this way:

> Nick took long strides and pumped his arms. He ran with more purpose than he ever had on the football field. He shot through the subdivision that quiet October morning as he kept aslant the windows of Julie's house. He rocketed through backyards, vaulted low fences, and ducked clothes lines. Though it roused dogs to clamorous barking, he stayed away from the street should Mr. Kelly decide to leave the house as unexpectedly as he'd arrived.

In fact, at the end of the chapter, Tom writes a paragraph that looks like my revision of the original running paragraph. When Nick reaches relative safety on the other side of town, Tom describes the scene in this way:

> Nick took a deep breath where he stood at the edge of uptown Medville. He looked up High Street. Cars waited at the light, ready to head his way. At the moment the light turned green and Nick instinctively stuck out his thumb, he felt something wrong. He patted his back pocket. Empty. Nick felt a sharp giving sensation in his bowels. His wallet was gone. And instantly he knew where it was—somewhere on the living room floor at Julie's.

Can you characterize the sentences in Tom's two paragraphs and explain why he wrote the sentences he did? Can you explain how the sentences in Tom's two paragraphs affect you as a reader and how they contribute to the meaning and movement of the first chapter in *Blindside*? Let's try to reflect on those questions, using our knowledge of grammar.

To begin with, the first paragraph from the novel contains only three sentences; but it has seven nonrestrictive present participial phrases. The present participles, because they are verbs and because present participles represent ongoingness, capture Nick's movement, making it appear both swift and instantaneous, as if it's occurring in front of our eyes. In the first two sentences, the participial phrases follow the main clauses, moving away from them. In the last sentence, the participles precede the main clause. The placement of the participles in relation to the main clause seems to show that Nick, moving from the Kellys' house as rapidly as possible, can't run from the image of Mr. Kelly, who can impose himself unexpectedly into Nick's life. Had Tom written this paragraph as I did, without all the present participial phrases, he would have produced acceptable sentences, but he would have created a conflict between the meaning of the paragraph and the structure of the sentences. The sentence structures wouldn't have supported the necessary movement of Nick's run. And they wouldn't have been nearly as effective as they are the way Tom crafted them, with the syntax commenting on and supporting the meaning.

If the first example paragraph from *Blindside* is about swiftness and movement, the second is about stasis, lack of movement. Nick stops. He assesses his situation. So the sentences have no present participles, no verbs as free modifiers. There are eight sentences and five free modifiers. These include an adverb clause **where he stood at the edge of uptown Medville**; a prepositional phrase with compound relative clauses embedded in the noun phrase object of the preposition, **at the moment the light turned green and Nick instinctively stuck out his thumb**; and an appositive adjective, **empty**, which is punctuated as a fragment to emphasize Nick's shock of recognition. There is a second appositive adjective phrase, **ready to head his way**, and another prepositional phrase, **somewhere on the living room floor at Julie's.** The free modifiers don't move, swiftly or otherwise. They make generalizations about the scene: Nick's pocket is empty, and cars are ready to head Nick's way. The free modifiers in this paragraph orient us to Nick's situation, to where he is in relation to traffic, and to where he is in town. A different set of circumstances demands a different set of sentence structures.

What we've done in this section is to use our conscious knowledge of grammatical structures and relationships to analyze literary style in selections from two novels and from a *National Geographic* article. Knowing how to do grammar has allowed us to understand how literary style is determined by the structures a writer chooses from among her options. And it has allowed us to reflect on how sentence structure can contribute to meaning.

Better Writers Match Sentence Structure with Content

In the mid 1960s, Kellogg Hunt conducted research which showed how the written sentence structure of students changes between fourth and twelfth grade. Hunt measured these changes, calculating the length of various grammatical constituents. In terms of grammatical skills, he summed up this growth with the statement "little sentences grow into big ones." What he meant was that as students develop more skills in writing, they embed more clauses into matrix clauses and produce, in stages, longer, more complex, grammatical structures. When they begin to write, they use single clauses or they conjoin clauses. Later they use relative clauses, embedding rather than simply conjoining. Next, they reduce many of those relatives to restrictive phrases. Finally, the better writers, in about ninth or tenth grade, begin using more and more nonrestrictive modifiers, and they generally employ a large repertoire of structures, restrictive and nonrestrictive. The sentences of the more effective student writers begin looking like the sentences of skilled adult writers. The less effective writers don't naturally develop all of these later skills; typically they employ a smaller repertoire of structures and use fewer nonrestrictive structures.

This is not to say that all you have to do to improve your writing is to use more nonrestrictive modifiers or to use a greater variety of syntactic structures. While it is true that you have to learn to judiciously employ a range of syntactic structures in order to improve your writing, what Hunt's research really points to is that the better writers are more aware of the options open to them and understand the necessity to match their syntax more closely with their content. They use a greater variety of grammatical structures—nonrestrictive modifiers, noun clauses, gerunds, passives—whatever they need to make their syntax reflect upon and enhance their content. They generally have more solid content as well.

Becoming a better writer is not simply a case of throwing more nonrestrictive modifiers into your own sentences willy-nilly; nor is it simply a case of gaining more awareness of your syntactic options. But improving your style, especially when you revise, is one step toward becoming a more effective writer. And some writing teachers believe that consciously using your stylistic options can enhance your content, making the improvement of style doubly effective. This was Francis Christensen's argument for making style the center of the writing curriculum. Whether you believe that stylistic concerns should be the core of the writing curriculum or an adjunct to other issues in the process of writing, it's hard to deny that effective student writers have mastered stylistic techniques.

Students Writing with Style

Students who understand how to use grammar and style do as well as Hemingway or Stephen King, Toni Morrison or Barbara Kingsolver. Here is Robert Koch, a Miami student who wrote a paper for his first-year writing class about writing narratives for college entrance exams. He briefly summarizes the high school to college changes. He wants to move his reader quickly.

> We grew up, things change, people move on, high school ends, college starts.

In six two- and three-word sentences separated by commas, Robert speeds you through high school to college. Could he have used more effective syntactic options for quick movement than short sentences and commas?

And here is Spencer Shadel in an open letter to his sister that summarizes his first semester—conjoining phrases without commas.

> I'm so excited with all my classes and running cross-country and meeting new people and starting my work with the other varsity teams as an athletic trainer and so many other things.

Spencer, of course, can use internal and external punctuation and restrictive and nonrestrictive modifiers. Here's a much more complex sentence about running a race.

As I take off my outerwear, I notice how sweaty my uniform is from only my warm-up jog—a good indication that my muscles are much more loose and relaxed than my mind.

Here is the writing of Marly Ellis, who submitted a portfolio of her writing to Miami University's portfolio assessment program. This is a program for high school students entering Miami to "test out of" first-year composition classes. Most of the students submitting portfolios have done well as writers in high school. The writing in Marly's portfolio shows why her teachers considered her a good writer—in no small part because she can write interesting sentences that make use of grammatical options to reflect upon their content. She is a good writer because she does what a writer must do: match grammatical structure and meaning. Her narrative called "Balance" is the story of an anorexic teenage girl named Mourning. The two example paragraphs that follow are from "Balance"; Mourning is in her bedroom, balancing herself between sanity and madness.

Looming ghost-like in the center of the room, she tells herself, "Mourning, you're gonna get your life together. But for now just fill yourself up, take in the air and hold it, or you'll just vanish in the sky like a sick helium balloon." So she counts her breath and lines up on the rug in her room, filling up with air so she won't whisper into nothing, wondering when it was that she lost sight of so much of herself. She hangs there, poised in air, taking in the breaths and feeling herself grow stronger. She needs the balance.

And maybe she would just stay there, suspended like a daydream personified, but her mother comes mincing up the stairs. Mourning can hear her creeping footsteps down the hallway, nervous and tight. A soft knock on the door confirms her guess. "Come in, Mother," Mourning whispers in her head, softly, breathlessly, "Come in." She doesn't speak out loud because she doesn't want to waste the air. Her mother bumps in anyway, face messy with nervous smiles and an overflowing breakfast tray in one pale hand. She hesitates imperceptibly when she sees her daughter wavering in the middle of her room as if there were a tightrope, body clenched and linear in the stillness.

We don't have to calculate the words per clause to see whether Marly has reached a "mature" level of sentence structure. She has. Anyone who reads her sentences knows she is a writer. She proves it in many ways. One way is how she uses nonrestrictive modifiers. Rewrite her second paragraph without the nonrestrictive modifiers if you want to see how much such modifiers add to her writing:

> And maybe she would just stay there, but her mother comes mincing up the stairs. Mourning can hear her creeping footsteps down the hallway. A soft knock on the door confirms her guess. "Come in, Mother," Mourning whispers in her head, "Come in." She doesn't speak out loud because she doesn't want to waste the air.

Or break down Marly's sentences into their underlying structures and then rebuild the paragraph with other options in order to see how the same content might have been said differently.

1. a. And maybe she would just stay there.
   b. She was suspended like a dream.
   c. The dream was personified.
   d. But her mother comes mincing up the stairs.
2. a. Mourning can hear her footsteps down the hallway.
   b. Her footsteps are creeping.
   c. Her footsteps are nervous.
   d. And her footsteps are tight.
3. a. A knock confirms her guess.
   b. The knock is soft.
   c. The knock is on the door.
4. a. Mourning whispers "Come in, Mother" in her head.
   b. Mourning whispers softly.
   c. And Mourning whispers breathlessly.
5. a. Mourning whispers "Come in" in her head.
6. a. She doesn't speak out loud for this reason.
   b. She doesn't want to waste the air.

If we can combine **It surprised me** and **Jane arrived late** in 467 different ways, how many ways could we combine those 17 sentences? More than we could count. Here is just one possible variation built from the sentences underlying Marly's paragraph:

And maybe she would just stay there and be suspended like a dream personified. But her mother comes mincing up the stairs. Mourning can hear her creeping, nervous, and tight footsteps down the hallway. Her guess is confirmed by a soft knock on the door. In her head, Mourning whispers softly and breathlessly, "Come in, Mother." Mourning whispers "Come in" in her head. In order not to waste the air, she doesn't speak out loud.

This version doesn't have the effect of Marly's original. It doesn't capture in syntax Mourning's attempt to balance reality and unreality. But if you understand that grammar gives you many options for revision, you might be able to work toward a more effective version in the way that Marly must have. If you see that you have to ask the same questions about your own sentences that you would ask about Hemingway's or Romano's, then you understand how reflecting about sentence structure can help you become a more effective writer. Will nonrestrictive modifiers help you produce the effects you need? Will a passive or active sentence make a better characterization? Do your sentences need to show movement or stasis? If you want to show a tenuous balance between reality and unreality, can you do it like Marly did, by having Mourning's mother perceive her on a tightrope, balanced in a nominative absolute?

She hesitates imperceptibly when she sees her daughter wavering in the middle of her room as if there were a tightrope, **body clenched and linear in the stillness**.

Did Marly put in the nonrestrictive modifiers or structure her sentences the way she did because she had a grammar course to show her how to do so? Probably not. I don't think Hemingway did either. Some people come to their knowledge of sentence structure and other attributes of writing through reading, through intuition, without a conscious knowledge of the terminology. But for those of us who want to learn how to write better, doing grammar can provide the kind of conscious awareness of our own language that will help us reflect on how to improve our sentences and to know that we can change them. A conscious knowledge of language might alert us to add a nonrestrictive modifier, or suggest that we might combine two sentences into one, or allow us to realize that we can make a passive into an active sentence. Doing grammar can help us see into our own writing, just as it can help us see into the writing of others.

Most Punctuation Can Be Addressed with Three Principles

When I was an undergraduate, one of my English teachers, Dr. Larkin, liked to refer her students to a handbook when we made an error in punctuation. In the margin of our paper might be written directions like "CS. 27c." With that cryptic note, Dr. Larkin was telling us that the handbook had a section 27c which would clear up our CS (comma splice) errors. Dr. Larkin assumed we could understand the instructions in the section. I never could, because they were couched in grammatical terminology that made no sense to me. Not only did the rules make no sense, but there seemed to be hundreds of them, unrelated to one another or to any pattern I could discern. Who could make sense of them all? Who wanted to? I didn't. With your working knowledge of grammar and mastery of terminology, you should now understand the hundreds of punctuation rules. But maybe you don't have to, since there are only a few principles that underlie all the rules, and the principles make sense once you understand the logic behind them. Most punctuation can be addressed in three principles. The first concerns end punctuation marks; the second and third concern internal punctuation marks. We can add a fourth and fifth principle to take care of exceptions.

The end punctuation marks refer to those marks that you put at the end of independent clauses—periods, semicolons, question marks, and exclamation points. The internal punctuation marks refer to those marks that you use to set off either compound phrases and clauses within sentences or nonrestrictive phrases and clauses within sentences—commas, dashes, colons, and parentheses. There are just a few end punctuation marks and a few internal punctuation marks, and the principles for using them are pretty straightforward.

1. End sentences (independent clauses together with their nonrestrictive modifiers, if any) with end punctuation marks. You may also separate independent clauses from one another by a comma and a coordinate conjunction.

   EXAMPLES:
   Though we have been deluged with reports and studies, backed by abundant anecdotes, documenting the academic deficiencies of our young people, most states have not yet implemented serious school

reforms. We continue to muddle along with old-fashioned schools and old-fashioned curriculums.

With each step on the moon, the Apollo 11 astronauts launched a perfect umbrella-shaped spray of dust particles. But the most amazing part of their moonwalk was the moon itself—an alien panorama of ashen rocks and forbidding craters.

OR

With each step on the moon, the Apollo 11 astronauts launched a perfect umbrella-shaped spray of dust particles, but the most amazing part of their moonwalk was the moon itself—an alien panorama of ashen rocks and forbidding craters.

2. Separate the phrases in a series of three or more compound phrases with commas. The last phrase in the series should be separated by a comma and a coordinate conjunction. This is true for subordinate clauses, too.

EXAMPLES:
Mom asked my new friend Rosa what her father did, where her family was from, **and** why they had moved to Springfield.

The Reds' new pitcher worked seven innings, struck out eight batters, **and** gave up three hits.

The Boy Scouts who trashed the old cemetery were **neither** brave, clean, **nor** reverent.

3. Separate nonrestrictive modifiers from main clauses and from other nonrestrictive modifiers by commas, dashes, parentheses, or colons. Separate conjunctive adverbs from main clauses with commas, and separate names in direct address with internal punctuation.

EXAMPLES:
Flies and aphids suck the juices from plants—preferring soft leaves, like those of basil, rather than the tough leaves of rosemary, thyme, or oregano.

When the Step Pyramid was built in 2630 BCE, it was the world's finest tomb; indeed, it was the world's largest building.

Probably the most quoted movie line is "Play it again, Sam." It even became the title of a Woody Allen film. But that's not what Humphrey Bogart's character Rick Blain actually said to the piano player in *Casablanca*. All he said was, "Play it!"

Those are the three standard principles. The fourth and fifth might read:

4. Use a comma when the reader might otherwise misread your sentence. This often relates to initial modifiers, when you might confuse the subject of the sentence with the object of the modifier's verb.

EXAMPLE:
As her parents watched, the toddler walked across the room.
                              NOT
As her parents watched the toddler walked across the room.

Another possibility for misreading occurs when a modifier follows a negative main clause, as in the examples below. The first example sentence implies that the Raiders lost for different reason than the referee's call. The second says that the Raiders didn't lose, and the reason they didn't lose was the referee's bad call.

EXAMPLE:
The Raiders didn't lose because the referee made a bad call.
                   DOES NOT MEAN
The Raiders didn't lose, because the referee made a bad call.

5. Ignore the first four principles for rhetorical reasons (for effect). But know that to ignore one of these principles puts you in jeopardy. Unless you've convinced your readers that you have both grammatical and rhetorical control of your text, many people (teachers included) will think you made a mistake.

Those five principles basically outline "correct" punctuation. But, since the principles provide you with options, you can use punctuation not only to make your writing correct but to make it more effective as well. To explore the rhetorical aspect of punctuation, I've taken some examples from the writing Shiri Frank submitted to Miami's portfolio assessment program several years ago. Shiri was a bright young woman, 18 years old and just about to enter Miami University when she was killed in an auto accident. In the following, Shiri was trying to communicate an experience she had had walking alone in the woods:

With my arms up, I coasted sideways through the path, doing goofy imitations of a Jane Fonda workout.

Shiri began the sentence with a nominative absolute separated from the main clause by a comma; she ended the sentence with a present participial phrase separated from the main clause in the same way. Commas are the normal internal punctuation mark; they don't call attention to themselves. If she had wanted to emphasize, say, the action in the participial phrase, Shiri might have used a dash or even a colon:

> With my arms up, I coasted sideways through the path—doing goofy imitations of a Jane Fonda workout.

OR

> With my arms up, I coasted sideways through the path: doing goofy imitations of a Jane Fonda workout.

The dash might have been a good choice; it makes the reader pause for a moment longer, adding emphasis. The colon would have been too formal for the breezy content of the sentence. The comma makes the participial phrase essentially equal to the absolute, probably the effect Shiri was after. She knew when to use the longer pause; she used dashes in several places throughout the portfolio. In her introduction, for instance, Shiri set off in dashes a comment about the paper she wrote on Eliot's "The Hollow Men":

> The last contribution to my assessment—an analysis of "The Hollow Men"—serves as a necessary and a universal message.

Commas would have sufficed, as in:

> The last contribution to my assessment, an analysis of "The Hollow Men," serves as a necessary and a universal message.

But commas wouldn't have foregrounded the appositive noun phrase in the way the dashes do. Shiri knew how to control punctuation marks, both internal and end marks. In one place in her woods piece, Shiri described a change of temperature caused by the thick foliage:

> Once inside the woods, I felt the cooler temperature; the light from the sun had been filtered by the canopy of new and old trees standing together.

Shiri used a semicolon to separate the two independent clauses. Look what would have happened had she used a period instead:

> Once inside the woods, I felt the cooler temperature. The light from the sun had been filtered by the canopy of new and old trees standing together.

The period would have nearly isolated the ideas in the two clauses from one another. The semicolon indicates they are both independent clauses but closely related to one another, close enough to be placed within the same sentence. Shiri understood how to vary end punctuation. She certainly used periods to separate sentences most of the time, as you would expect. But when the occasion called for a different option, she didn't hesitate. In another place in the woods, she sat behind a waterfall and put her hand in the water.

> I stuck my hand through the water, and the power of the fall pushed it downward.

What if she had separated these two sentences differently? Shiri could have written:

> I stuck my hand through the water. And the power of the fall pushed it downward.

> OR

> I stuck my hand through the water. The power of the fall pushed it downward.

Either of these options would have been perfectly acceptable. But they would have made the separation between the ideas greater and more abrupt. The conjunction and the comma make a gentle segue. A more abrupt transition might have disrupted the misty vision Shiri attempted to portray here.

There are two main points in this discussion of punctuation. The first is that, once you understand how to analyze sentences, a confusion of punctuation rules can be reduced to a few understandable principles. The second point is that when you understand how to punctuate, you can use punctuation rhetorically, in order to enhance the effect of your writing, just as you use grammatical structures for effect. Shiri was a good writer—which means that she knew more about writing than simply how to do it correctly. She obviously knew more than grammar and punctuation rules as well. But her ability to use punctuation for rhetorical effects enhanced her writing. It showed how much control she had over the written word, and it added a sophisticated dimension to her writing. Dr. Larkin may have gotten us to punctuate correctly through her handbook instructions. I don't remember, though, that she ever showed us how punctuation could have a positive effect on our writing.

Teachers Should Point Out Interesting and Effective Student Sentences

Many of the students who study grammar from this book plan to be English teachers. So, how teachers can show students the positive effects of grammatical choices is the final point about what you can do now that you can do grammar. In one study of writing, Don Daiker asked 24 English professors to read and comment on a single freshman paper. Using the results of his and similar studies, Daiker concluded that English teachers are better trained to spot errors in student papers than to recognize strengths, "especially on the sentential and lexical levels. Daiker showed a number of instances in which the English professors overlooked well-written sentences. In one such case, "many instructors pointed out the dangling modifier in the next-to-last sentence of the first paragraph . . . but no one applauded the effective use of appositive adjectives . . . in the following sentence." What a shame!

When she was in the ninth grade, my older daughter, Ara, "discovered" nonrestrictive modifiers. As kids learning to swim, to play tennis, or to dance tend to do when they begin to master new techniques, she overused present participial phrases and appositives and absolutes, making almost every sentence long and dense, a syntactic thicket. Her English teacher commented on one excessively florid paper, "Write shorter sentences. Write more like Hemingway." Actually, she had written "like Hemingway," at least in terms of being able to add nonrestrictive modifiers to sentences. I wrote back to the teacher, comparing my daughter's sentences with Hemingway's in his nonfiction *Death in the Afternoon,* which is narrative and descriptive and has fewer short, choppy dialogue sentences than his novels, more sentences with nonrestrictive modifiers. What that teacher should have done was praise my daughter for using nonrestrictive modifiers, and then he should have shown her how to use them effectively, how to trim the growth back. To craft sentences like Hemingway's and Faulkner's and Maya Angelou's.

Imagine how much more productive English classes are when teachers point out interesting and effective sentences in the writing of their students and in the literature they're reading for class. Perhaps students would become not only more skilled writers but better readers of literature as well. Understanding how language works, after all, connects writing, reading, and literature study. Traditionally, doing grammar—becoming aware of language structure—was the core of composition and literature instruction.

Before the First World War, an American educator named Rollo Brown spent a year observing classrooms throughout France, which was then thought to have the best educational system in the world. His book *How the French Boy Learns to Write* (badly titled for our more gender-sensitive age) explains his observations. One thing that surprised Brown was how much French students understood of how sentences worked in novels, short stories, and poetry and how little time French teachers spent in grammar book lessons. They taught grammar mostly out of literature texts and out of the students' own writing: "The grammar lesson itself is based upon some more or less complete passage of prose that is drawn from the boy's reading. . . . In truth, the French teacher seems to increase the boy's interest distinctly by helping him to see the structure of what he reads."

Those pre-WWI French teachers taught their students to see grammatical structures in literature and their own writing. In *Wondrous Words*, a contemporary book on teaching writing and reading, Katie Wood Ray returns to the idea that students have to become grounded in language issues, but in order to learn better how to read and write, not simply how to parse sentences. She teaches her students to read like writers, to recognize sentences and larger text structures, and to understand the craft that writers use to produce text. Ray wants students to incorporate into their writing the craft techniques that drive the work of Cynthia Rylant or Kenneth Mallory or Mem Fox—more compelling goal for a language arts teacher than sentence recognition or correctness, and certainly more interesting and productive for students. Ray understands that teachers must learn to see craft in writing, because "the more you know, the more you see in your students' writing."

Chapter Summary: Good Writers, Good Readers, and Good Teachers Understand the Options Grammar Gives Us to Construct Sentences

This chapter started out with a question: *What #@!$% good is knowing how to do grammar?* I hope the chapter has been a satisfactory, if incomplete, answer. The basis of the answer is that good writers, good readers, and good teachers are aware of the options grammar gives us to construct sentences, to clarify them, to punctuate them, and to choose the most effective among them. Studying grammar makes that knowledge conscious. It gives us a language with which to think about language. And it gives us an entryway into other craft issues in writing. You don't learn grammar simply to parse sentences or to draw diagrams. You learn grammar so that you can understand how language works. If you are interested in the structure of language, as a linguist is, you build on that knowledge of how your language works and look at how other languages work, in order to discern basic principles of language or to investigate how the mind processes language, or to view language in a social context. If you're not a linguist, you likely want to learn grammar so that you will have the means to reflect on your writing and on the writing of others.

EXERCISES

I. Take a paragraph or two from a writer you like a lot and analyze the writing's sentence structure. Then break the sentences down into their underlying components and write them in a way different from the original. What have you discerned about the author's style with this exercise? Write a one- or two-page paper in which you relate the author's sentence structure to his or her content, in effect analyzing the author's style. You can analyze the writing in a novel, a short story, a poem, or a magazine or newspaper article.

II. Take a paper that you are writing for this or any other class. Revise it using your knowledge of grammatical options. You may want to add free modifiers, to revise sentences, or to punctuate it anew. Keep notes on the changes you make, and write a one- or two-page reflection on how your changes made the paper more effective—or on why you went back to the original versions.

III. In an article entitled "Grammars of Style: New Options in Composition," Winston Weathers explores what he calls Grammar B. In short, Weathers asks you to perceive your text in other than standard ways. For instance, he suggests using fragments or arranging comparisons on the page in columns rather than in paragraphs that follow one after another. Read Weathers' article and write a paper using the principles of

Grammar B. Add a brief reflection on the Grammar B processes you used and how they affect your content. An abridged version of "Grammars of Style" appears in Richard L. Graves, ed., *Rhetoric and Composition: A Sourcebook for Teachers* (Upper Montclair, NJ: Boynton/Cook, 1984), pp. 133–147; the original article appeared in *Freshman English News* 4 (Winter 1976): 1–4, 12–18.

***

Finally, a note about relying on technology: In 2004, Microsoft Word's grammar checker found "Microsoft the company should big improve Word **grammar** check" perfectly grammatical. It found other ungrammatical sentences like that acceptable. You can see the errors accepted by the grammar checker at *http://faculty.washington.edu/ sandeep/check*, part of the University of Washington faculty website.

ANSWER KEY

....

Introduction to Answer Key

In order to save space, I haven't drawn tree diagrams for the Answer Key. Instead, I've used lines and labels to define constituents and hierarchies. The lined diagrams are like upside down tree diagrams. Once students get used to these diagrams, they generally find them as useful as tree diagrams. I hope you find them clear and easy to follow.

Here's how to set up a lined diagram.

The first thing you have to do is space between the words then label the individual parts.

The	Model T's	engine	produced	20	horsepower.
D/Art	GenN	N	VT	CardNo	N

Next you label constituents and hierarchies, one line at a time.

Det	——NP——	MV:Past	Det
——NP:Subj——		—— NP:DObj ——
		——————VP:Pred ————————

Your final lines should always indicate an NP:Subj on the left and a VP:Pred on the right.

Chapter 1   Identifying Verb Types

1. VT
2. BE
3. Vg
4. Vc
5. VL
6. Vc
7. VI

8. BE
9. VT
10. VI
11. Vg
12. Vc
13. VL
14. VT
15. VL
16. Vc
17. BE
18. VT
19. Vc
20. VT
21. Vc
22. Vg
23. VI
24. VI
25. VL

Chapter 2   Relating Words, Phrases, and Slots

1. The boiler exploded with   a   loud bang.
   Art   N   VI   Prep   Art Adj   N
   └─NP:Subj─┘   └──── NP ────┘
                                  └──NP:Obj/Prep──┘
                            └──PrepPh:Adv-manner──┘
                    └────────── VP:Pred ──────────┘

2. A dancer's body is her   living voice.
   Art PossPr   N   BE PossPr   Adj   N
       └── NP ──┘   └───── NP ─────┘
   └── NP:Subj ─┘   └── NP:PredN ──┘
                       └──────── VP:Pred ────────┘

3. Americans love informal dining.
      N   VT   Adj   N
                              └─NP:DObj─┘
   └─NP:Subj─┘   └───── VP:Pred ──────┘

4. The aircraft commander behaved prudently.
   Art   N:Adj   N   VI   Adv-manner
        └───── NP ──────┘
   └──── NP:Subj ────────┘ └───── VP:Pred ──────┘

5. Sagebrush carpets western terrain.
      N   VT   Adj   N
                              └─NP:DObj─┘
   └─NP:Subj─┘   └───── VP:Pred ──────┘

6. Dr. Jekyll became   a   different person after   his   experiment.
      N   VL   Art   Adj   N   Prep PossPr   N
                                                            └── NP:ObjPrep ──┘
                            └───────── NP ─────────┘ └── PrepPh:Adv-time ──┘
                            └──────── NP:PredN ──────┘
   └─NP:Subj─┘   └────────────── VP:Pred ──────────────────────────────┘

7. The groom showed up in a brocade tuxedo
   Art N VI Prep Art Adj N
   —NP:Subj—
   NP
   NP:Obj/Prep
   PrepPh:Adv-manner
   VP:Pred

8. Stephen King gives readers scary stories.
   N N Vg N Adj N
   —NP:Subj— NP:IObj —NP:DObj—
   VP:Pred

9. Our local yards turned brown because of the drought.
   PossPr Adj N VL Adj Prep Art N
   AdjPh:PredAdj NP
   NP:Obj/Prep
   PrepPh:Adv-cause
   —NP:Subj—
   VP:Pred

10. Literary historians call Joel Chandler Harris an American regionalist.
    Adj N Vc N Art Adj N
    —NP:Subj— NP:DObj NP:ObjComp
    VP:Pred

11. The International Olympic Committee returned Jim Thorpe's medals to his family in 1938.
    Art Ad Adj N Vg PossN N Prep PossPr N Prep N
    —NP:Subj— NP:DObj NP:Obj/Prep NP:ObjPrep
    PrepPh:Adv-reception PrepPh:Adv-time
    VP:Pred

12. Holocaust Museum visitors find their experience unsettling.
    N N N Vc PossPr N Adj
    —NP:Subj— NP:DObj Adj:ObjComp
    VP:Pred

13. Amelia Earhart disappeared in 1937 during a global flight.
    N   VI   Prep N   Prep Art Adj   N
    NP:Subj   MV:Past   NP:Obj/Prep   ——NP——
                                     PrepPh:Adv-time   ——NP:Obj/Prep——
                                                         ——PrepPh:Adv-time——
                              ——————————VP:Pred——————————

14. Spring is hiking season in Idaho.
    N   BE N:Adj   N   Prep   N
    NP:Subj ——NP:PredN—   NP:Obj/Prep
                             PrepPh:Adv-place
            ——————————VP:Pred——————————

15. The chef made the young couple a mango-basil soup.
    Art N   Vg Art Adj   N   Art N:Adj   N
    —NP:Subj—   ——————NP——————   ——————NP——————
                ——————NP:IObj——   ——————NP:DObj——
                ——————————————VP:Pred——————————————

16. The Senate came up with a compromise bill despite White House opposition.
    Art   N   VT   Art   Adj   N   Prep   N   Adj   N
    —NP:Subj—   ——————————NP——————————   ————————NP:Obj/Prep————————
                          ——————————NP:DObj——————   ——PrepPh:Adv-contrary cond——
                          ————————————————————VP:Pred————————————————————

17. AIDS was a big city plague until the 1990s.
    N   BE Art Adj N   N   Prep Art   N
    NP:Subj ——————NP——————   NP:Obj/Prep
            ——————NP:PredN——   —PrepPh:Adv-time—
            ——————————VP:Pred——————————

18. The 1948 Chrysler Town and Country makes an unforgettable impression at   car shows.
    Art   N   VT Art   Adj   N   Prep N:Adj N
    ——————————N——————————   MV:Pres   ——————————NP——————————   ——NP:Obj/Prep——
    ——————————NP:Subj——————   ——————————NP:DObj——————   — PrepPh:Adv-pl —
                                                   ————————————————VP:Pred————————————————

19. New York's Cotton Club made African-American entertainment popular during the 1920s.
    PossN   N   N   Vc   Adj   N   Adj   Prep   Art   N
    ——NP:Subj——   ————————NP:DObj————————   ObjComp   Np:ObjPrep
                                                                                 —PrepPh:Adv time—
                        ————————————————————VP:Pred————————————————————

20. Early TV sitcoms seem naive nowadays.
    Adj   N:Adj N   VL   Adj   Adv-time
         ——NP——   AdjPh:PredAdj
    ——NP:Subj——   ————VP:Pred————

21. The Blue Ridge Parkway runs through a magic land.
           N   VI   Prep   Art Adj   N
                                      ——— NP ———
                                      —NP:Obj/Prep—
                                      —PrepPh:Adv-place—
    ——NP:Subj——   ————————VP:Pred————————

22. Nepal's government declared their nation a republic in 2008.
    PossPr   N   Vc   PossPr   N   Art   N   Prep   N
    ——NP:Subj——   ——NPDObj—— — NP:ObjComp PrepPh:Adv-time
                            ————————————VP:Pred————————————

23. Huck is an unreliable narrator.
     N   BE Art   Adj   N
                 ————— NP —————
     NP:Subj   ——NP:PredN——
                 ————VP:Pred————

24. Midwesterners moved to California in large numbers after World War II.
          N   VI Prep   N   Prep Adj   N   Prep   N
    ——NP:Subj——   NP:Obj/Prep   ——NP:Obj/Prep——   —NP:Obj/Prep—
                        PrepPh:Adv-place —PrepPh:Adv-extent— —PrepPh:Adv-time—
                        ————————————————VP:Pred————————————————

25. A   peaceful world proved a   fleeting dream in   the 1990s.
    Art Adj   N   VL   Art Adj   N   Prep Art N
         ——NP——   ——NP——   NP:Obj/Prep
    ——NP:Subj——   ——NP:DObj——   PrepPh:Adv-time
                         ————————————VP:Pred————————————

Chapter 3   Expanding Verb Phrases

1. The state legislature might offer parents school vouchers soon.
   Art N:Adj N   M   Vg   N   N:Adj   N   Adv-time
        ——NP——   Aux   Inf   NP:IObj ——NP:DObj——
   ——NP:Subj——   MV:PastCond
                                   ————————————VP:Pred————————————

2. Student Senate denied funding to   the gay   rights organization.
   N:Adj   N   Vg   N   Prep Art N:Adj N
   ——NP:Subj——   MV:Past NP:DObj   ——NP——
                                                       ——NP:Obj/Prep——
                                           ——PrepPh:Adv-reception——
                            ————————————VP:Pred————————————

3. Females are initiating dates   nowadays.
   N   BE   VT   N   Adv-time
   NP:Subj Aux PresPart   NP:DObj
            ——MV:PresProg——
            ————————VP:Pred————————

4. Daiker College will have a splendid chemistry building next year.
   N   M   VT   Art   Adj   N:Adj   N   Art   N
   —NP:Subj—   Aux Inf   NP:Adv-Time
               MV:PresCond
                                              ——— NP ———
                                       ——— NP:DObj ———
                             ——— VP:Pred ———

Note: **Have** is more properly a semi-transitive verb.

5. Springfield would have built a police station with the federal grant.
   N   M   HAVE   VT   Art N:Adj   N   Prep Art   Adj   N
   NP:Subj   ——— Aux ——— PastPart   ——— NP ———
                — MV:PastPerfCond—   ——— NP ———   — NP:Obj/Prep —
                                          ——— NP:DObj———   — PrepPh:Adv-instrument—
                                      ——— VP:Pred ———

6. The Navy can finance your   college education.
   Art   N   M   VT   PossPr   N:Adj   N
   NP:Subj   Aux Inf   ——— NP ———
               MV:PresCond   ——— NP:DObj ———
                            ——— VP:Pred ———

7. Edna Buchanan has   set   her   novels in   south Florida.
   N   HAVE VT   PossPr N   Prep Adj   N
   —NP:Subj—   Aux   PastPart   —NP:DObj—   — NP:Obj/Prep —
                  —MV:PresPerf—   PrepPh:Adv-place—

8. Winston Churchill was a   complicated giant on   the world stage.
   N   BE   Art Adj   N   Prep Art N:Adj N
   —NP:Subj—   MV:Past   ——— NP ———   ——— NP ———
                                     ——— NP:PredN ———   —NP:Obj/Prep—
                                                              PrepPh:Adv-place—
                                 ——— VP:Pred ———

9. Franklin Roosevelt had understood the Nazi threat before World War II.
   N — HAVE VT — Art N:Adj N — Prep — N
   —NP:Subj— Aux PastPart — NP — NP:Obj/Prep
   —MV:Past Perf— NP:DObj — PrepPh:Adv-time
   —VP:Pred—

10. Elvis may be history's biggest star.
    N M BE PossN Adj N
    NP:Subj Aux Inf — NP —
    MV:PresCond —NP:PredN—
    —VP:Pred—

11. My history class is reading The Diary of Anne Frank.
    PossPr N:Adj N BE VT N
    NP — Aux PresPart —NP:DObj—
    —NP:Subj— MV:PresProg
    —VP:Predicate—

12. Stingrays could have been cruising near the beach.
    N M HAVE HAVE Pastrt VI Prep Art N
    NP:Subj —Aux— PresPart —NP:Obj/Prep
    —MV:Past Perf Prog Cond— —PrepPh:Adv-place—
    —VP:Pred—

13. The prince may complete his education at Harvard.
    Art N M VT PossN N Prep N
    —NP:Subj— Aux Inf —NP:DObj— PrepPh:Adv-place
    —MV:Pres Cond—
    —VP:Pred—

14. Paul Simon's lyrics have become political.
    PossN N HAVE VL Adj
    —NP:Subj— Aux PastPart AdjPh:PredAdj
    —MV:PresPerf—
    —VP:Pred—

15. The environment will suffer because of rising temperatures.
   Art   N   M   VI   Prep   Adj   N
  —NP:Subj— Aux Inf   —NP:Obj/Prep—
          MV:PresCond —PrepPh:Adv-reason—
                  —VP:Pred—

16. The silo might have blown up.
   Art N   M   HAVE   VI
  NP:Subj   Aux —   PastPart
        —MV:PastPerfCond—
          —VP:Pred—

17. Lawsuits can cripple medical practices.
   N   M   VT   Adj   N
  NP:Subj Aux Inf   —NP:DObj—
      MV:Pres Cond

18. My roommate's nervousness was becoming a burden.
  PossPr PossN   N   BE   VL   I/Art N
     —NP—   Aux PresPart NP:PredN
    —NP:Subj—   —MV:PastProg—
               —VP:Pred—

19. Eddie Murphy was being vulgar during the interview.
   N   N   BE   BE   Adj   Prep Art   N
  —NP:Subj— Aux PresPart AdjPh:PredAdj   —NP:Obj/Prep—
        —MV:Past Prog—   —PrepPh:Adv-time—
                 —VP:Pred—

20. A poor Christmas season could shut down smaller stores.
  Art Adj N:Adj N   M   VT   Adj   N
      —NP—   Aux Inf   —NP:DObj—
     —NP—   —MV:Past Cond—
    —NP:Subj—   —VP:Pred—

21. Miami Beach has turned into the American Riviera.
    N   HAVE   VL   Art   Adj   N
    NP:Subject Aux PastPart
               ——MV:PresPerf——
                            ————NP————
                            ——NP:PredN——
               ——————————VP:Pred——————————

22. Cable outlets are challenging phone companies for computer hookups.
    N:Adj   N   BE   VT   N:Adj   N   Prep   N:Adj   N
    —NP:Subj—   Aux   —PresPart—   —NP:DObj—   ——NP:Obj/Prep——
                  —MV:PresProg—   —PrepPh:Adv-goal—
                            ——————————VP:Pred——————————

23. The architecture students have to come up with a functional home design.
    Art   N:Adj   N   M   VT   Art   Adj   N:Adj   N
                                —Aux—   ——Inf——
    ————NP:Subj————   —MV:PresCond—
                ———NP———   ——————NP——————
                                      ——————NP:DObj——————
                            ——————————VP:Pred——————————

24. Education can be a potent weapon.
    N   M   BE   Art Adj   N
    NP:Subj   Inf
              MV:PresCond
                   ————NP————
                   ——NP:PredN——

25. Suburbanites are pouring their creative juices into Halloween celebrations.
    N   BE   VT   PossPr   Adj   N   Prep   N:Adj   N
    —NP:Subj—   Aux PresPart   ————NP————   ————NP:Obj/Prep————
                 MV:Pres Prog   ——NP:DObj——   ——PrepPh:Adv-place——
                            ——————————VP:Pred——————————

Chapter 4   Exploring Noun Phrases

1. Bruce Wayne will turn eighty in 2019.

Bruce Wayne	will	turn	eighty	in	2019.
PropN	M	VL	N	Prep	N
NP:Subj	Aux	Inf	NP:PredN	Prep	NP:Obj/Prep
		MV:PresCond			PrepPh:Adv-time
			VP:Pred		

2. The torte recipe required a cup of almonds.

The	torte	recipe	required	a	cup	of	almonds.
D/Art	N:Adj	N	VT	PreArt	N		
Det	NP		MV:Past	Det			
Det—NP				Det—NP:DObj			
NP:Subj				VP:Pred			

3. Kwanzaa celebrates the heritage of African Americans.

Kwanzaa	celebrates	the	heritage	of	African Americans.
PropN	VT	D/Art	N	Prep	PropN
NP:Subj	MV:Pres	Det			NP:Obj/Prep
					PrepPh:Gen
					NP
					NP:DObj
					VP:Pred

4. Cell phones outsell all other media now.

Cell	phones	outsell	all	other	media	now.
N:Adj	N	VT	PreArt	Det	N	Adv-time
NP:Subj		MV:Pres	Det		NP	
					NP	
					VP:Pred	

5. The Cat in the Hat uses a vocabulary of 225 words.

The Cat in the Hat	uses	a	vocabulary	of	225	words.
PropN	VT	I/Art	N	Prep	CardN	N
NP:Subj	MV:Pres	Det			NP:Obj/Prep	
					PrepPh:Gen	
					NP	
					NP:DObj	
					VP:Pred	

6. No   comics   craft   ballets   of   abuse   like   the Three Stooges.
   PreArt   N   VT   N   Prep   N   Prep   ———PropN———
   ——NP:Subj—   MV:Pres   NP:Obj/Prep   ——NP:Obj/Prep——
                                               PrepPh:Gen   ——PrepPh:Adv-manner——
                                               ——NP:DObj——
                                               ————VP:Pred————

7. The   oil   industry's   misjudgments   have   scarred   Alaska   deeply.
   D/Art   GenN   N   HAVE   VT   PropN   Adv-manner
   Det   ——NP——   Aux   PastPart   NP:DObj
   ——NP:Subj——   —MV:PresPerf—
                                                                ——VP:Pred——

Note: **Oil industry's** is more correctly a genitive noun phrase composed of the genitive noun **industry's** and the noun **oil**, which functions as an adjective.

8. Stephen Jay Gould's   books   address   the   question   of   evolution.
   ——GenN——   N   VT   D/Art   N   Prep   N
   ——NP:Subj——   MV:Pres   Det   NP:Obj/Prep
                                                                      PrepPh:Gen
                                                               ——NP——
                                           ——NP:DObj——
                                           ————VP:Pred————

9. Umpires   must   administer   the   rules   of   the   game   fairly.
   N   M   VT   D/Art   N   Prep   D/Art   N   Adv-manner
   NP:Subj   Aux   Inf   Det   Det   PrepPh:Gen
   ——MV:PastCond—   ——NP——
                                                         ——NP:DObj——
                                                 ——NP:DObj——
                                                 ————VP:Pred————

10. My   father's   surgeon   plopped   herself   into   a   plastic   chair.
    PossPron   GenN   N   VT   ReflexPron   Prep   I/Art   Adj   N
    Det   ——NP——   MV:Past   NP:DObj   Det   ——NP——
    ——NP:Subj——   ——NP:Obj/Prep——
                                                                   ——PrepPh:Adv-place——
                                      ——————————————VP:Pred——————————————

11. Antismoking   activists   are   dancing   on   the   Marlboro Man's   grave.
    Adj   N   BE   VI   Prep   D/Art   GenN   N
    ——NP:Subj——   Aux   PresPart   ——NP——
                              —MV:PresProg—   ——NP:Obj/Prep——
                                                              ——PrepPh:Adv-place——
                                       ——————————VP:Pred——————————

12. No one   answered   the   phone   at   your   house   last   night.
    IndefPron   VT   D/Art   N   Prep   PossPron   N   OrdN   N
    NP:Subj   MV:Past   Det   NP:Adv-time
                           —NP:DObj—   —NP:Obj/Prep—
                                                  ——PrepPh:Adv-place——
                                       ——————————VP:Pred——————————

    I   called   four   times.
    PersPron   VI   CardN   N
    NP:Subj   MV:Past Det
                        NP:Adv-frequency
                        ——VP:Pred——

13. John Kennedy   was   a   magnetic   politician.
    PropN   BE   D/Art   Adj   N
    —NP:Subj—   MV:Past   ——NP——
                           ——NP:PredN——
                           ——VP:Pred——

    The   media   made   him   a   shining   knight.
    D/Art   N   Vc   PersPron   I/Art   Adj   N
    ——NP:Subj——   MV:Past   NP:DObj   ——NP——
                                                 ——NP:ObjComp——
                              ——————————VP:Pred——————————

14.

The	five	Shiites	found	themselves	on	the	wrong	side	of	Kurdistan	during	the	shelling.
D/Art	CardN	PropN	VT	ReflexPron	Prep	D/Art	Adj	N	Prep	PropN	Prep	D/Art	N

MV:Past
NP:DObj
——— NP ———
——— NP:Subj ———
PrepPh:Gen
——— NP ———
——— NP:Obj/Prep ———
——— NP:Obj/Prep ———
——— PrepPh:Adv-place ———
——— PrepPh:Adv-time ———
——— VP:Pred ———

15.

Pep	rallies	serve	several	purposes.
N:Adj	N	VT	PreArt	N

MV:Pres
——— NP:Subj ———
——— Det ———
——— NP:DObj ———
——— VP:Pred ———

They	give	teams	support.
PersPron	Vg	N	N

NP:Subj   MV:Pres   NP:IObj   NP:DObj
——— VP:Pred ———

And	they	give	students	a	sense	of	togetherness.
Conj	PersPron	Vg	N	PreArt	N	Prep	N

NP:Subj   MV:Pres   NP:IObj
——— Det ———
——— NP:DObj ———
——— VP:Pred ———

Note: The conjunction is properly a constituent of the clause, not of the noun phrase subject.

16.

Pennsylvania's	Longwood	Gardens	unfold	in	four	miles	of	paths.
GenN	PropN		VI	Prep	PreArt		N	

MV:Pres
——— NP:Subj ———
——— Det ———
——— NP:Obj/Prep ———
——— PrepPh:Adv-extent ———
——— VP:Pred ———

Note: Rather than separate **four miles of** into two constituents, it seemed more appropriate to consider **four and miles of** a single prepositi...

17. One Japanese honeysuckle may produce 30 feet of vine in a single year.
CardN Adj   N   M   VT   —PreArt— N Prep I/Art Adj N
Det   Aux Inf   Det   NP
    —NP:Subj—   MV:PresCond —NP: DObj—   —NP:Obj/Prep—
                                                        —PrepPh:Adv-duration—
                                         —VP:Pred—

18. Helsinki is   full of offbeat charm.
    PropN   BE   PreArt Adj   N
    PropN   MV:Pres   —NP—
                         —NP:PredN—
                         —VP:Pred—

19. The Internet makes everyone   equal.
    PropN   Vc   IndefPron Adj
    NP:Subj   MV:Pres NP:DObj AdjPh:ObjComp
                         —VP:Pred—

20. Lisa Henson was   the   first woman president of the Harvard Lampoon.
    PropN   BE   D/Art OrdN   N:Adj N   Prep   PropN
    NP:Subj   MV:past Det   —NP:Obj/Prep—   PropN
                                                            —PrepPh:Gen—
                                                          —NP—
                                            —NP—
                                            —NP:PredN—
                                            —VP:Pred—

21. The   modern study of   linguistics began with Noam Chomsky's Syntactic Structures in   1957.
    D/Art Adj   N   Prep N   VI   Prep GenN   PropN   Prep N
    Det   —NP:Obj/Prep—   MV:Past   GenN   PropN   —NP:Obj/Prep—
                  —PrepPh:Gen—   —NP:Obj/Prep—   —PrepPh:Adv-time—
                —NP—   —PrepPh:Adv-source—
              —NP:Subj—   —VP:Pred—

22. Computers perpetuate a two-tiered system of education in our country.
N   VT   I/Art Adj   N   Prep   N   Prep PossPron N
NP:Subj   MV:Pres   Det   NP:Obj/Prep   NP:Obj/Prep
                                                         —PrepPh:Gen—   —PrepPh:Adv-place—
                                                         —NP—
                                              —NP:DObj—
                                              ——VP:Pred——

23. Most of California was rain-free last month.
PreArt   PropN   BE   Adj   OrdN N
Det   MV:Past AP:PredAdj Det
—NP:Subj—   —NP:Adv-time—
                       ——VP:Pred——

24. Lack of money fuels divorce.
PreArt   N   VT   N
Det   MV:Pres NP:DObj
—NP:Subj—   ——VP:Pred——

25. Boredom is contagious.
N   BE   Adj
NP:Subj MV:Pres AP:PredAdj
         ——VP:Pred——

It   can cause a   chain reaction in   a   dorm.
PersPron M   VT   I/Art N   Prep I/Art N
NP:Subj MV:PresCond Det   Det
                     —NP:DObj—   —NP:Obj/Prep—
                                              —PrepPh:Adv-place—
                     ——VP:Pred——

Note: Though **chain reaction** is two words, it acts as if it were a single word, like **Statue of Liberty**. Some grammar books might call **chain reaction** a collocation. Labeling it a noun seems sufficient for our purposes.

Chapter 5 Rearranging and Compounding

1. Marco Polo might not have reached China on his Asian trip.
   PropN | M | Neg | HAVE | VT | PropN | Prep | PossPr | Adj | N
   NP:Subj | ——Aux—— | PastPart | NP:DObj | | Det | ——NP——
   ——MV: PastPerfCond—— | | | | NP:Obj/Prep
   | | | | | ——PrepPh: Adv-place——
   ——————————VP:Pred——————————

2. There are several Democratic candidates at this point.
   Expl | BE | PreArt | Adj | N | Prep | Demon | N
   NP:GramSubj | MV:Pres | | ——NP—— | | | Det
   | | ——NP:PredN/LogSubj—— | | NP:Obj/Prep
   | | | | ——PrepPh:Adv-time——
   ——————————VP:Pred——————————

3. Why do school buildings sit empty most of the day?
   Adv-reason | DO | N:Adj | N | VI | Adj | PreArt | D/Art | N
   | Aux | ——NP:Subj—— | Inf | Adv-manner | | ——Det——
   | | | | | | ——NP:Adv-time——
   ———MV:Pres Int———

   Note: The predicate is **do ... sit empty most of the day.**

4. The Sox couldn't put together a rally in the fifth.
   PropN | M/Neg | VT | I/Art | N | Prep | D/Art | N
   NP:Subj | Aux | Inf | Det | ——NP:DObj—— | -Det-
   ——MV:PastCond—— | | | | NP:Obj/Prep
   | | | | | PrepPh:Adv-time
   ——————————VP:Pred——————————

5. Fingernails   are   scrutinized   by   nutritionists   for   vitamin   deficiencies.
   N   BE   VT   Prep   N   Prep   N:Adj   N
   NP:GramSubj Aux   PastPart   NP:Obj/Prep/LogSubj   —— NP:Obj/Prep ——
            —MV:Pres Pass—   —PrepPh:Adv-agency—   —— PrepPh:Adv-reason ——
                                                            VP:Pred

6. The Marx Brothers   were   funny   and   progressive   and   creative.
   PropN   BE   Adj   Conj   Adj   Conj   Adj
   —NP:Subj—   —MV:Past—   —AdjPh:Pred Adj—
                                            VP:Pred

7. Dutch New Amsterdam   became   English   New York.
   Adj   VL   Adj   PropN
                        —MV:Past—   —NP:PredN—
   ——NP:Subj——   VP:Pred

   But   Dutch Breukelen   remained.
   Conj   Adj   PropN   VI
                            MV:Pat
          ——NP:Subj——   VP:Pred

8. Homer   and   Marge Simpson   and   their   three   kids   put   the   fun   in   dysfunctional.
   PropN   Conj   PropN   Conj   PossPron   CardN   N   VT   D/Art   N   Prep   N
   NP   —NP—   Det   —— NP ——   MV:Pres Det   -NP:Obj/Prep-
           ——————NP:Subj——————   —NP:DObj— —PrepPh:Adv-place —
                                                                                            VP:Pred

9. One-third of   American   households   sort   their   garbage   now.
   —Fraction—   Adj   N   VT   PossPron   N   Adv-time
   —PreArt—   ——NP——   MV:Pres   Det
   — Det —   —NP:DObj—
            ——NP:Subj——   VP:Pred

So   40 million tons of   garbage   is   recycled   yearly.
ConjAdv PreArt   N   BE   VT   Adv-frequency
         Det   Aux   PastPart
                                        MV:PresPass
      ———— NP:GramSubj ————   ———— VP:Pred ————

Note: The agent phrase **(by cities)** has been deleted. The underlying active sentence is
Cities recycle 40 million tons of garbage yearly.

10. The   tarot cards   were   set out   by   the   fortune-teller.
     D/Art N:Adj N   BE   VT   Prep D/Art N
     Det   NP   Aux   PastPart   Det
     —— NP:GramSubj ——   MV:PastPass   NP:Obj/Prep/LogSubj
                                               ——PrepPh:Adv-agency——
                         ————————— VP:Pred —————————

11. Homeowners shouldn't keep firewood close to   the   house.
     N   M/Neg   VT   N   Prep D/Art N
     NP:Subj   Aux   Inf NP:DObj   Det
     —— MV:PastCond ——   NP:Obj/Prep
                                       ——— PrepPh:Adv-place ———
                         —————————— VP:Pred ——————————

12. There   are   thousands of   Harry Potter fans throughout   the   world.
     Expletive BE   PreArt   N:Adj   N   Prep   DefArt N
     GramSubj MVpres   NP:Obj/Prep
                      ———— NP:LogSubj ————   ——— PrepPh:Adv-place ———
                      ————————— VP:Pred —————————

13. What   influenced Dr. King's   dream?
     IntPron VT   GenN   N
     Subj   MV:PastInt   NP:DObj
             ———— VP:Pred ————

14.

MV:PastPerfCondInt

Could	the	pioneers	and	the	Native Americans	have	coexisted	without	violence?
M	D/Art	N	Conj	D/Art	PropN	HAVE	VI	Prep	N
	Det			Det		Aux	PastPart		

Aux

——— NP ——— | ——— NP ———

NP:Subj

PrepPh:Adv-manner

NP:Obj/Prep

Note: The predicate is **could . . . have coexisted without violence. Could . . . have** is the Aux.

15.

MV:Past Passive

Julia Child's	first	TV	show	was	called	*The French Chef.*
GenN	OrdN	N:Adj	N	BE	Vc	PropN
				Aux	PastPart	NP:Obj Comp

——— NP ———

——— NP ———

NP:Gram Subj

VP:Pred

Note: The agent phrase (**by producers/someone**) has been deleted. The underlying active sentence is **Producers/Someone called Julia Child's first TV show** *The French Chef.*

CorrConj

But	she	was	neither	French	nor	a	chef.
Conj	PersPron	BE		Adj		I/Art	N
	NP:Subj	MV:Past		AP:PredAdj		NP:PredN	

SubjComplement

VP:Pred

Note: The phrase **neither French nor a chef** compounds a predicate adjective and a predicate noun. Together they compose a single constituent which functions as a subjective complement. Remember that both predicate adjectives and predicate nouns are subjective complements.

16.

MV:Past Int

Why	didn't	George Washington	free	his	slaves	after	the	Revolution?
Adv-reason	DO/Neg	PropN	VT	PossPron	N	Prep		PropN
	Aux	—NP:Subj—	Inf	Det				NP:Obj/Prep
				—NP:DObj—		—PrepPh:Adv-time—		

Note: The predicate is **didn't . . . free his slaves after the Revolution [why]**. The proadverb **why** replaces an adverb like **for some reason**.

17.

MV:Pres Perf Int

How often	has	genocide	reared	its	ugly	head	since	the	Holocaust?
Adv-frequency	HAVE	N	VT	PossPron	Adj	N	Prep		PropN
	Aux	NP:Subj		—NP—					NP:Obj/prep
				—NP:DObj—			—PrepPh:Adv-time—		

Note: The predicate is **has . . . reared its ugly head since the Holocaust [how often]**. The proadverb **how often** replaces an adverb like **frequently**.

18.

Bake	the	mixture	in	the	oven	for	20	minutes.
VT	D/Art	N	Prep	D/Art	N	Prep	CardN	N
MV:Imp	—NP:DObj—		NP:Obj/Prep			—NP:Obj/Prep —		
			PrepPh:Adv-place			—PrepPh:Adv-duration—		

19.

Trinidad's	mud	volcanoes	don't	spew	lava.
GenN	N:Adj	N	DO/Neg	VT	N
—NP—			Aux	Inf	NP:DObj
—NP:Subj—			MV:PresCond		
			—VP:Pred—		

They	belch	mud.
Perspron	VT	N
NP:Subj	MV:Pres	NP:DObj
—VP:Pred—		

CorrConj

20. Some   Southern   states   honor   both   Robert E. Lee   and   Martin Luther King Jr.   on   Martin Luther King Day.
    PreArt   Adj   N   VT   —PropN—   —PropN—   Prep   PropN
    ————NP————   MV:Pres   ————NP————   ——NP——   ———NP:Obj/prep———
    ——NP:Subj——   ————————NP:DObj————————   ———PrepPh:Adv-time———
                                                                                               ————————VP:Pred————————

21. Macbeth   is   consumed   by   ambition,   deceit,   and   remorse.
    PropN   BE   VT   Prep   N   N   Conj   N
    NP:GramSubj Aux PastPart   NP   NP   NP
                MV:PresPass   ——NP:Obj/Prep/LogSubj——
                                              ———PrepPh:Adv-agency———
                                           ————————VP:Pred————————

22. Gunfire   could   be   heard   throughout   Jerusalem.
    N   M   BE   VT   Prep   PropN
    NP:GramSubj —Aux— PastPart   NP:Obj/Prep
                —MV:PastCondPass—   —PrepPh:Adv-place—
                               ————————VP:Pred————————

Note: The agent phrase has been deleted. The underlying active sentence is **Someone heard gunfire throughout Jerusalem.**

23. Diet   and   exercise   can   lower   cholesterol.
    N   Conj   N   M   VT   N
    NP   NP   MV:PresCond NP:DObj
    ———NP:Subj———   ————VP:Pred————

24. Boys   don't   read   Nancy Drew.
    N   DO/Neg VT   PropN
    NP:Subj Aux   Inf   NP:DObj
            —MV:Pres—
           ————VP:Pred————

25. Churchill, Stalin, and Roosevelt created modern Europe at Yalta in 1945.
PropN   PropN   Conj   PropN   VT   Adj   PropN   Prep PropN Prep   N
NP   NP   NP   MV:Past —— NP:DObj ——   NP:Obj/Prep NP:Obj/Prep
——————— NP:Subj ———————   PrepPh:Adv-place PrepPh:Adv-time
                                                        ———————————— VP:Pred ————————————

Chapter 6   Constructing Relative Clauses

1. My   folks don't   like the   guy   I   'm   dating   now.
PossPr   N   DO/Neg   VT   D/Art   N   PersPr   BE   VT   Adv-time
Det   Aux   Inf Det   NP:Head NP:Subj Aux PresPart
—— NP:subj —— —— MV:Pres - ——   MV:PresProg
                                                    ———————— VP:Pred ————————
                                              ———————————— RelCl:Adj ————————————
                                              ———————————————— NP:DObj ————————————————
                                    ———————————————————————— VP:Pred ————————————————————————

Note: The relative clause **I'm dating now** derives from **whom I'm dating now** < **I'm dating** *someone* **now**. **Whom,** the direct object of **dating,** has been deleted.

2. Lucille Ball was   a   glamour girl   who   became   a   clown.
PropN   BE   I/Art   Adj   N   RelPr   VL   I/Art   N
NP:Subj   MV:Past Det   —— NP ——   NP:Subj MV:Past Det
                    —— NP:Head ——   —— NP:PredN ——
                                                    ———————— VP:Pred ————————
                                              ———————————— RelCl:Adj ————————————
                            ——————————————————— NP:PredN ———————————————————
                    ———————————————————————— VP:Pred ————————————————————————

3. The   drug   epidemic   is   a   cancer   which   threatens   the   nation's   survival.
   D/Art   N:Adj   N   BE   I/Art N   RelPr   VT   D/Art GenN   N
   Det   ——NP——   MV:Pres Det   NP:Subj MV:Pres   Det   ——NP——
   ————NP:Subj————   ——NP:Head——   ——NP:DObj——
                                                                             ————VP:Pred————
                                                         ——————RelCl:Adj——————
                                                     ——————NP:PredN——————
                                            ————————————VP:Pred————————————

4. Countries whose   energy   consumption does   not   decrease   will   suffer   during   the   next   decade.
   N   RelDet   N:Adj   N   DO   Neg   VI   M   VI   Prep   D/Art OrdN   N
   NP:Head   Det   ——NP——   ——Aux——   Aux   Det   ——NP——
              ——NP:Subj——   ——MV:Pres——   MV:PresCond   ——NP:Obj/Prep——
                       ————NP:Subj————   ————VP:Pred————   ——PrepPh:Adv:duration——
                       ——————RelCl:Adj——————   ————————VP:Pred————————

5. Dad   wanted   the   subwoofer system   which   Mom   considered   overpriced.
   N   VT   D/Art   N:Adj   N   RelPron N   Vc   Adj:ObjComp
   NP:Subj   MV:Past   Det   ——NP——   NP:DObj NP:Subj   MV:Past
                       ——NP:Head——   ——NP:DObj——   ————VP:Pred————
                                                             ——————RelCl:Adj——————
                       ————————NP:DObj————————
             ————————————VP:Pred————————————

6. Elephants are   complex   social   animals   that   can   feel   compassion.
   N   BE   Adj   Adj   N   RelPr   M   VT   N
   NP:Subj   MV:Pres   ——NP——   NP:Subj Aux   NP:DObj
                        ————NP:Head————   MV:PresCond
                                                             ————Pred————
                                                     ——————RelCl:Adj——————
                        ——————————NP:PredN——————————
             ————————————————VP:Pred————————————————

7.

The	American	soldiers	met	Afghan	children	who	had	overcome	the	squalor	that	surrounded	them.
D/Art	Adj	N	VT	Adj	N	RelPron	HAVE	VT	D/Art	N	RelPron	VT	PersPron
Det	—	NP —	MV:Past	—	NP:Head —	NP:Subj	Aux	PastPar	—	NP:Head —	NP:Subj	MV:Past	NP:DObj

(NP:Subj)
(MV:PastPerf)
(NP:DObj)
(VP:Pred — RelCl:Adj)
(NP:DObj)
(VP:Pred)
(RelCl:Adj)

8.

The	cows	that	were	stolen	from	Colorado	ranches	wound	up	in	Utah.
D/Art	N	RelPr	BE	VT	Prep	N:Adj	N	VI	—	Prep	PropN
Det	— NP:Head —	NP:GramSubj	Aux	PastPart	—	NP:Obj/Prep —	—	MV:Past		NP:Obj/Prep	

(MV:PastPass)
(PrepPh:Adv-source)
(PrepPh:Adv-place)
(VP:Pred)
(RelCl:Adj)
(VP:Pred)
(NP:Subj)

Note: The relative clause is in passive form. The agent phrase **by rustlers** has been deleted. The independent clause underlying the relative clause would be **The cows were stolen (by rustlers) from Colorado ranches.**

9.

The	university	dismissed	the	coach	whose	recruiting	practices	the NCAA	questioned.
D/Art	N	VT	D/Art	N	RelDet	Adj	N	PropN	VT
Det	— NP:Subj —	MV:Past	Det	— NP:Head —	Det	—	NP	NP:Subj	MV:Past

(NP:DObj)
(NP:DObj)
(RelCl:Adj)
(VP:Pred)

Note: The NP **whose recruiting practices** is the object of the main verb of the relative clause. If you made the relative clause into an independent clause, it would become **The NCAA questioned his recruiting practices.** The predicate of the relative clause is **questioned whose recruiting practices**, though the object noun phrase is disjoined to the front of the clause.

10. The   joyous Cubs' fan   rang   a   bell   that   rivaled Big Ben.
    D/Art   Adj   GenN   N   VT   I/Art N   RelPron VT   PropN
    Det   ——NP——   MV:Past Det   —NP:Head— NP:Subj MV:Past   NP:DObj
           ————NP————   ——————VP:Pred——————
    ————NP:Subj————   ————————RelCl:Adj————————
                                                ———————NP:DObj———————
                                       ———————————————VP:Pred———————————————

11. The   best   fiction comes from   writers who   have   a   sensitive vision of   the   world.
    D/Art Adj   N   VI   Prep   N   RelPr   VT   I/Art Adj   N   Prep D/Art N
    Det   ——NP——   MV:Pres   NP:Head NP:Subj MV:Pres Det   Det
    ——NP:Subj——   NP:Obj/Prep
                                                                                         PrepPh:Gen
                                                                                   ——NP——
                                                                          ——NP——
                                                                    ——NP:DObj——
                                                              ————VP:Pred————
                                                  ————RelCl:Adj————
                                         ————NP:Obj/Prep————
                                ————PrepPh:Adv-source————
                         ————VP:Pred————

12. The   warden opened the   gray   steel door   that   connects death row   to   the   execution chamber.
    D/Art N   VT   D/Art Adj   N:Adj N   RelPr   VT   N:Adj N   Prep D/Art N:Adj   N
    Det   MV:Past Det   NP:Subj MV:Pres   ——NP:DObj——   Det   ——NP——
    ——NP:Subj——   ——NP——   NP:Obj/Prep
                          ——NP:Head——   PrepPh:Adv-place
                                                                              ————VP:Pred————
                                                           ————RelCl:Adj————
                                  ————NP:DObj————
                          ————————VP:Pred————————

13. Jerry Springer | interviewed | parents | whose | authority | had | been | questioned | by | their | children.
 - Jerry Springer — PropN — NP:Subj
 - interviewed — VT — MV:Past
 - parents — N — NP:Head
 - whose — Rel/Det — NP:GramSubj
 - authority — N
 - had — HAVE BE — Aux PastPart
 - been — BE — MV:PastPerfPass
 - questioned — VT — PastPart
 - by — Prep — PrepPh:Adv-agency
 - their — PossPron — NP:Obj/Prep/logSubj
 - children — N

NP:DObj · VP:Pred · RelCl:Adj · VP:Pred

14. Mercer Sullivan | is | an | anthropologist | who | studies | youth | crime | on | the | streets | of | Brooklyn.
 - Mercer Sullivan — PropN — NP:Subj
 - is — BE — MV:Pres
 - an — I/Art — Det
 - anthropologist — N — NP:Head
 - who — RelPr — NP:Subj
 - studies — VT — MV:Pres
 - youth — N:Adj
 - crime — N — NP:DObj
 - on — Prep
 - the — D/Art — Det
 - streets — N
 - of — Prep — PrepPh:Gen
 - Brooklyn — PropN — NP:Obj/Prep

NP:Obj/Prep · PrepPh:Adv-place · NP · NP:Obj/Prep · PrepPh:Adv-place · VP:Pred · RelCl:Adj · VP:Pred

Note: I analyzed the prepositional phrase in the relative clause, **on the streets of Brooklyn,** as an adverb of place, a constituent of the relative clause's verb phrase. It's possible to see it as a constituent of the noun phrase **youth crime on the streets of Brooklyn,** where it would function as an adjective. But that would get us into the next chapter on reducing relative clauses to hrases.

15.

The	new	mall	established	a	climate	in	which	high-class	stores	could	thrive.
D/Ar	Adj	N	VT	I/Art	N	Prep	RelPron	Adj	N	M	VI
Det	—NP—		MV:Past	Det			NP:Obj/Prep	NP:Subj		Aux	
—NP:Subj—				—NP:Head—		PrepPh:Adv-place			—MV:PastCond—		
										—VP:Pred—	
							—RelCl:Adj—				
					—NP:DObj—						
					—VP:Pred—						

Note: The predicate of the relative clause is **could thrive in which.** The sentence underlying the relative clause is **High-class stores could thrive in the climate.**

16.

Woody Allen	is	the	vulnerable	artist	who	takes	things	personally.
PropN	BE	D/Art	Adj	N	RelPr	VT	N	Adv-manner
NP:Subj	MV:Pres	Det	—NP—		NP:Subj	MV:Pres	NP:DObj	
		—NP:Head—				—VP:Pred—		
					—RelCl:Adj—			
		—NP:PredN—						
		—VP:Pred—						

17.

Senior	citizens	who	have	suffered	strokes	come	to	the	clinic	for	speech	therapy.
Adj	N	RelPr	HAVE	VT	N	VI	Prep	D/Art	N	Prep	N:Adj	N
—NP:Head—		NP:Subj	—MV:PresPerf—		NP:DObj	MV:Pres		Det			—NP:Obj/Prep—	
—NP:Head—				—VP:Pred—				NP:Obj/Prep		PrepPh:Adv-reason		
			—RelCl:Adj—					—PrepPh:Place—				
—NP:Subj—								—VP:Pred—				

18.

We	rode	whitewater	rapids	that	battered	our	raft	perilously.
PersPr	VT	N:Adj	N	RelPr	VT	PossPr	N	Adv-manner
NP:Subj	MV:Past	—NP:Head—		NP:Subj	MV:Past	Det		
		—NP:Subj—				—NP:DObj—		
						—VP:Pred—		
				—RelCl:Adj—				
				—NP:DObj—				
				—VP:Pred—				

19.

Special-education	teachers	succeed	with	students	for	whom	there	has	been	no	hope.
N:Adj	N	VI	Prep	N	Prep	RelPr	Expl	HAVE	BE	PreArt	N
		MV:Pres		NP:Head		NP:Obj/Prep	NP:GramSubj	Aux	PastPart	Det	NP/LogSubj

— NP:Subj —
MV:PresPerf
PrepPh:Adv-source
RelCl:Adj
NP:Obj/Prep
PrepPh:Adv-goal
VP:Pred

Note: The predicate of the relative clause is disjoined. The prepositional phrase has been moved to the front of the clause. The predicate of the relative clause is **has been no hope**. The predicate of the main clause is **there has been no hope for whom**. With **students for whom** is rather like an abstract place: in what area do special-education teachers succeed? I chose to call that area their goal; it seemed strange to call it a place adverb, though I suppose you could.

20.

Our	Zagreb	trip	was	complicated	by	a	taxi	driver	who	spoke	no	known	language.
PosPron	N:Adj	N	BE	VT	Prep	I/Art	N:Adj	N	RelPr	VT	PreArt	Adj	N
Det			Aux	PastPart		Det			NP:Subj	MV:Past	Det		

— NP —
— NP:Subj —
MV:PastPass
NP:Head
NP:Obj/Prep/LogSubj
PrepPh:Adv-agency
NP:DObj
VP:Pred
RelCl:Adj
VP:Pred

21.

There	are	several	ornamental	grasses	that	will	flourish	in	partial	shade.
Expl	BE	PreArt	Adj	N	RelPr	M	VI	Prep	Adj	N
NP:GramSubj	MV:Pres	Det			NP:Subj	Aux				

— NP —
— NP:Head —
MV:PresCond
PrepPh:Adv-place
VP:Pred
NP:PredN/LogSubj
RelCl:Adj
VP:Pred

22. Ginger Rogers and Fred Astaire tapped and shimmied through ten movies that define Hollywood's romantic heyday.

Ginger Rogers	and	Fred Astaire	tapped	and	shimmied	through	ten	movies	that	define	Hollywood's	romantic	heyday.
PropN	Conj	PropN	VI	Conj	VI	Prep	CardN	N	RelPr	VT	GenN	Adj	N

NP — NP — NP:Subj — MV:Past — Det — NP:Head — NP:Subj MV:Pres — NP:DObj — VP:Pred — RelCl:Adj — NP:Obj/Prep — PrepPh:Adv-place — VP:Pred

23. Mountain bikers race on courses that screech up rock-strewn passes and scream down log-infested trails.

Mountain	bikers	race	on	courses	that	screech	up	rock-strewn	passes	and	scream	down	log-infested	trails.
N:Adj	N	VI	Prep	N	RelPr	VI	Prep	Adj	N	Conj	VI	Prep	Adj	N

NP:Subj — MV:Pres — NP:Head — NP:Subj MV:Pres — NP:Obj/Prep — PrepPh:Adv-place — VP — MV:Pres — NP:Obj/Prep — PrepPh:Adv-place — VP — VP:Pred — RelCl:Adj — NP:Obj/Prep — PrepPh:Adv-Place — VP:Pred

24. The new tech school provides classrooms in which every student has a computer.

The	new	tech	school	provides	classrooms	in	which	every	student	has	a	computer.
D/Art	Adj	Adj	N	VT	N	Prep	RelPr	PreArt	N	VT	I/Art	N

Det — NP — NP:Subj — MV:Pres — NP:Head — NP:Obj/Prep — Det — NP:Subj — NP:DObj — VP:Pred — PrepPh:adv-pl — RelCl:Adj — NP:DObj — VP:Pred

Note: The predicate of the relative clause is disjoined; the prep phrase **in which** has been moved to the front of the clause. The underlying sentence would be **Every student has a computer in the classrooms**.

25. Gospel singer Fontella Bass' voice bursts with a spirit that seems to come from a different world.

Gospel — N:Adj
singer — N:Adj
Fontella Bass' — GenN
voice — N — NP — NP:Subj
bursts — VI — MV:Pres
with — Prep
a — I/Art — Det
spirit — N — NP:Head
that — RelPr — NP:Subj
seems to — M — Aux
come — VI — MV:PresCond
from — Prep
a — I/Art — Det
different — Adj
world. — N — NP — NP:Obj/Prep — PrepPh:Adv-source — VP:Pred — RelCl:Adj — NP:Obj/Prep — PrepPh:Adv-manner — VP:Pred

Chapter 7 Reducing Relative Clauses to Phrases

1. Foreigners traveling in Russia should drink bottled water.

Foreigners — N — NP:Head
traveling — VI — PresPart
in — Prep
Russia — PropN — NP:Obj/Prep — PrepPh:Adv-place — PresPartPh:Adj — NP:Subj
should — M — Aux
drink — VT — MV:PastCond
bottled — Adj
water. — N — NP:DObj — VP:Pred

2. Most of the doctors trained in Ohio practice in other states.

Most of — Pre-Art — Det
the — D/Art — Det
doctors — N — NP — NP:Head
trained — VT — PastPart
in — Prep
Ohio — PropN — NP:Obj/Prep — PrepPh:Adv-place — PastPartPh:Adj — NP:Subj
practice — VI — MV:Pres
in — Prep
other — Adj
states. — N — NP:Obj/Prep — PrepPh:Adv-place — VP:Pred

264 ANSWER KEY

Note: Students sometimes have a difficult time determining whether a prepositional phrase is adjectival or adverbial. The answer, of course, is constituency. If the prepositional phrase sembedded within a noun phrase immediately to the right of a noun phrase head, as in sentences 3 and 4 (a monk **in prayer** and our national frustration **with welfare**), it functions as an adjective. If it is part of a verb phrase, as are the two prep phrases in sentence 2 (trained **in Ohio** and practice **in other states**), then it is an adverb, even if the verb phrase is itself embedded as an adjective within a noun phrase. Since prep phrases that function as adjectives always derive from relative clauses, you can often put the relative clause parts back in as a test: "George Harrison posed as a monk **who was** in prayer."

3.
George Harrison	posed	as	a	monk	in	prayer.
PropN	VI	Prep	I/Art	N	Prep	N
NP:Subj	MV:Past		Det			NP:Obj/Prep
			NP:Head			—PrepPh:Adj—
					NP:Obj/Prep—	
				PrepPh:Adv-manner—		
			VP:Pred—			

4.
Our	national	frustration	with	welfare	is	exploited	by	some	politicians.
PossPr	Adj	N	Prep	N	BE	VT	Prep	PreArt	N
Det				NP:Obj/Prep	Aux	PastPart		Det	
	—NP:Head—		—PrepPh:Adj—		—MV:PresPass—		NP:Obj/Prep/LogSubj		
	NP:GramSubj—						—PrepPh:Adv-agency—		
							VP:Pred—		

5.
The	books	sold	at	this	sleazy	newsstand	are	not	available	in	the	city	library.
D/Art	N	VT	Prep	Demon	Adj	N	BE	Neg	Adj	Prep	D/Art	N:Adj	N
Det		PastPart				NP	MV:Pres—		PredAdj		Det		—NP—
—NP:Head—					—NP:Obj/Prep						NP:Obj/Prep		
				—PrepPh:Adv-place—						—PrepPh:Adv-place—			
			—PastPartPh:Adj—							VP:Pred—			
			NP:Subj—										

6. Wall Street traders investing in foreign markets have earned 6 percent interest this year.

Wall Street	traders	investing	in	foreign	markets	have	earned	6	percent	interest	this	year.
N:Adj	N	VI	Prep	Adj	N	HAVE	VT	CardNum	N	N	Demon	N
		PresPart					PastPart				Det	

— NP:Head —
— NP:Obj/Prep —
— PrepPh:Adv-place —
— PresPartPh:Adj —
— NP:Subj —
— PastPart · MV:PresPerf —
— NP:DObj —
— NP:Adv-time —
— VP:Pred —

Note: I've called "6 percent" a cardinal number for the sake of simplifying the diagram. Actually it's the cardinal number 6 plus the noun **percent**.

7. The restaurant served shrimp boiled in a special creole sauce.

The	restaurant	served	shrimp	boiled	in	a	special	creole	sauce.
D/Art	N	VT	N	VT	Prep	I/Art	Adj	Adj	N
Det		MV:Past	NP:Head	PastPart		Det			

— NP:Subject —
— NP —
— NP:Obj/Prep —
— PrepPh:Adv-place —
— PastPartPh:Adj —
— NP:DObj —
— VP:Pred —

8. Astronomers have identified a new class of gamma rays coming from a mysterious source.

Astronomers	have	identified	a	new	class	of	gamma	rays	coming	from	a	mysterious	source.
N	HAVE	VT	I/Art	Adj	N	Prep	N:Adj	N	VI	Prep	I/Art	Adj	N
NP:Subj		MV:PresPerf											

— NP:Subj —
— MV:PresPerf —
— NP —
— PrepPh:Gen —
— NP —
— NP:Head —
— NP:Obj/Prep —
— PrepPh:Adv-source —
— PresPartPh:Adj —
— NP:DObj —
— VP:Pred —

9. Rural communities across America lack physicians.

Rural	communities	across	America	lack	physicians.
Adj	N	Prep	PropN	VT	N
			NP:Obj/Prep	MV:Pres	NP:DObj
			—PrepPh:Adj—		
—NP:Head—				—VP:Pred—	
—NP:Subj—					

10. The police scattered the young men loitering outside the convenience store.

The	police	scattered	the	young	men	loitering	outside	the	convenience	store.
D/Art	N	VT	D/Art	Adj	N	VI	Prep	D/Art	N:Adj	N
Det		MV:Past	Det		—NP—	PresPart		Det		—NP—
—NP:Subj—			—NP:Head—						NP:Obj/Prep	
								PrepPh:Adv-place		
							PresPartPh:Adj			
					—NP:DObj—					
				—VP:Pred—						

11. Bighorn Canyon National Park contains multilayered canyons blanketed by juniper woodlands and rolling prairies.

Bighorn Canyon National Park	contains	multilayered	canyons	blanketed	by	juniper	woodlands	and	rolling	prairies.
PropN	VT	Adj	N	VT	Pepp	N:Adj	N	Conj	Adj	N
—NP:Subj—	MV:Pres	—NP:Head—		PastPart		—NP—				—NP—
							NP:Obj/Prep/LogSubj			
						PrepPh:Adv-Agency				
					PastPartPh:Adj					
				—NP:DObj—						
				—VP:Pred—						

12. The New York Philharmonic aims at lucid performances filled with orchestral detail polished to a high sheen.

The New York Philharmonic	aims	at	lucid	performances	filled	with	orchestral	detail	polished	to	a	high	sheen
PropN	VI	Prep	Adj	N	VT	Prep	Adj	N	VT	Prep	I/Art	Adj	N
NP:Subj	MV:Pres			NP:Head	PastPart			NP:Head	PastPart		Det		NP

- NP:Obj/Prep
- PrepPh:Adv-goal
- PastPartPh:Adj
- NP:Obj/Prep
- PrepPh:Adv-manner
- PastPartPh:Adj
- NP:Obj/Prep
- PrepPh:Adv-place
- VP:Pred

Note: I've called *with orchestral detail polished to a high sheen* an adverb of manner. You might consider it an instrument. *To a high sheen* might also be called an adverb of aim or result, as could *at lucid performances ... sheen.* Adverbs, as we know, are often tough to label.

13.

There	are	no	quick	fixes	for	broken	children
Expl	BE	PreArt	Adj	N	Prep	Adj	N
NP:GramSubj	MV:Pres	Det		NP			NP
				NP:PredN/LogSubj			

- NP:Obj/Prep
- PrepPh:Adv-goal
- VP:Pred

Note: You might consider *for broken children* a prepositional phrase functioning as an adjective and embedded in the NP *no quick fixes.* It matters whether you derive this sentence from *no quick fixes are for broken children* (with *are* meaning something like "exist") or you consider the sentence to have no underlying form that could possibly be a surface form, something like *no quick fixes for broken children are.* My own answer wavers.

14. Dr. Putman's cosmetic dentistry will give you a face with a great smile
    GenN   Adj   N   M   Vg   PersPr Art N   Prep Art Adj   NH
                      ———— NP ————   MV:PresCond NP:IndObj NP:Head   —— NP ——
    ———— NP:Subj ————   — PrepPh:Adj —
                                                                          ——— NP:DirObj ———
                                                              ———————————— VP:Pred ————————————

15. Hungarian cooks serve   a   garlicky cucumber salad called uborka salata.
    Adj   N   VT   I/Art   Adj   N:Adj   N   Vc   Adj   N
    — NP:Subj —   MV:Pres   PastPart PastPartPh:Adj —
                               —— NP ——   —— NP ——
                                              —— NP:Head ——   — NP:ObjComp —
                                                        ——— NP:DObj ———
                                              ————————— VP:Pred —————————

Note: The past participial phrase **called *uborka salata*** derives from the passive sentence **the cucumber salad is called *uborka salata* by Hungarians**. Ultimately it derives from the active sentence **Hungarians call the cucumber salad *uborka salata***. That's why *uborka salata* is an object complement, even in the past participial phrase.

16. Salvador Dali made   the   world beyond the rational seem real in   his   paintings.
    PropN   VC   D/Art N   Prep   D/Art N   VL   Adj Prep PossPr N
    NP:Subj   MV:Past — NP:Head —   — NP:Obj/Prep — Inf AdjPh:PredAdj   — NP:Obj/Prep —
                                              — PrepPh:Adj —   — InfPh —   — PrepPh:Adv-place —
                          —————— NP:DObj ——————   — NP:ObjComp —
                          —————————————————————— VP:Pred ——————————————————————

17. NASA   draws upon   knowledge   accumulated   over   decades.
    PropN   VT   N   VT   Prep   N
              MV:Pres   NP:Head   PastPart   NP:Obj/Prep
    NP:Subj   PrepPh:Adv-time
                                         —— PastPartPh:Adj ——
                                         —— NP:DObj ——
                           —— VP:Pred ——

Note: I've called **draws upon** a two-word transitive verb. You could call **upon** a preposition and **draws** an intransitive verb. Then **knowledge accumulated over decades** would function as the object of a preposition, and **upon knowledge accumulated over decades** would be a source adverb.

18. Children   are   unnerved   by   parents   suffering   job   distress.
    N   BE   VT   Prep   N   VT   N:Adj   N
    NP:GramSubj Aux   PastPart   NP:Head   PresPar   — NP:DObj —
                                                                 —— PresPartPh:Adj ——
                                                       —— NP:Obj/Prep/LogSubj ——
                                             —— PrepPh:Adv-agency ——
                                  —— VP:Pred ——

19. The   first   city   destroyed   by   an   atomic   bomb   was   Hiroshima.
    D/Art   OrdNum   N   VT   Prep   I/Art   Adj   N   BE   PropN
                        —— NP —— PastPart   — NP — MV:Past NP:PredN
             —— NP:Head ——   —— VP:Pred ——
                                                   —— NP:Obj/Prep ——
                                             —— PrepPh:Adv-agency ——
                                  —— PastPartPh:Adj ——
                        —— NP:Subj ——

20.

The	land	around	this	church	was	the	first	property	blacks	owned	in	our	town	after	the	Civil War.
D/Art	N	Prep	Demon	N	BE	D/Art	OrdN	N	N	VT	Prep	PossPr	N	Prep	D/Art	PropN
Det			Det		MV:Past	Det	Det		NP:Subj	MV:Past						

—NP:Head—
——NP:Obj/Prep——
———PrepPh:Adj———
————NP:Subj————

——NP:Head——
————NP:PredN————
————VP:Pred————
————RelCl:Adj————
——NP:Obj/Prep—— —PrepPh:Adv-time—
—PrepPh:Adv-place—
——VP:Pred——
——NP:PredN——

Note: The independent clause underlying the relative clause **blacks owned in our town after the Civil War** is **Blacks owned the property in our town after the Civil War**. The object noun phrase has been deleted from the relative clause.

21.

There	are	several	Vietnamese	dishes	on	the	restaurant's	menu.
Expl	BE	PreArt	Adj	N	Prep	D/Art	GenN	N
NP:GramSubj	MV:Pres	Det				Det		

——NP——
——NP:Obj/Prep——
——PrepPh:Adj——
——NP:PredN/LogSubj——
——VP:Pred——

Note: I've analyzed the prepositional phrase **on the restaurant's menu** as an adjective, That explains the example sentence. But it doesn't explain how the example sentence can be derived from **several Vietnamese dishes are on the restaurant's menu**. I'm torn between the two analyses.

22.

I	ate	cold	pizza	under	the	gaze	of	the	Malibu Barbie	sitting	on	my	date's	dining-room	table.
PersPr	VT	Adj	N	Prep	D/Art	N	Prep	D/Art	PropN	VI	Prep	PossPr	GenN	N:Adj	N
NP:Subj	MV:Past				Det			Det		PresPart		Det			

NP:DObj
NP:Head
NP
— NP —
NP:Obj/Prep
PrepPh:Adv-place
PresPartPh:Adj
NP:Obj/Prep
Prep Ph:Gen
NP
NP:Obj/Prep
PrepPh:Adv-place
VP:Pred

23. Companies advertising in *Vogue* aim toward women in their thirties.

Companies	advertising	in	*Vogue*	aim	toward	women	in	their	thirties.
N	VI	Prep	PropN	VI	Prep	N	Prep	PossPr	N
NP:Head	PresPart		NP:Obj/Prep MV:Pres					Det	

PrepPh:Adv-place
PresPartPh:Adj
NP:Subj
NP:Head
NP:Obj/Prep
PrepPh:Adj
NP:Obj/Prep
PrepPh:Adv-place
VP:Pred

24. The three teenage girls admitted to the hospital yesterday had attempted suicide.

The	three	teenage	girls	admitted	to	the	hospital	yesterday	had	attempted	suicide.
D/Art	CardNo	Adj	N	VT	Prep	D/Art	N	Adv-time	HAVE	VT	N
Det	Det	NP		PastPart		Det			Aux	PastPart	NP:DObj

NP:Head
NP:Obj/Prep
PrepPh:Adv-place
PastPartPh:Adj
MV:PastPerf
VP:Pred
NP:Subj

25. Major dance companies throughout the world still perform Balanchine's ballets.

Major	dance	companies	throughout	the	world	still	perform	Balanchine's	ballets.
Adj	N:Adj	N	Prep	D/Art	N	Adv-duration	VT	GenN	N

NP:Head
NP
PrepPh:Adj
NP:Obj/Prep
NP:Subj
MV:Pres
NP:DObj
VP:Pred

Note: The adverb **still** is a constituent of the predicate. Like a lot of adverbs, it can precede the verb, but some would argue that it's not a constituent of the main verb.

Chapter 8   Making Noun Clauses, Gerunds, and Infinitives

1. Robert Kennedy said we need love, wisdom, and compassion in · the U.S.

Robert Kennedy	said	we	need	love,	wisdom,	and	compassion	in	·	the	U.S.
PropN	VT	PersPr	VT	N	N	Conj	N	Prep		D/Art	PropN
NP:Subj	MV:Past	NP:Subj	MV:Pres		NP		NP				NP:Obj/Prep

NP:DObj
NCl
NP:DObj
VP:Pred
PrepPh:Adv-place
VP:Pred

2. James Cagney is remembered for playing gangsters on the screen.

James Cagney	is	remembered	for	playing	gangsters	on	the	screen.
PropN	BE	VT	Prep	VT	N	Prep	D/Art	N
NP:GramSubj	Aux	PastPart	*Sub*	V:Head	NP:DObj		Det	

MV:PresPass
NP:Obj/Prep
PrepPh:Adv-place
GerPh
NP:Obj/Prep
PrepPh:Adv-reason
VP:Pred

Note: In this sentence and others like it, the superscripted **sub** means subordinator; it indicates here that **-ing** is a subordinator and is attached to the gerund phrase.

But — Conj — NP:Subj
he — PersPr — NP:Subj
considered — Vc — MV:Past
himself — ReflPr — NP:DObj
a — I/Art — Det
singer — N — NP
and — Conj
dancer — N — NP
— NP —
— NP:ObjComp —
— VP:Pred —

3. That — Subord
the Raiders — PropN — NP:Subj
returned — VI — MV:Past
to — Prep
Oakland — PropN — NP:Obj/Prep
— PrepPh:Adv-place —
— VP:Pred —
— NCl —
— NCl —
— NP:Subj —
angered — VT — MV:Past
LA — N:Adj
football — N:Adj
fans. — N — NP
— NP:DObj —
— VP:Pred —

4. It — Expl — NP:GramSubj
angered — VT — MV:Past
LA — N:Adj
football — N:Adj
fans — N — NP
— NP:DObj —
that — Subord
the Raiders — PropN — NP:Subj
returned — VI — MV:Past
to — Prep
Oakland. — PropN — NP:Obj/Prep
— PrepPh:Adv-place —
— VP:Pred —
— NCl —
— NCl —
— NP:LogSubj/ComptoNP —
— VP:Pred —

5.

The	journalism	class	asked	the	visiting	reporter	why	she	prefers	the	police beat.	...
D/Art	N:Adj	N	Vg	D/Art	Adj	N	Subord	PersPr	VT	D/Art	N:Adj N	Adv-reason
Det	—NP—		MV:Past	Det	—NP—			NP:Subj	MV:Pres	Det	—NP—	
—NP:Subj—				—NP:IObj—						—NP:DObj—		
										—VP:Pred—		
								—NCl—				
							—NP:DObj—					
							—VP:Pred—					

Note: Wh-noun clauses diagram like that-clauses. That is, I show **why she prefers the police beat** as both a noun clause and a noun phrase. My justification is consistency: a noun clause is a clause that fills a noun phrase slot. **Why** is a proadverb of reason, moved to the front of its clause.

6.

			Sub		
America	cannot	postpone	confronting	environmental	problems.
PropN	M/Neg	VT	VT	Adj	N
NP:Subj	Aux		V:Head	—NP:DObj—	
—MV:PresCond—			—GerPh—		
			—NP:DObj—		
—VP:Pred—					

7.

Psychologists	who	study	aphasia	want to	understand	how	memory	works	...
N	RelPr	VT	N	M	VT	Subord	N	VI	Adv-manner
NP:Head	NP:Subj	MV:Pres	NP:DObj	Aux	VT		NP:Subj	MV:Pres	
	—VP:Pred—			—MV:PresCond—			—VP:Pred—		
	—RelCl:Adj—					—NCl—			
—NP:Subj—						—NP:DObj—		
						—VP:Pred—		

```
                              Sub
8. The     defense   attorney's   probing     displeased    the      judge.
   D/Art    N:Adj     GenN         VI           VT           D/Art     N
   Det     ————      ——NP——       PartPred     – MV:Past –   Det
           ——GerNP——                                         —— NP:DObj ——
           ——NP:Subj——                                       ————VP:Pred————
```

Remember that the phrase **The defense attorney's** is the subject of the gerund phrase. And **Probing** is the partial predicate.

```
9. Doctors   know      that      certain   hormones   can    intensify   depression.
   N          VT        Subord    PreArt    N          M      VT          N
   NP:Subj    MV:Pres             ——NP:Subj——          Aux                NP:DObj
                                                       MV:PresCond
                                                       ————VP:Pred————
                                              ——————————NCl——————————
                                     ————————————————NCl————————————————
                                     ————————————————NP:DObj——————————————
                         ————————————————————————VP:Pred——————————————————————
```

```
10. The    basic   rule    in      the White House   is       that      debate    should   be    internal.
    D/Art   Adj     N       Prep    ——PropN——         BE       Subord    N         M        BE    Adj
    Det    ——NP——          —NP:Obj/Prep—             MV:Pres             NP:Subj   Aux            PredAdj
           ——NP:Head——     ——PrepPh:Adj——                                         MV:PastCond
           ————NP:Subj————                                                        ————VP:Pred————
                                                                          ——————————NCl——————————
                                                               ————————————————NP:PredN————————————
                                                               ——————————————————VP:Pred——————————————
```

11. The Nicaraguan refugee went to Los Angeles to join her sister.

- The — D/Art — Det
- Nicaraguan — Adj — NP
- refugee — N — NP:Subj
- went — VI — MV:Past
- to — Prep
- Los Angeles — PropN — NP:Obj/Prep — PrepPh:Adv-place
- to — Subord
- join — VT — V:Head
- her — PossPr — Det
- sister — N — NP:DObj
- InfPh
- InfPh:Adv-reason
- VP:Pred

12. Some book reviewers criticize Pat Conroy for retelling the story of his dysfunctional family in each of his novels.

Sub

- Some — PreArt — Det
- book — N:Adj — NP
- reviewers — N — NP:Subj
- criticize — VT — MV:Pres
- Pat Conroy — PropN — NP:DObj
- for — Prep
- retelling — VT — V:Head
- the — D/Art — Det
- story — N
- of — Prep
- his — PossPr — Det
- dysfunctional — Adj — NP — NP:Obj/Prep — PrepPh:Gen — NP — NP:DObj — GerPh — NP:Obj/Prep — PrepPh:Adv-reason — VP:Pred
- family — N
- in — Prep
- each of — PreArt — Det — NP — NP:Obj/Prep — PrepPh:Adv-place
- his — PossPr — Det
- novels — N — NP

13. It doesn't take long for Crystal Gayle's audience to understand that she is Loretta Lynn's sister.

- It — Expl — GrSubj
- doesn't — Aux/Neg VL — MV:Pres
- take — VT — MV:Pres
- long — Adj — PredAdj
- for — Subord

Subord

- Crystal Gayle's — GenN — NP:Subj
- audience — N
- to understand — VT — V:Head
- that — Subord
- she — PersPr — NP:Subj
- is — BE — MV:Pres
- Loretta Lynn's — GenN — NP:PredN — VP:Pred — NCl
- sister — N
- NCl
- NP:DObj

———VP:PartPred———
——InfPh——
——InfPh——
——NP:LogSubj——
——VP:Pred——

Note: I've defined **long** as an adjective, which makes **take** a linking verb like **become**. **Take** seems to have a sense of becoming in this sentence: "it doesn't 'become' long before.... "If you consider **long** as a substitute for the whole phrase "a long time," you might analyze **take** as transitive, in the sense of "It doesn't take a long time."

14. Psychiatrists   have   not   shown   why   Freudian   therapy   works   . . .
    N   HAVE   Neg   VT   Subord   Adj   N   VI   Adv-reason
    NP:Subj   —Aux— —PastPart—   —NP:Subj—   MV:Pres
               —MV:PresPerf—   —VP:Pred—
                                                       ——NCl——
                                              ——NCl——
                                              ——NP:DObj——
              ——VP:Pred——

15. The British   revere   Winston Churchill   for   rallying   their   country   against   Nazi   aggression.
    PropN   VT   PropN   Prep   VT   PossPr   N   Prep   N:Adj   N
    NP:Subj   MV:Pres NP:DObj   V:Head   Det   Sub
                                                      —NP:DObj— —PrepPh:Adv-opposition— —NP:Obj/Prep—
                                                      ——GerPh——
                                                      ——NP:Obj/Prep——
                                                      ——PrepPh:Adv-reason——
              ——VP:Pred——

16. Internet surfers use electronic bulletin boards to swap software.
    N:Adj   N   VT   Adj   N:Adj   N   Subord VT   N
    ——NP:Subj——   MV:Pres   V:Head NP:DObj
                                       ————NP————   ——InfPh——
                       ————————NP:DObj————————   ——InfPh:Adv-reason——
                       ——————————————————VP:Pred——————————————————

17. The   Israeli press chided the   Syrians for   what   they   called .... unfriendly activity.
    D/Art Adj   N   VT   D/Art PropN   Prep Subord PersPr Vc   Adj   N
    Det   ——NP——   MV:Past Det   ——NP——   NP:Subj MV:Past   ——NP:ObjComp——
    ——NP:Subj——   ——NP:DObj——   ——VP:Pred——
                                                                                    ——NCl——
                                                         ——————————————NCl——————————————
                                                         ——————————NP:Obj/Prep——————————
                                                   ——————————————PrepPh:Adv-reason——————————
                          ——————————————————————————VP:Pred——————————————————————————

                        Sub
18. Helping fat   children lose weight means   walking an   emotional tightrope.
    Vc   Adj   N   VT   N   VT   VT   I/Art   Adj   N
    V:Head   ——NP:DObj——   V:Head ——NP:DObj——   MV:Pres V:Head Det   ——NP——
                             ——InfPh——   V:Head   ——NP:DObj——
             ——NP:ObjComp——   ——GerPh——
    ——————GerPh——————   ——————NP:DObj——————
    ——————NP:Subj——————   ——————————VP:Pred——————————

19. Computer companies haven't shown teachers how they can use technology .... in the classroom.

Computer	companies	haven't	shown	teachers	how	they	can	use	technology	....	in	the	classroom.
N:Adj	N	HAVE/Neg	Vg	N	Subord	PersPr	M	VT	N	Adv-manner	Prep	D/Art	N
		Aux	PastPart	NP:IObj	Subord	NP:Subj	Aux		NP:DObj			Det	

— NP:Subj —
—— MV:PresPerf ——
MV:PresCond
———— NP:Obj/Prep ——
———— PrepPh:Adv-place ——
———— VP:Pred ——
———— NCl ——
———— NCl ——
———— NP:DObj ——
———— VP:Pred ——

20. It takes skill and luck for a gambler to win at blackjack.

It	takes	skill	and	luck	for	a	gambler	to	win	at	blackjack.
Expl	VT	N	Conj	N	I/Art		N		VI	Prep	N
NP:GramSubj	MV:Pres	NP		NP	Det				V:Head		NP:Obj/Prep

—— NP:DObj ——
Subord
—— NP:Subj ——
PrepPh:Adv-place
PartPred
InfPh
InfPh
NP:LogSubj/ComptoNP
—— VP:Pred ——

21. Thomas Edison became famous for inventing the light bulb.

Thomas Edison	became	famous	for	inventing	the	light	bulb.
PropN	VL	Adj	Prep	VT	D/Art	N:Adj	N
NP:Subj	MV:Past	PredAdj		V:Head	Det		NP

—— NP:DObj ——
GerPh
—— NP:Obj/Prep ——
—— PrepPh:Adv-reason ——
———— VP:Pred ————
Sub

22.

Sub

Scientists	take	wondering	as	a	course	of	action.
N	VT	VI	Prep	I/Art	N	Prep	N
NP:Subj	MV:Pres	GerPh		Det			NP:Obj/Prep
		NP:DObj					

PrepPh:Gen — NP — NP:Obj/Prep — PrepPh:Adv-manner — VP:Pred

23.

Sub

Calling	a	Texan	a	liar	will	usually	provoke	a	fight.
Vc	I/Art	N	I/Art	N	M	Adv-frequ	VT	I/Art	N
V:Head	Det		Det	NP:ObjComp	Aux			Det	
		NP:DObj							NP:DObj

NP:DObj — GerPh — NP:Subj

MV:PresCond — VP:Pred

Note: **Usually** is attached to a verb phrase but not to the main verb, though it interrupts it. It might, for instance, be moved to the end of the verb phrase: **will provoke a fight usually.**

24.

Twenty percent	of	Americans	don't	believe	that	murderers	should	be	executed	by	the	state.
PreArt		PropN	Aux/Neg	VT	Subord	N	M	BE	VT	Prep	D/Art	N
Det		NP:Subj	MV:Pres			NP:GramSub	Aux		PastPart		Det	
NP:Subj							MV:PastPassCond				NP:Obj/Prep	

PrepPh:Adv-agency

VP:Pred

NCl

NCl

NP:DObj

VP:Pred

25. Martin Luther King, Jr. wondered whether the United States was a just country.

```
Martin Luther King, Jr.   wondered   whether   the United States   was      a      just   country.
        PropN                VT       Subord        PropN           BE      I/Art   Adj      N
        NP:Subj            MV:Past                  Subj           MV:Past   Det ———————————— NP
                                                                           ———— NP:PredN ————
                                                                           ———————— VP:Pred ————————
                                                     ———————————————————— NCl —————————————————————
                           —————————————————— NCl ——————————————————————
                           —————————————————— NP:DObj ——————————————————
        —————————————————————————— VP:Pred ——————————————————————————————
```

Chapter 9 — Adding Modifiers to Sentences

```
                                          MClause                                              NonrestrictictiveMod

1. Romans believed   the   appearance of   Sirius  ... made   the   weather   hotter.    known   as    the Dog Star,
   PropN    VT       D/Art    N    Prep     PropN      Vc     D/Art    N'       Adj       VT     Prep   PropN
   NP:Subj MV:Past   Det              NP:Obj/Prep    MV:Past   Det  NP:DObj AdjPh:ObjComp  PastPart      NP:Obj/Prep
                                      PrepPh:Gen               ———— NP:DObj ——             ——— PrepPh:Adv-manner ———
                           ———————————— NP ————————             ————— VP:Pred ——————        ———————— PastPartPh ————————
                           ——————— NP:DObj ————————
                     ———————— NP:Subj ————————
   ————————————————————————————— VP:Pred —————————————————————————
```

Note: Remember that a past participial phrase derives from a passive clause, which must have a transitive verb.

2. **Many Bronx buildings have been abandoned and torched, leaving streets barren and empty.**

MClause

NonrestrictiveMod

3. **Buried in a remote Guatemalan rain forest, the ancient city of Tikal contains thousands of Mayan structures.**

NonrestrictiveMod

MClause

Note: I've labeled *of Tikal* a phrasal genitive. Some students want to call **city of** a prearticle, like, say, **jar of**. The construction seems to me more like **the Queen of England** than **a jar of plums**. But their analysis seems worth considering.

4. **As I walk to my car, I can see the snow-filled mountains that brought me to Wyoming.**

AdvCl

MClause

Note: The adverb clause probably originates within the predicate of the main clause and is moved to the front of the sentence. It's simply an adverb of time.

5.

MClause   NonrestrictictiveMod

```
The J.B. Ford  ...  steams     no more.    the      freighter  I       worked on    as     a        teenager
PropN               VI         Adv-frequency D/Art   N          PersPr  VT           Prep   I/Art    N
NP:Subj             MV:Pres                  Det                NP:Subj MV:Past              Det
       ——— VP:Pred ———                ——— NP:Head ———                                       NP:Obj/Prep
                                                                                     ——— PrepPh:Adv-time ———
                                                                             ——————— VP:Pred ———————
                                                                        ——————————— RelCl:Adj ———————————
                                                          ————————————————————————— NP —————————————————————
```

6.

NonrestrictiveMod

```
Hoping    to    catch    a       last    glimpse    of      their     families,
M         Sub   VT       I/Art   OrdN    N          Prep    PossPr    N
PresPart        V:Head   Det     Det     Det                Det
                                                                       NP:Obj/Prep
                                                            ——— PrepPh:Gen ———
                                                    ————————— NP —————————
                                 ——————————————————— NP ———————————————————
                      ————————————————————————— NP:DObj —————————————————————
                ——————————————————————————————— InfPh ———————————————————————
          ————————————————————————————————————— NP:DObj ———————————————————————
    ——————————————————————————————————————————— PresPartPh ———————————————————————
```

Note: I've called **hoping** a verb and **to catch** ... **families** an infinitive phrase functioning as a direct object. Some students call **hoping to** a semimodal. That seems defensible, though it demands that you make the semimodal the head of the verb phrase. That's possible, since semimodals, unlike modals, can be made into present or past participles (**is hoping to**, had **hoped to**), but we haven't discussed this issue, which complicates the main verb more than I had cared to.

MClause

Sub

the   children   lingered   for   a   moment   before   boarding   the   camp   bus.
D/Art   N   VI   Prep   I/Art   N   Prep   VT   D/Art   N:Adj   N
Det   MV:Past   Det   V:Head   Det ——NP——
——NP:Subj——   NP:Obj/prep   ——NP:DObj——
PrepPh:Adv-duration   ——GerPh——
——NP:Obj;Prep——
——PrepPh:Adv-time——
——VP:Pred——

NonrestrictictiveMod

MClause

7. Bruce Springsteen … has   become   a   political   symbol.   who   exemplifies   intelligent rock and roll
PropN   HAVE   VL   I/Art   Adj   N   RelPr   VT   Adj   N
NP:Subj   PastPart   Det ——NP——   NP:Subj   MV:Pres ——NP——
MV:PresPerf   ——NP:PredN——   ——NP:DObj——
——VP:Pred——   ——VP:Pred——
——RelCl——

MClause

NonrestrictictiveMod

8. Pelted   by   wind   and   rain,   we   struggled   with   the   tent   flaps   in order to   keep   dry.
VT   Prep   N   Conj   N   PersPr   VI   Prep   D/Art   N:Adj   N   Subord   VL   Adj
PastPart   NP   NP   NP:Subj   MV:Past   Det ——NP——   AdjPh:PredAdj
——NP:Obj/Prep——   —NP:Obj/Prep—
— PrepPh:Adv-instrument—   PrepPh:Adv-instrument   ——InfPh——
——PastPartPh——   InfPh:Adv-reason
——VP:Pred——

Note: I've called **struggled** intransitive. Some students analyze **struggle with** as a two-word transitive. Either analysis seems defensible to me.

NonrestrictiveMod

MClause

9. The   camera-toting tourists   swarmed from   the   monorail,   joining   Epcot's   early morning rush.
   D/Art   Adj   N   VT   VI   Prep   D/Art   N   VT   GenN   Adj   N
   Det   ——— NP ———   MV:Past   Det   PresPart   ——— NP ———
   ——— NP:Subj ———   ——— NP:Obj/Prep ———   ——— NP:DObj ———
                                       —PrepPh:Adv-source—   ——— PresPartPh ———
                                       ——— VP:Pred ———

MClause

10. When   I   think of   my   grandfather   now,   I   see   him   on   a   tractor,   N
    Subord PersPr   VT   PossPr N   Adv-time PersPr   VT   PersPr Prep I/Art   N
            NP:Subj MV:Pres   Det   NP:Subj MV:Pres NP:DObj   Det   NP:Obj/Prep
                    ——— NP:DObj ———   ——— PrepPh:Adv-place ———
                    ——— VP:Pred ———   ——— VP:Pred ———
                    ——— Cl ———
            ——— AdvCl:Adv-time ———

NonrestrictiveMod

tilling   ground   in   wind   that   cuts   a   bitter   day.
VT   N   Prep N   RelPr   VT   I/Art Adj   N
PresPart   NP:DObj   NP:Head NP:Subj MV:Pres Det   ——— NP ———
                                                         ——— NP:DObj ———
                                                         ——— VP:Pred ———
                                           ——— RelCl:Adj ———
                           ——— NP:Obj/Prep ———
                           ——— PrepPh:Adv-place ———
——— PresPartPh ———

Note: The adverb clause probably originates within the predicate of the main clause and is moved to the front of the sentence.

11.

MClause / NonrestrictiveMod

The lions rose, yawning and stretching, as they began their search for the day's first meal.

The	D/Art — Det
lions	N
rose	VI — MV:Past
	NP:Subj — VP:Pred
yawning	VI — PresPart
and	Conj
stretching	VI — PresPart
	PresPartPh
as	Subord
they	PersPr — NP:Subj
began	VT — MV:Past
their	PossPr — Det
search	N — NP:Head
for	Prep
the	D/Art — Det
day's	GenN — Det
first	OrdN
meal	N

Higher nodes: NP, PrepPh:Adj, NP:DObj, VP:Pred, Cl, AdvCl:Adv-time

Note: The adverb clause probably originates within the predicate of the main clause, from which it is disjoined by the present participial phrase.

12.

MClause / NonrestrictiveMod

Several dozen boats sit on the dry bed of the Aral Sea their anchors buried in the sand.

Several	PreArt — Det
dozen	CardN — Det
boats	N
	NP — NP:Subj
sit	VI — MV:Pres
on	Prep
the	D/Art — Det
dry	Adj
bed	N
of	Prep
the Aral Sea	PropN
their	PossPr — Det
anchors	N — NP:Subj
buried	PastPart — VI
in	Prep
the	D/Art — Det
sand	N

Higher nodes: NP:Obj/Prep, PrepPh:Gen, NP, NP:Obj/Prep, PrepPh:Adv-place, VP:Pred, NP:Obj/Prep, PrepPh:Adv-place, VP:PartPred, NomAbs

13.

NonrestrictiveMod

The Range Rover sat near the salt lick, lights off and engine silent, concealing three hunters and their equipment.

MClause — NonrestrictiveMod — NonrestrictiveMod

D/Art PropN VI Prep D/Art N:Adj N N Adv-cond Conj N Adj VT PresPart CardN N Conj PossPr N

Det — NP:Subj — MV:Past — Det — NP — NP:Subj PartPred NP:Subj PartPred PresPart Det Det

— NP:Obj/Prep — — NomAbs — — NomAbs — — NP — — NP —

— PrepPh:Adv-place — — NomAbs — — NP:DObj —

— VP:Pred — — PresPartPh —

14.

MClause — NonrestrictiveMod

It stood for hours at Cincinnati's riverfront dock, awaiting the arrival of a Mississippi steamboat

PersPr VI Prep N Prep GenN N:Adj N VT D/Art N Prep I/Art N:Adj N

NP:Subj MV:Past NP:Obj/Prep — NP — PresPart Det — NP —

PrepPh:Adv-duration — NP:Obj/Prep — — NP:Obj/prep —

— PrepPh:Adv-place — — PrepPh:Gen —

— VP:Pred — — NP —

— NP:DObj —

— PresPartPh —

NonrestrictiveMod

a paddlewheeler named the Memphis Queen.

I/Art N Vc PastPart PropN

Det — NP:Head — PastPart — NP:ObjComp —

— NP — — PastPartPh:Adj —

— NP —

MClause

The	mother	bear	curled up	beside	a	tree,	while	the	cub	grazed	on	grass,
D/Art	N:Adj	N	—VI—	Prep	D/Art	N	Subord	D/Art	N	VI	Prep	N
Det	—NP—		MV:past		Det			Det		MV:Past		
	NP:Subj				NP:Obj/Prep			NP:Subj				NP:Obj/Prep
					PrepPh:Adv-place							PrepPh:Adv-goal
				VP:Pred							VP:Pred	
									Cl			
									AdvCl:Adv-time			

15.

NonrestrictiveMod

an	important	part of	a	young	bear's	diet.
I/Art	Adj	PreArt I/Art	Adj	Adj	GenN	N
Det		Det Det			NP	
					NP	
			NP			
		NP				
	NP					
NP						

Note: I've called **on grass** an adverb that states a goal. It could be called a place adverb, though goal seems more apt to me.

MClause

NonrestrictiveMod

The	mayor	of	Djénné	pointed	to	the	town's	masterpiece	of	Muslim	architecture,	the	great	mosque	in	the	city	square.
D/Art	N	Prep	PropN	VI	Prep	D/Art	GenN	N	Prep	Adj	N	D/Art	Adj	N	Prep	D/Art	N:Adj	N
Det		Obj/Prep	PropN	MV:Past	Det						NP:Obj/Prep	Det	NP		Det		NP	
		PrepPh:Gen								PrepPh:Gen			NP:Head			NP:Obj/Prep		
	NP								NP							PrepPh:Adj		
NP:Subj								NP:Obj/Prep						NP				
								PrepPh:Adv-place										
								VP:Pred										

16.

17.

MClause

I	hit	the	gas	pedal	instead of	the	brake,
PersPr	VT	D/Art	N:Adj	N	— Prep —	D/Art	N
NP:Subj	MV:Past	Det	—NP—			Det	
						NP:Obj/Prep
		—NP:DObj—			—PrepPh:Adv-contrast —
				——VP:Pred ——

NonrestrictiveMod

the	policeman	on	the	corner	staring	as	I	ran	the	red	light.
D/Art	N	Prep	D/Art	N	VI	Subord	PersPr	VT	D/Art	Adj	N
Det			Det		PresPart		NP:Subj	MV:Past	Det		—NP —
—NP:Head —			NP:Obj/Prep							NP:DObj —
			—PrepPh:Adj—						—VP:Pred —
—NP:Subj —							—AdvCl:Adv-time —
				—PresPartPh:PartPred —
			—NomAbs —

MClause   NonrestrictiveMod

18. Canyon Ranch ... is   not   a   fat-farm for   the   rich,   a   former dude ranch converted into   a   fitness spa
    PropN   BE   Neg   D/Art N   Prep D/Art N   I/Art Adj   N:Adj N   VT   Prep   I/Art N:Adj   N
    NP:Subj   MV:Pres   Det   NP:Obj/Prep   Det   PastPart   Det   NP —
                                   — NP:Head —— — PrepPh:Adj —   — NP —   — NP:Obj/Prep —
                                          — NP:PredN —   — NP:Head —   — PrepPh:Adv-place —
                                   ——— VP:Pred ———   — PastPartPh:Adj —
                                                                                                  — NP —

                                                        MClause

19. It   's   easy   to   write about Cajun   culture   when   you   're   living   in   that   world
    Expl   BE   Adj   Subord VT   N:Adj   N   Subord PersPr BE   VI   Prep Demon N
    NP:GramSubj MV:Pres PredAdj   V:Head   — NP:DObj —   NP:Subj Aux   PresPart   — NP:Obj/Prep —
                                            ——— InfPh ———   MV:PresProg   — PrepPh:Adv-place —
                                    ——— InfPh:LogSubj/ComptoAdj ———   ——— VP:Pred ———
                                                                                                         ——— Cl ———
                                                                                                  ——— AdvCl:Adv-time ———
                                                                                                  ——— VP:Pred ———

NonrestrictiveMod   NonrestrictiveMod

eating   seafood gumbo, listening to swamp pop   on   the   radio.
VT   N:Adj   N   VT   N:Adj N   Prep D/Art N
PresPart   PresPart   — NP:DObj —   NP:Obj/Prep
V:Head   — NP:DObj —   V:Head   — PrepPh:Adv-place —
— PresPartPh —   — PresPartPh —

MClause

20. Harlem Renaissance writers were important for their own words and because they built an African-American literary tradition.

Harlem Renaissance	writers	were	important	for	their	own	words	and	because	they	built	an	African-American	literary	tradition.
N:Adj	N	BE	Adj	Prep	PossPr	PossPr	N	conj	Subord	PersPr	VT	I/Art	Adj	Adj	N

—— NP:Subj ——
—— MV:Past AdjPh:Pred

Det Det

—— NP ——
—— NP ——
—— PrepPh:Adv-reason ——

NP:Subj MV:Past

—— NP ——
—— NP:DObj ——
—— VP:Pred ——
—— Cl ——
—— AdvCl:Adv-reason ——
—— AdvCl:Adv-reason ——
—— VP:Pred ——

MClause

21. Stately and erect, the United Artists Tower looms prominent along the skyline overlooking Nashville's Music Row.

NonrestrictiveMod

Stately	and	erect,	the	United Artists Tower	looms	prominent	along	the	skyline	overlooking	Nashville's	Music Row.
Adj	Conj	Adj	D/Art	PropN	VL	Adj	Prep	D/Art	N	VT	GenN	PropN
AdjPh		AdjPh		NP:Subj	MV:Pres	Adj:PredAdj				PresPart		

—— AdjPh ——
—— NP:Subj ——
—— NP:Head ——
—— PresPartPh:Adj ——
—— NP:Obj/Prep ——
—— PrepPh:Adv-place ——
—— NP:DObj ——
—— PresPart ——
—— VP:Pred ——

22.

NonrestrictiveMod

As   Caribbean   cooking   becomes   popular
Subord   Adj   N   VL   MV:Pres   Adj
                              AdjPh:PredAdj
—NP:Subj—   —————VP:Pred—————
            ——————————Cl——————————
            ——————————AdvCl:Adv-time——————————

MClause

plantains … may   replace   potatoes   at   the   American   table.
N   M   VT   N   Prep   D/Art   Adj   N
NP:Subj   Aux   NP:DObj   Det   —NP—
         MV:PresCond   —NP:Obj/Prep—
                              ——PrepPh:Adv-place——
                    ——————————VP:Pred——————————

exotic bananas   eaten   as   a   starch
Adj   N   VT   Prep   D/Art   I/Art   N
            PastPart   Det
—NP:Head—   —NP:Obj/Prep—
                    —PrepPh:Adv-manner
            ——PastPartPh:Adj——
——————————NP——————————

23.

MClause

To   defend   the   government   of   South Vietnam,   American   forces   tore   the   country   apart.
VT   D/Art   N   Prep   PropN   Adj   N   VT   D/Art   N   Part
Subord   Det   —NP:Obj/Prep—   NP:Subj   MV:Past   Det
                    PrepPh:Gen   —NP:DObj—
            ————NP————   ——————VP:Pred——————
         ——NP:DObj——
         ——InfPh——
——InfPh:Adv-reason——

Note: **Tore apart** is a two-word verb; the particle **apart** has been disjoined, moved around the direct object NP. The adverbial infinitive, like other adverbs, is derived within the verb phrase of the main clause and moved to the front of the sentence.

24.

MClause

One of the strangest comic book villains is Catwoman, whose heart belongs to crime and to Batman.

NonrestrictiveMod

PreArt — One of / the — D/Art / strangest — Adj / comic book — N:Adj / villains — N / is — BE MV:Pres / Catwoman, — PropN / whose — RelDet / heart — N / belongs — VI MV:Pres / to — Prep / crime — N / and — Conj Prep / to — Conj / Batman. — N

Det; Det; NP; NP:PredN; RelDet Det; NP:Subj; NP:Obj/Prep; NP:Obj/Prep

VP:Pred; NP; NP; NP:Subj; PrepPh; PrepPh; PrepPh:Adv-goal; VP:Pred; RelCl

25.

NonrestrictiveMod   MClause

Barefoot and disheveled, my son stood shamefaced before me, as I had once stood before my father.

Barefoot — Adj AdjPh / and — Conj / disheveled, — Adj AdjPh / my — PossPr Det / son — N / stood — VL MV:Past / shamefaced — Adj AdjPh PredAdj / before — Prep / me, — PersPr NP:Obj/Prep / as — Subord Subord / I — PersPr NP:Subj / had — HAVE Adv-time / once — Adv-time MV:PastPerf / stood — VI / before — Prep / my — PossPr Det / father. — N

AdjPh; NP:Subj; PrepPh:Adv-place; VP:Pred; NP:Obj/Prep; PrepPh:Adv-place–; VP:Pred; PrepPh:Adv-place–; Clause; AdvC l:Adv-manner

Note: I called **stood** a linking verb, making **shamefaced** an adjective. In the last edition of the book, I called **stood** intransitive, making **shamefaced** an adverb of manner. I changed my mind essentially because the sentence is introduced by an adjective phrase, and I decided **shamefaced** should be parallel. It seems to me that you can argue either way. I did.

GLOSSARY

....

Absolute phrase: a nominative absolute that contains both a noun phrase subject and a partial predicate, a predicate lacking finiteness. To construct an absolute, you generally delete BE from a clause, the verb BE or the auxiliary BE. In the following example, the auxiliary BE is deleted to leave an absolute with a past participial partial predicate: "At the Parisian chocolatier, I discovered the *macarolat,* a version of the macaroon, **its dark chocolate shell filled with almond and hazelnut praline.**"

Absolute phrases are the only structures in English that allow you to narrow in on a scene as if you were using a zoom lens on a camera. And they can sometimes be introduced by the word **with.**

Adjective: a content word that generally limits, qualifies, or specifies characteristics of nouns, as in a **small** chair or **beige** paint. Most adjectives are gradable. So you can often compare or intensify them.

Adverb clause: a subordinate clause that functions in the full range of adverb roles, including manner, place, time, reason, and condition. The following is an adverb clause of time: *The U.S. seaman was taken hostage **after pirates hijacked his ship**.* Adverb clauses have similar freedom of movement around and within a main clause as nonrestrictive modifiers, though they are not additional comments separate from the main clause. They are introduced with subordinators like **because, if,** and **before**, often the same as the prepositions that precede noun phrases to make prepositional phrases.

Adverbial: shows many relationships, including time, place, reason, means, extent, and frequency and can be realized by many structures, including single-word adverbs, prepositional phrases, and clauses. Adverbials help to orient readers and listeners to what is going on in a sentence.

Adverbial infinitive: functions as an adverb of reason and can always be introduced by the subordinator **in order to,** though it sometimes uses just **to**. For example, "Many alcoholics drink **in order to** medicate their depression" or "Many alcoholics drink **to** medicate their depression." The subordinator **in order to** identifies adverbial infinitives.

Appositive: noun phrase or adjective phrase used as nonrestrictive modifier. Appositive noun phrases are placed next to other nouns and explain them, as in "Churchill regarded Gandhi as a fakir, **a street magician and beggar**," where the appositive noun phrase defines a fakir. Appositives derive from predicate nouns or predicate adjectives. Appositive adjectives identify or define noun phrases: "The kindergarten kids, **cute and bright,** won over the new teacher."

Aspect: indicates that the action of a verb is completed or continuing, the action flows or it stops. Aspect occurs in two varieties, perfect (HAVE plus a past participle, **have eaten**) or progressive (Aux BE plus a present participle, **is eating**).

BE verb: As the main verb of a sentence, it is a stative verb followed by a predicate noun, a predicate adjective, or a predicate adverb. BE has eight principal parts: **be, is, am, are, was, were, been, being**.

Clause: dependent or independent, a clause contains a noun phrase subject and a finite verb phrase predicate.

Common noun: names general things, like **boy, refrigerator, president**, or **office building**.

Complement: refers to a constituent that completes a phrase or clause. For example, "Europeans thought the Chinese **backward**" (Obj Comp).

Conditional mood: a modal auxiliary plus an infinitive; shows possibility: **will escape**.

Conjunctive adverb: connects sentences and marks discourse. The most common conjunctive adverbs are words and phrases like **besides, furthermore, first, for, finally, however, in the first place, in the meantime, likewise, moreover, nonetheless, on the other hand,** and **rather**. They typically show comparison, contrast, cause/effect, and sequence. When you connect sentences with them, you punctuate with periods or semicolons, as in:

Brand-name cereals are expensive. **Nonetheless,** they appeal to kids.

OR

Brand-name cereals are expensive; **nonetheless,** they appeal to kids.

Coordinate conjunctions: the single words **and, but, or**. They can conjoin words, phrases, and clauses, including sentences, with different kinds of punctuation schemes.

Core verbs: intransitive (VI), linking (VL), transitive (VT), Vg, Vc, and BE.

Correlative conjunctions: join words and phrases within clauses. They are pairs of words, like **both . . . and, either . . . or, neither . . . nor**, and **not only . . . but also**. Correlative conjunctions are more emphatic than coordinate conjunctions.

Definite article: a determiner that indicates shared (old) information. **The** is the only definite article in English.

Demonstrative: a determiner that points to things—**this, that, these**, and **those**. A demonstrative is deictic.

Dependent clauses (also called subordinate clauses): are embedded within larger clauses as nouns, adjectives, or adverbs.

Determiners: function words that include articles, demonstratives, numbers, possessive pronouns, and prearticles. They precede and form phrases with nouns.

Diagram: a drawing or chart that shows how you parse a phrase or clause, naming the structures and functions of constituents and showing their hierarchal relationships.

Direct object: a function of a noun phrase that follows a transitive verb, as in, "*Time*'s photo editors selected **these photos**." A direct object is affected by the verb in some way.

Embedded structures: phrases or clauses that that fit into larger, matrix structures.

Existential-there sentence: has an expletive **there** that functions as the grammatical subject, and a logical subject following a verb BE, as in "**There are 25 students in this class**." Most existential-there sentences seem to be made from core sentences like "**Twenty five students are in the class**," with the original subject moved around the BE and then replaced by the expletive **there.**

Expletive: has a grammatical function but no meaning of its own. The existential **there** and the existential **it** fill noun phrase subject slots. The expletive DO holds tense in negative and question sentences. **It, there**, and **DO** are the three expletives in English.

Finiteness: the characteristic of a verb or auxiliary that "shows" past or present tense. A conjugated verb or auxiliary is finite.

Function: what a word or phrase does in a larger constituent, a relation it has with another grammatical component. A constituent may function as a subject, a direct object, an indirect object, an oblique object (the object of a preposition), an object complement, a predicate, a predicate adjective, or a predicate noun.

Function word: a determiner, auxiliary, pronoun, conjunction, or preposition. Function words are closed classes.

Genitives: occur as -'s nouns and as **-of** phrases, and even as uninflected phrases. Since many so-called possessives show relationships like actor, object, or measure, *genitive* is a more accurate term than *possessive*.

Gerund: an **-ing** verb form that fills a noun phrase slot. **Meeting Joseph Stalin** is a gerund phrase which fills the direct object slot in "Winston Churchill disliked **meeting Joseph Stalin**." A gerund looks like a present participle; but it does not derive like one nor function like one. Gerunds always fill noun phrase slots; present participles never do. Moreover, the **-ing** of a gerund is a subordinator. And a gerund phrase, like an infinitive phrase, can contain an inflected subject, making a gerund with genitive phrase, as in, "**Laura's drinking** destroyed her family."

Grammar: a system that puts words together into meaningful units. It builds constituents into hierarchies.

Head: a head and its attributes compose a phrase. Linguists argue over definitions of heads in technical treatises. For our purposes, the head of a phrase is central to the phase. It is always a word that the phrase is named for: the head of a noun phrase is a noun; the head of a verb phrase is a verb; the head of an adjective phrase is an adjective; the head of a prepositional phrase is a preposition.

Hierarchy: a pattern in which structures fit within structures. Hierarchies define the basic structural principle of clauses and phrases. Grammar builds constituents as hierarchies.

Imperative mood: the mood or modality of a verb phrase that makes a command or request.

Imperative sentence: has no subject. Nor does it display a finite verb phrase. It begins with an infinitive: "**Take the next bus to Manhattan**."

Indefinite article: a determiner that does not express shared information. The indefinite articles are **a** and **an**.

Indefinite pronoun: ends in **-body**, **-thing**, or **-one**—e.g., **everybody**, **something**, or **no one**. The indefinite pronouns don't refer to specific nouns. As the name suggests, the meaning of an indefinite pronoun is indefinite or general.

Independent clause: see *Sentence*.

Indicative mood: the normal (unmarked) mood; it indicates an opinion or fact, a statement.

Indirect object: the function of a noun phrase that either follows a Vg verb immediately or as part of a **to** or **for** prepositional phrase in a clause with a Vg verb. It typically receives and perceives, as in "The teacher gave a book to **the student**" or "The teacher gave **the student** a book."

Infinitive: one of the five principal parts of a verb. It is the base form of the verb. It is often shown with the subordinator **to,** as **to go** or **to bedazzle.** But the **to** does not have to appear for a verb form to be an infinitive.

Infinitive phrase: can fill a noun phrase slot, as in "Laura's goal should be **to reduce her wine consumption,**" where the verb phrase **to reduce her wine consumption** functions as a predicate noun, filling a noun phrase slot. Infinitive phrases can fill many different noun phrase slots. An infinitive phrase can occur without the subordinator **to,** and can occur with a subject within a **for . . . to** phrase, e.g., "**For home foreclosures to rise above a certain level** frightens economists."

Interrogative mood: the mood or modality of a verb phrase that asks a question.

Intransitive verb (VI): can end sentences or may be followed by adverbs: "Hurricanes **rotate** around an eye."

Irregular verb: either does not have a past tense that ends in **d** or **-ed**, or its past participle is not the same as its past tense form. There are fewer than one hundred irregular verbs in English.

Linking verb (VL): must be followed either by a noun phrase that functions as a predicate noun or an adjective phrase that function as a predicate adjective. Linking verbs constitute a small class of no more than a few dozen or so verbs, including **seem, remain, appear, become,** and the verbs of the senses. Here is an example: "Lance Armstrong's Tour de France wins **remain** impressive."

Main verb: the verb that is central to a predicate, along with the forms that show its tense, mood, and aspect.

Matrix structures: phrases or clauses that embed structures within them.

Modal auxiliaries: indicate conditional mood (possibility). The modal auxiliaries are **can, could, shall, should, may, might, will, would,** and **must.** There are also several semi-modals.

Mood: denotes the purpose of a clause. This book explains the conditional, indicative, interrogative, and imperative moods.

Multiple-word verb (phrasal verb): a single verb constituent that contains more than one word, a verb like **tick off** or **put up with.**

Negative sentence: displays a **Not** after the first Aux element, or it inserts an expletive DO to "hold" the tense and negative, as in "**Educators don't know the effects of video games on children.**"

Nominative absolute: see *Absolute phrase.*

Nonrestrictive modifier: a phrase or clause added to another clause parenthetically, not bound within it. Nonrestrictive structures, like appositives, participial phrases, relative clauses, prepositional phrases, and absolute phrases, are set off by internal punctuation: commas, dashes, parentheses, or colons.

Noun: a content word that does more than name people, places, or things; it can follow determiners and form plurals.

Number: if it precedes a noun, a number is a determiner. Numbers occur as cardinal (**one, two, three**) or ordinal (**first, second, last**).

Open classes: nouns, verbs, adjectives, and adverbs. They are content words.

Parsing: analyzing clauses and phrases, breaking them down into structures and functions and naming the structures and functions.

Particles: like **off, over, up**, and **with**, make phrasal verbs, for example, "General Schwarzkopf added **up** the Iraqi losses" or "General Schwarzkopf added the Iraqi losses **up**."

Though often confused with prepositions, particles make constituents with verbs, not noun phrases.

Parts of speech: word categories: noun, verb, adjective, adverb, determiner, auxiliary, pronoun, conjunction, and preposition.

Passive sentence: the rearrangement of a sentence with a transitive verb—a VT, a Vg, or a Vc. The original direct object is moved to the front, as a grammatical subject. The core subject is moved into a prepositional phrase with **by**, an agent phrase, and the verb is turned into a past participle, while auxiliary BE is added to the verb phrase: "**Our habitat is threatened by toxic wastes.**"

Past participle: one of the five principal parts of a verb. Past participles of regular verbs end in **-d** or **-ed**. Past participles of irregular verbs have different forms. The auxiliary HAVE followed by a past participle shows perfect aspect. A past participle can head a past participial phrase, either restrictive or nonrestrictive.

Past participial phrase: a verb phrase (what's left of a passive clause when you delete the grammatical subject and BE) that's headed by a past participle. It is either bound or not bound (nonrestrictive) into another clause.

Past tense: one of a verb's principal parts. It generally means something has happened in the past. For all regular verbs, it is formed with a **-d** or **-ed**. Irregular verbs usually form past tense in different ways.

Perfect aspect: indicates that the action of a verb is completed. Perfect aspect is shown by the auxiliary HAVE followed by a past participle.

Personal pronoun: **I, you, they, me, us**, and **them**. Personal pronouns fill noun phrase slots, occur in subject and object forms, and refer to previously mentioned nouns.

Phrasal verb: See *Multiple-word verb.*

Possessive pronouns: **my, his, her, its, your**, and **their** are determiners; they form phrases with the nouns they precede. **Mine, ours, his, hers, its, yours**, and **theirs** are independent; they fill noun phrase slots. Many possessives pronouns, like inflective or phrasal genitives, show relationships other than possession, including actor, object, or measure.

Prearticles: determiners that include several categories that occur before articles or possessives: partitives and quantifiers (**some of, any of, a little of**), multipliers (**twice**), and fractions (**one third of**).

Predicate: one of the two basic constituents of a clause. It is a finite verb phrase and generally makes a comment about the subject, the topic of the clause.

Predicate adjective: the function of an adjective phrase that follows a BE verb or a linking verb: "Fresh roses seem **hardy**."

Predicate adverb: the function of an adverb phrase that follows a BE verb immediately in its nucleus: "That condo is **in the most expensive building in town**."

Predicate noun: the function of a noun phrase that follows a BE verb or a linking verb: "The Internet has become **a mass of undifferentiated data**."

Preposition: a part of speech that precedes a noun phrase and makes a prepositional phrase with it. Prepositions are usually single words, like **in, up, for**, or **below**. But they can be multiple words, like **in front of, thanks to**, or **apart from**.

Present participle: an -**ing** form of a verb. It is one of the five principal parts. Together with an auxiliary BE, it makes present progressive aspect. A present participle can head a present participial phrase, either restrictive or nonrestrictive.

Present participial phrase: a verb phrase (what's left of the predicate of a relative clause) that's headed by a present participle. It is either bound (restrictive) or not bound (nonrestrictive) into another clause.

Present tense: a principal part of a verb. It has both form and meaning. It basically means habitual, like "My neighbors **drive** to work every day." Or it states a general truth, like "The sun **sets** in the west." For most verbs, except with third-person singular subjects, the form is the same as the infinitive form. With third person singular subjects (he, she, it), it adds an -**s** or -**es**—as in **throw/throws** and **pitch/pitches**. The most obvious exception is BE—**am, is, are**.

Principal part: one of the five forms of a verb: present tense, past tense, present participle, past participle, or infinitive/base.

Progressive aspect: indicates that the action of a verb is continuous. Progressive aspect is shown by the auxiliary BE plus a present participle.

Proper noun: a noun that refers to unique people, places, or things; a proper noun is a set of one and typically names something or someone, like **the Statue of Liberty, Bobby**, or **Ohio**.

Reflexive pronoun: a pronoun that ends in -**self** or -**selves** (as **himself** or **themselves**) and refers to the subject of the clause it is in: "The president walked the dog **himself**."

Regular verb: a verb that has a past tense form that ends in -**d** or -**ed** and a past participle that shows the same form as its past tense. Regular verbs make up all but a hundred or so verbs in the language.

Relative clause: a dependent clause, restrictive or nonrestrictive. A relative clause has an antecedent noun phrase in a matrix clause for one of its own noun phrases. It relativizes that noun phrase and moves the relative pronoun to the front of the relative clause. When a relative pronoun is the object of a preposition, you can front the noun phrase alone or the whole prepositional phrase. Though you can delete a relativized direct object noun phrase from a relative clause, a relative clause normally displays its relative pronoun.

Relative determiner: whose, which replaces only a possessive pronoun or a genitive noun in a relative clause.

Relative pronouns: that, which, who, and **whom,** which replace different kinds of noun phrases in relative clauses. **Who** replaces a human subject; **whom** replaces a human object; **which** replaces a nonhuman subject or object; **that** replaces a human or nonhuman subject or object.

Restrictive modifier: an embedded phrase or clause that typically implies a larger group exists. For instance, the restrictive relative clause in the sentence "The candidates **who support the tax increase** came to the rally tonight" implies there are candidates who don"t support the tax increase. Restrictive modifiers are said to be bound into matrix structures.

Restrictive prepositional phrase: a prepositional phrase (what's left of a relative clause after you delete its subject and BE). It is embedded into a matrix noun phrase and functions as an adjective.

Restrictive relative clause: is embedded within matrix noun phrases as an adjective.

Sentence: an independent clause, a clause that is not included in another constituent; it stands alone.

Sentence nucleus: defined by the six core verbs and the slots associated with them. A nucleus is the minimum sentence built from a core verb, without additional structures and functions added to it.

Slot: a space in a clause that holds a structure and its function. The slot immediately following a transitive verb is an NP:DObj (noun phrase: direct object) slot.

Status: the totality of the tense, modality, and aspect of the main verb; for instance, the past perfect progressive.

Structure: what a constituent is, the physical category it falls into (like noun phrase, verb phrase, adjective phrase) rather than the relation it has with other constituents. We label both structures and functions, like NP:Subj, VP:Pred.

Subject: is one of the two basic constituents of a clause. It is a function that fills a noun phrase slot and typically precedes a verb phrase predicate. It generally defines the topic of the clause.

Subordinator (also called a subordinate conjunction): introduces noun and adverb clauses and phrases. Adverb clauses are introduced with words and phrases like **until, after, because,** and **whenever**; many subordinate conjunctions that introduce adverb clauses are prepositions when they make phrases with nouns. Noun clauses are introduced by words like **that, who, when, where, how, how often, why,** and **whether. To** and **in order to** function as subordinators with infinitive phrases. And this book considers the -**ing** of a gerund as a subordinator.

Tag question: repeats the subject and auxiliary of a sentence in an added tag phrase. To make a tag phrase, you take the first word in AUX, make it negative (if it is positive), and add the subject of the sentence; if the subject is a personal pronoun, simply copy the pronoun. Otherwise, turn the noun phrase subject into a pronoun: "The Spanish Department will change the curriculum next year, **won't it?**"

Tense: determines the physical form of a verb or auxiliary, the first word in the main verb. English grammar names the two tenses *past* and *present,* though they do not relate exactly to real-world time.

That-clause: a noun clause that can fill almost any noun slot in a sentence—subject, direct object, object complement, or predicate noun. Here is a that-clause functioning as the subject of a sentence: "**That a Yankee wrote "Dixie"** surprised my students." The word **that,** which often introduces such noun clauses, is a subordinate conjunction, not a pronoun.

Transitive verb: must be followed by a noun phrase that functions as a direct object. Often the object of a transitive verb has something "done" to it by the subject. Vg, Vc, and VT verbs are all transitive. A clause with a transitive verb can almost always be inverted to form a passive.

Vc verb: a two-place transitive followed by a direct object and an object complement—either a noun phrases, an adjective phrase, or an infinitive phrases that completes the meaning of the verb: "Many Americans **find** Abe Lincoln inspirational."

Vg verb: a two-place transitive verb followed by both an indirect and a direct object. Here is an example: "The elementary teacher **read** the class *Horton Hears a Who!*"

VT verb: a one-place transitive. The verb is followed by a noun phrase that functions as a direct object.

Wh-clauses: noun clauses introduced by subordinators like **who(m), which, what, when, where, how, how often, why, whose, if,** or **whether.** Except for **if**

and **whether**, the Wh-subordinators also have a function within the clause. Wh-clauses can function as subjects, objects, predicate nouns, complements, and objects of prepositions. They are also called indirect questions. Here is one example: "The article explains **why Henry VIII's arrogance renders him attractive.**"

Wh-question sentence: queries some content constituent of a sentence—a noun phrase, an adverb phrase, or a determiner: "**Why does cancer frustrate microbiologists?**" The queried constituent is moved to the front of the sentence, along with the first auxiliary or DO.

Yes/no question: a sentence which asks a question that demands a yes or no for an answer: "**Did you wreck your mother's car last night?**" The first auxiliary or DO is moved around the subject noun phrase.

INDEX

....